W9-AYA-449

PROPHETIC MINISTRY

OTHER BOOKS BY MORTON T. KELSEY:

God, Dreams and Revelation:
A Christian Interpretation of Dreams

Encounter with God:
A Theology of Christian Experience

Healing and Christianity

Myth, History and Faith:
The Remythologizing of Christianity

The Christian and the Supernatural

The Other Side of Silence:
A Guide to Christian Meditation

Can Christians Be Educated? A Proposal
for Effective Communication of our Christian Religion

The Cross: Meditations on the
Seven Last Words of Christ

Discernment: A Study in Ecstasy and Evil

Dreams: A Way to Listen to God

Tales to Tell: Legends of the Senecas

The Age of Miracles: Seven Journeys to Faith

Afterlife: The Other Side of Dying

Adventure Inward:
Christian Growth through Personal Journal Writing

Reaching for the Real

Caring: Can We Love One Another?

Transcend: A Guide to the Spiritual Quest

Tongue Speaking: The History
and Meaning of Charismatic Experience

PROPHETIC MINISTRY
The Psychology and Spirituality of Pastoral Care

MORTON T. KELSEY

CROSSROAD · NEW YORK

1982
The Crossroad Publishing Company
575 Lexington Avenue, New York, NY 10022

Copyright © 1982 by Morton T. Kelsey

All rights reserved. No part of this book may be reproduced, stored in a retrieval system,
or transmitted, in any form or by any means, electronic, mechanical, photocopying,
recording, or otherwise, without the written permission of
The Crossroad Publishing Company.

Printed in the United States of America

Library of Congress Cataloging in Publication Data

Kelsey, Morton T.
  Prophetic ministry.

  Bibliography: p.
  1. Pastoral counseling — Addresses, essays, lectures.
  2. Jung, C. G. (Carl Gustav), 1875-1961 — Addresses, essays, lectures. I. Title.
BV4012.2.K435   253.5   81-17471
ISBN 0-8245-0441-0   AACR2

ACKNOWLEDGMENTS

"Jung as Philosopher and Theologian" first appeared in *The Well-Tended Tree*, ed. Hilde
Kirsch, reprinted here with permission of the C. G. Jung Foundation for Analytical Psychology, Inc., New York, N.Y.

"Faith and the Healing Ministry" reprinted from *Dimensions in Wholistic Healing*, edited by
Herbert A. Otto and James W. Knight. Copyright © 1979 by Herbert A. Otto and James W.
Knight. Used by permission of Nelson-Hall Publishers, Chicago.

"Aggression and Religion" reprinted from the May/June 1937 issue of *Religious Education*, by
permission of the publisher, The Religious Education Association, 409 Prospect Street, New
Haven, CT 06510.

"Confronting Inner Violence" originally published in the *Journal of Pastoral Counseling*, Vol.
VIII, No. 1, Spring/Summer 1973 at Iona College, Graduate Division of Pastoral Counseling,
New Rochelle, N.Y.

"Facing Death and Suffering" first published in *Lumen Vitae*, Vol. XXVII (1973), No. 2, pp.
281-295 in Brussels, Belgium.

CONTENTS

To Ollie Backus

Prophetic spirit, gifted teacher
and friend

THE MEANING OF PROPHETIC MINISTRY

Prophets speak to the needs of their times. Most times are out of joint in one way or another. These seers speak from the point of view of ultimate meaning, of eternal values, of God. Chinese sages are prophetic in that they try to see the conditions around them as related to *Tao*. Prophets are trying to apply a vision of God to the present situation; they are trying to make the general principles of the universe specific to here and now.

If they have caught a true picture of the eternal purpose and will of God, they have stepped beyond space and time. They can see that certain paths that the people are taking will lead to disaster. Sometimes they can foretell the future because they have a vision that is beyond the common perception of ordinary people. Many of us are given a touch of this gift of seeing beyond time and space, but these glimpses happen only on rare occasions. Prophets live so close to God or are so open to the Divine Purpose that one of their main vocations is to speak forth what they have come to know. Their most essential task is forth-telling, which is predicting the future. As the practice of prophecy developed in the history of the Hebrew people, the emphasis was more and more on telling forth, speaking out against those actions of men and women that were against the nature and purpose of God.

Amos, one of the first great Hebrew prophets, was a sheepherder, from a little south of Bethlehem. Like many of the other great prophets, he did not particularly want to speak his message. He was not a member of the "guild" of prophets. In the middle of the eighth century before Christ he thundered against social injustice in Israel. He warned that the greed of the rich and their lack of concern for the poor would lead to disaster. (The people thought that all God wanted from them was their sacrifices and burnt offerings. They believed that the gods were amoral and could be manipulated like oriental despots.) Isaiah continued the tradition of Amos with great power.

These prophets did not need to speak of the reality of God and the spiritual world. The people of that time never doubted the existence of a nonphysical realm and the existence of many gods. They would even sacrifice their firstborn to the god Molech, one of the many gods of Canaan called Baal.

Hosea and Ezekiel also spoke out against injustice in Israel. They also spoke of Yahweh's love for his people Israel and how unfaithful they were to him. They compared the people with harlots as the nation followed the amoral gods of Canaan and so did not live out Yahweh's will for justice, righteousness, and lovingkindness within the nation.

In many ways Jesus followed the tradition of the prophets and was the greatest of the prophets. From a Christian perspective, he incarnated or embodied the reality that touched and communicated with the other great prophets. Like the other great prophets, Jesus did more than just speak forth. He also taught and healed. Indeed, as I shall show later on, a larger proportion of the Gospel narrative is concerned with healing than with preaching or teaching. Prophetic ministry requires actions as well as words.

Within the Christian tradition there is little need for totally new insights, and so the role of the prophet has become one of seeing into the message of Jesus and bringing one aspect of it after another before the people. It is difficult to believe, but true, that it took seventeen hundred years before *Christian* nations began to see the implications of Christ's teaching in regard to slavery. John Woolman and William Wilberforce brought this home in America and in Great Britain. It took nearly nineteen hundred years before the vision of Christ was extended so that women were believed to have the same value as men.

Francis of Assisi lived the love that Jesus said was central to the nature of God more fully than any other major saint. He also saw the implications of Jesus' concern for the poor. He took a vow of poverty so that he might better minister to the oppressed. Florence Nightingale was touched by the plight of the wounded and sick, Father Damien by that of the lepers, Martin Luther King by the discrimination against the blacks. The list is endless. Often there is a need to change the structures of society before the prophetic goal is accomplished. In recent years the Church has come alive with a renewed concern and activity in the area of social action.

NEW AREAS OF PROPHETIC MINISTRY

Each age brings its new needs, and truly prophetic ministry deals with these. In Jesus' time most people were just struggling to survive. In our time whole nations are prosperous, and prosperous people have their own problems. Indeed, when we are no longer struggling to make a living other concerns emerge. One social worker used to remind some of his colleagues that the rich had problems as well as the poor. Often great wealth is more than people can bear.

As human beings grow in consciousness, they grow in conflicts and tensions. In our highly specialized civilization people have more and different problems. Men and women will often come to churches for counsel and help when they would not consider going to a social agency. The Church, in providing pastoral care or pastoral counseling, is providing prophetic ministry for those with need. The leaders of the movement that led to a new understanding of pastoral care, like Anton Boisen, were prophets in the best sense of that word.

Many people will come to a psychologist or a minister when they are hurting and in trouble. Often they stop when the pain goes away. John Sanford, one of the finest counselors I know, has worked as a minister in the Church and as a secular counselor. He has commented that people frequently just begin on their inner way to wholeness and integration, and then they stop because they don't hurt any more. There is need for healing beyond the quieting of pain.

Beneath much of the distress and anguish of our present age is the lostness and meaninglessness of a people cut off from their religious roots. Most people in our culture with an education have drunk deeply of the naturalism and materialism which started to grow in Western civilization in the sixteenth century and took over that civilization in the nineteenth and early twentieth centuries. The "death of God" theology of the nineteen sixties was an honest attempt to deal with this fact, but one which helped very few human beings in their quest for meaning.

If men and women are merely material things in a purely material world, then they have a right to be discouraged. Under those circumstances religion is an illusion, society is created for the convenience of the powerful, and morality and human values evaporate. Human freedom and dignity disappear, as B.F. Skinner states quite frankly in *Beyond Freedom and Dignity*. From this point of view human life is meaningless, and if we don't accept that fact we just aren't very bright.

There are a number of prophetic voices speaking out against this naturalistic view. Teilhard de Chardin, for one, shows that quite a different interpretation can be given to the facts of evolution. However, no one of our time has dealt with this pervasive problem of our time better than C.G. Jung. As a psychiatrist and philosopher of great originality, he shows that meaninglessness can destroy as effectively as arsenic. He also provides a new, yet old, understanding of the universe in which God is not dead and in which we human beings find meaning by our contact with him.

In the chapters that follow I shall, first of all, describe at some length Jung's suggestions for finding a way out of meaninglessness. Then I shall go on to describe the importance of religion and meaning for both pyschological and physical health. I shall then show how important Jung's understanding of life is for the teaching of religion. Violence is a major worldwide problem. I hope to show how we can begin to deal with our own violence and that of others using the same framework. And then there is the finality of death, which in a naturalistic world is simply the end of the road. Jung's view of the universe gives us a new way of believing that the traditional view of the Church has a real validity; he provides a way of helping people to accept this prospect and to prepare for a life beyond.

THE WAY BACK

Before I begin I would like to add a personal note. I am very much a child of our age. I was raised in a family with one parent a materialistic agnostic and the other ridiculed for a religious faith for which there was no firm foundation. The church I attended as a child and youth was a conventional one, and it never suggested that I could have a meaningful relationship with a real God. With the death of the one parent to whom I was very close, I found my emotional underpinnings swept out from under me. At Princeton Graduate School I studied Immanuel Kant's *Critique of Pure Reason,* and because of this had my intellectual reasons for belief swept away. After a period of deep despair, I finally decided to go to seminary to see if the Church provided any answers to the question of meaning. I emerged from a liberal seminary with the conviction that there were as good reasons for believing in some purpose in the universe as not believing in such purpose. With this "solid" foundation I went out into parish life.

During this period I was touched by Charles Whiston's book on

prayer, and began practices that no one had suggested in the seminary. After that I met Agnes Sanford, first in her books and later in
person, and through her met the reality of the healing ministry in the
Church. I began to practice this ministry. And then, paradoxically, I
came to another crisis. The skeptic within kept whispering that I had
no basis for real belief. Von Hügel had provided a theological framework, but I had no personal experience to verify it. I entered Jungian
analysis and soon discovered people who believed that God was real
and still spoke to human beings through dreams and as one listened
deeply in the depth of the night. Max Zeller and Hilde and James
Kirsch each gave uniquely of themselves and gave me new understandings.

I decided that the way of salvation was through counseling and went
to the C.G. Jung Institute in Zurich. But I discovered that my way was
not to become an analyst, but to remain within the Church as a priest
and to bring to the Western Church the Greek understanding of Christianity (so much like that of Jung in many ways). As I made that decision, I continually dreamed of building Byzantine churches.

I returned to my parish and, as I began to preach with the aid of a
new point of view, found that people were touched. More and more
came to me with their pastoral problems. In order to meet this need,
the parish of which I was rector started a psychological clinic staffed
by trainees of the Jung Institute in Los Angeles.

With the help of Ollie Backus we started a program of religious education based on this worldview. It was incredibly effective. I began to
write out the new insights that had come to me, and their implications
for the life of the Church. One of my books came to the attention of
the Department of Graduate Studies in Education at the University of
Notre Dame. I went there as a visiting professor in 1969, became a
member of that department, and later a member of the Department
of Theology.

As a teacher of graduate students in religious education, mostly
nuns, brothers, and priests, I found that nothing was more important
for religious educators than a worldview that touched the educated
modern mind. I also began to teach a course entitled "Death, Dying
and Suffering" for a group of premedical students, and later taught
courses in the Nonviolence Program. I met some of the brightest and
most capable minds that I had ever encountered, many of them floun-
dering because of a loss of meaning. I discovered that the point of view
that Jung proposed revitalized their religious belief and practice.

During the last five years I have lectured widely throughout this country and beyond its borders. Again I have found clergy and lay groups eager to find a way to make religious belief sound and religious practice relevant.

I have written books about some of the subjects covered in the following pages, but I had never addressed the pastoral implications of these aspects of the Church's ministry. Some of these papers were written for various religious and psychological journals, and others were lectures given during my residence at Notre Dame. My friends and editors, Richard Payne and Caroline Whiting, suggested that these papers would present an aspect of my work and interest that had not been previously published in book form. Although the material has been carefully edited, it is impossible to eliminate all repetition, as many of the issues with which we are dealing are closely interrelated and overlapping.

Several people have been of great help in writing the original papers and in putting them together. Paisley Brown Roach did research and edited many of the original papers. Leo Froke introduced me to many of the psychological materials. John Sanford has been a constant friend with whom I have discussed these ideas over thirty years. Andy Canale, a former student, now a psychologist in private practice in the Boston area, has helped me in many, many ways. I have already expressed my debt of gratitude to Max Zeller and Hilde and James Kirsch. Cindy Wesley was of great help in typing the final manuscript and preparing bibliographies.

There have been a host of others who have contributed to the development of this book. The people of St. Luke's Church, Monrovia, where I was rector, responded to much of this material and gave me great encouragement. Ollie Backus was director of religious education there for many years. We had come independently to the same worldview and the same appreciation of C.G. Jung. I learned much from her educational expertise. The students and faculty at Notre Dame gave me the opportunity to test this material on a far different group than is found in the ordinary parish. And then there have been those who have come to lectures and workshops and have given me numerous suggestions and new ideas.

Most of all, my wife and children have been an enduring support and have given me the most important understandings about pastoral care. In addition, during the period in which these papers were written my wife, Barbara, served as secretary, researcher, and editor. Without her help this book could never have come into existence.

PROPHETIC MINISTRY

Chapter 1

REDISCOVERING THE MINISTRY THROUGH THE UNCONSCIOUS: A PERSONAL JOURNEY

In the past thirty years my conception of the priesthood and ministry has undergone a drastic change. Starting from a warmed-over intellectual approach, I have to come to the deep conviction that this profession is urgently needed by men and women today, and that the value of ministry and religion can be rediscovered in modern life through an understanding of the unconscious. This part of the human psyche has been discovered and described by one particular branch of psychological thought. The change has occurred, in fact, as I have worked with the findings of Carl Gustav Jung and his associates, first in my own pastoral ministry in the Episcopal Church, then with the leaders and clergy of several denominations all over the world, and finally with educators in the Catholic Church at the University of Notre Dame.

Others, of course, have investigated the unconscious, but they have considered mostly aspects exposed by some special point of view. It is no wonder the Church has felt that psychology offered little to religious understanding. Most schools of psychological thought have either shunned religion and the priesthood or dismissed them as simply unimportant to the mature life.

This is certainly not true of Dr. Jung and his followers. On the contrary, the school of analytical or Jungian psychology has come to see that religion is an essential part of mature living. The priesthood, which is the profession concerned with religion and its mediation, thus is seen as necessary to human development. In fact Jung's understanding that the individual psyche must find its way among a vast complex of unconscious realities gives the priesthood a unique importance. It is

1

the only profession committed to helping people deal religiously with these primary realities and is needed by them even when they would like to deny it.

This has not always been my understanding. A discovery took place in my own life, and since then I have talked with other ministers who have had similar experiences and who found other lives touched once this had happened. I shall first suggest the change that took place in my own life and how it occurred, and then discuss the implications of Jung's thought for the priesthood (or ministry) and religion. The subject is a complex one, and there is much that we shall leave to be investigated by the individual reader.

A CHANGING ATTITUDE

When I first became active in the Church, my view of the priesthood was greatly influenced by the humanistic point of view. Looked at from this position, ministers are the leaders of the religious activities of the community. They stand for moral order and are responsible for moral teaching. They are the community service experts. They deal with people in trouble. They are also authorities on religious ideas and the philosophy of meaning, and they organize and run the religious institution and its public and private services.

Such a role is a valuable one, as anyone would agree, except certain people who view any religious or moral influence as destructive. But even so, the ministry is not indispensable, or even central to the social structure. Priests are nice to have around, but doctors and lawyers and dentists, even scientists and school teachers, seem to be more important. Ministers add a sweet savor to society (and sometimes feelings of a different kind), but they are far from being at the heart of things.

This point of view has become far more pervasive than we ordinarily realize. It is widely held inside the Church, as reflected in clergy salaries, as well as out of it. Although few clergy would agree intellectually with such a formulation, nonetheless this is precisely the way many of us act. For instance, when it comes to valuing ourselves, most of us have avoided the real needs of our being like a plague. We have tried instead to put ourselves into a socially acceptable straitjacket. Yet how are people to value the priesthood, these human beings who are the carriers of the Church's message, if the ministers do not value themselves?

I now view this profession in a very different light. I have come to see that the role of the priest is the most essential in society. Unless we regain our position in the very heart and center of society, I question whether this civilization of ours can hold together and not collapse. The priest is the one who is, or should be, mediator of a vast realm of reality that relates to a spiritual or nonphysical dimension, rather than to the outer physical world, and thus exerts the final and most significant influence for good or evil on human life and destiny. It is this realm that some psychologists have called the unconscious.

Unless we consciously relate to this part of reality, usually only the negative aspects, the demonic element of spiritual reality, break through. What happened in Nazi Germany, in Russia, in Iran, and increasingly on our own streets, is only a foretaste of things to come unless men and women can once again come to a serious consideration of nonphysical reality. Ministers are most urgently needed. They are the ones who should be the experts in this realm, the mediators of it to mankind, just as scientists become the experts who mediate the physical world to us.

This change of attitude began in an attempt to solve some of my own problems, and I became deeply concerned with the psychology of Dr. Jung. There was a time when I was quite hesitant about mentioning the fact that I had become interested because I had personal problems. But as I have come to know more people well, I find that most of us have inner problems just about as difficult as my own. The important consideration is not that people have problems, but what they are doing about them.

This interest in Jung's thought increased as the problems began to disappear. This healing was not brought about by argument and logic. Instead, it was accomplished by an honest sharing of my life with another person, by allowing this relationship to become very real, by an attempt to understand my dreams, by a use of imagination and introspection under guidance and direction, by recording these experiences in a journal, and then by using my best rational powers to make some sense of what happened. Through this experience in analysis I came into contact with parts of my being, with levels and layers within myself that I had never known existed.

I found, first of all, layers of darkness and ugliness from which I had been hiding. But more important, I also found elements wiser than I touching me, impinging upon the depth of my being; these were elements that seemed bent on bringing me to a less one-sided and less neurotic adjustment. In other words, by looking deeply and directly within, I came into contact with positive as well as negative elements of the unconscious. Although they were found "within," these elements can by no means be described as "only psychological." The term *unconscious* is applied to them simply because they are elements of which we had not been aware. But this, of which we shall say more later, does not limit the kind of element that may be perceived, or where it may come from.

As I came into contact with this vast realm of the unconscious that had been troubling me, learned a little about it, and related my life to it, I was amazed and delighted to find problems disappearing. While certainly I became no paragon of maturity, yet there was a real change. Not only did my inner difficulties grow far less intense, but I found myself functioning better than I ever had before. My analysis took the place of spiritual direction, for I could find no spiritual director in the Church who knew both the depth of the human soul or psyche and the spiritual realities that influence it. At the same time there were two very specific results that had a profound effect on my outlook and ministry.

SPECIFIC RESULTS

First of all, once I had begun to handle my own problems, I found that people began knocking at my door with their problems. I hung out no shingle; the way I had come to my new-found knowledge was still an embarrassment. But people can tell when someone among them is trying to deal with the depths of him- or herself. When people begin to seek us out because we understand, it is hard to resist the temptation to move primarily into a counseling ministry. So much of our effort as ministers seems to have little effect in changing lives; the preaching, teaching, and even our sacramental actions appear to touch people so little, and yet one can see individuals changed in intensive, long-range counseling. Priests who have any flair for it may find their time almost totally absorbed in this work.

While taking a rather extensive detour into counseling, I became certain of one thing. It is not wise for the clergy, unless they are in a special situation, to become too deeply involved in long-range, purely psychological counseling. It is not that the clergy are incapable of doing the job, but that they are needed as ministers and mediators. If they abandon this role and its function, for whatever reason, then the priestly role is not expressed, and a function of the greatest importance is left unfulfilled in our society. And there was another, equally important result of my encounter with the unconscious that added conviction to this understanding.

This came as I returned to a consideration of the New Testament, and discovered that everything I learned in analysis was to be found there if I took it seriously. In order to give some talks on the healing ministry of Jesus and the early Church, I began to study the New Testament intensively. I was dumbfounded to realize the depth of insight in it that had escaped me when I studied it before. And I was not the only blind one; the understanding found in Jesus and Paul of the nature of human beings, their view of the depth and complexity of people, were rarely discussed.

It is clear what had happened. In the process of getting rid of my problems, I had had to put away the rationalistic point of view and the essentially materialistic philosophy that had been very much a part of me. In order to get well, I had had to lay these prejudices aside, and once they were at least partially gone, I could listen to the New Testament and hear what it had to say. And this was quite different from what most of contemporary Christianity said about human nature and the universe.

All of the realities experienced in the analytical situation — the same realities Jung had written of from a scientific point of view — were discussed and dealt with in the New Testament. In fact, the very parts of the New Testament that the rationalistic Church had avoided or even denied, for fear of making Jesus look silly, were the interest and concern of Jungian psychologists as they attempted to make sick people well.

Listening seriously to Jesus and Paul, one realizes that they were speaking of a realm of reality that they had experienced when they spoke of God, demons, the devil, angels, the Law, dominions, principalities, and powers. These things were just as real as the physical world — more real, in fact, for they could influence physical reality. They could affect the lives of men and women, corrupting them in sin and sickness, or breaking through in revelations, in visions, dreams, ecstatic utterances and experiences, and in physical and mental healings. Far from considering these things silly, Jung and his followers.

with no special religious interest, but with a passion to heal that allowed them to look in this area for help, had discovered experiences that were a large part of what the New Testament writers were describing. Although Jung called them by other names, the realities were clearly the same. Yet the Church and its priesthood, as I knew them, had avoided coming to know this realm of reality and helping people deal with it.

One of the most important areas the Church has avoided is the whole matter of the healing ministry, which plays such a significant part in the New Testament. (We shall describe it at greater length later on.) This ministry forces us to realize that our minds and bodies can be influenced by another realm of reality, and this means that the spiritual can influence the material, that the nonmaterial is real and can play upon our lives. The healing ministry forces us to take spiritual reality seriously, and we are afraid to deal with this reality, often for good reason. But if Jung is right, this is one real function of the priesthood that is needed today as never before. My analyst friend Hilde Kirsch once commented to me: "You know, Morton, there is no reason that there can't be healing in the Church as well as in the psychologist's office." Let us look at some of Jung's basic understanding.

THE THINKING OF DR. JUNG

Jung's basic premise is that human beings cannot be studied adequately by using the ordinary scientific method. The most important part of us, according to Jung, cannot be objectively verified. Consciousness cannot be directly observed. It can be studied only by listening to what people say goes on in it. But this fact has been ignored by most scientific psychologies. They start by ruling out the most important data about men and women, and so they come up with the most distorted views about people, views which either ignore their religious life entirely or are actively hostile to it.

Jung's views, and his method, were quite different from this. He started with the idea that human beings are somewhat more complex than other things. He observed what people said about their conscious lives, listened to what they expressed about themselves and their actions, and then studied these data scientifically. We shall describe Jung's method and worldview more fully in the next chapter. What is more than a little surprising is the fact that so few intelligent thinking people today have realized the need to observe themselves and other individuals in this way. This failure of most people, church people included, is one indication of how deeply the materialistic ideas of our time have cut into our ability to think about certain things.

Applying this method, Jung learned to free himself to listen objectively, without "scientific" prejudices. He was able to consider empirically what people said about themselves, about their dreams and subliminal experiences. As these data accumulated, he came to the conclusion that the human being has not only a conscious mind (which is even dismissed by some psychologies), but also a personal unconscious in which are deposited forgotten or repressed memories that can be called forth under the right circumstances. In addition, he found experiences of another sort that seemed to cross space and time, and appeared to come from what he called the collective unconscious — from an inner inexhaustible reservoir of psychic reality that impinges upon the human psyche and has a very real influence on it. Freud, in one of his last published papers, came close to the same formulation.

Because this is known through the inner activity of our minds, it is easy to assume that it is just mental activity, a final spinning out of cerebration. But this, Jung found, is anything but true. On the contrary, just as our physical senses bring us into contact with a real, but imperfectly known, external world of matter, so our inner, psychological faculties bring us into touch with a real, but imperfectly known, nonmaterial, nonphysical world. It is called "unconscious" because we are unconscious of it for the most part. Most of the time we are aware only of bits and pieces that often seem foolish to us, unless a larger experience of this world comes through to show that it is far from being our own creation.

While Jung became aware of such experiences early in his practice, he did not investigate this realm out of curiosity, but because he had to in order to help certain neurotically sick people get well. Most often, he found, those who became sick were the very ones who had no way to deal with this part of reality, and they did not recover until they had dealt with it in a satisfactory way. Once the patient had encountered this deep level of reality with the help of the therapist as intermediary, there were often dramatic experiences of the collective unconscious that offered new meaning in their lives, and their health improved, often physically as well as mentally. It was clear that the nonmaterial, the nonphysical realm has a very real effect on the physical world in human beings.

Jung recognized that historically it was the priesthood who helped

humankind deal with such nonmaterial realities, and he also saw that
people had begun to pay a price for trying to live by the material and
the rational alone. They needed a religious approach to this other
reality of spirit. As early as 1928 he made a plea for clergy equipped to
help meet "the urgent psychic needs of our age," adding, "It is indeed
high time for the clergyman and the psychotherapist to join forces to
meet this great spiritual task."[1] Jung suggested to Archbishop Temple
that he send clergy to be trained, but Temple did not see the relevance
of such training.

Jung did not come by this view just "naturally." Starting practice at
the turn of the century, he accepted as axiomatic the rational
materialism of the medical school. Like most of us, he seriously
doubted that any other reality existed. But unlike most of us in the
Church, he looked carefully at his own experiences—particularly his
dreams—as well as those of his patients, and noted their effect on the
outer, conscious life. These experiences forced him to take very
seriously communications coming into the psyche from the deep level
of our being. Among them were certain profound spiritual experiences that had a tremendous effect on his own life.

He also found that such things sometimes happened among his
seriously ill patients—experiences which they were not able to integrate into their lives, but which, because they were deficient in control, they could not shut out and were not ashamed to talk about. Certain of these, as Jung said, "bit him," in particular one vision which a
psychotic patient in a mental hospital in Zurich described and tried to
show him. The man pointed to the sun and, in awed tones, told him to
watch the tube swinging from it, for this was the origin of the wind,
the breath of God. A little later, in a journal inaccessible to the
patient, indeed in a language he did not know, Jung came across a
description of the same vision in practically identical phrases, translated from a mystical Greek papyrus unearthed from the sands of
Egypt.

It is no wonder Jung's eyes were opened. He broadened his studies to
include religion and mythology, and also fairy tales and folklore, finding the same basic images and ideas running through the stories of
diverse peoples having no communication among each other. As
patients began coming to him from all over the world, he found that
similar imaginings, dreams, and visions occurred to many of these
individuals, widely separated by distance, culture, and race. He also
found the same contents in his own dreams.

This variety of experience convinced Jung that when human beings withdraw their attention from exclusive preoccupation with the outer material world, they come into contact with a reality through the inner one. Ordinarily people discovered this other world in their dreams, but it could also be encountered in visions, and Jung helped many of his patients to experience it through a process very similar to religious meditation. I have described this correspondence in my book *The Other Side of Silence*. Thus, although he had started with a definitely negative view of religious reality, his medical and scientific work forced him to see the existence of this part of reality.

He discovered further that individuals, particularly in the second half of life, run the risk of neurosis when they become cut off from this realm of the unconscious, of nonphysical, nonrational reality. In other words, neurosis—which may be caused by many different things—can also result simply from a lack of religious roots, a failure to adjust to the whole of reality. A person may have been adequately reared, may learn and be very successful, without major sexual hang-ups, and still find his life falling to pieces if he has not taken this realm of spiritual being into account. The results in physical as well as mental illness can be just as disastrous as if one had developed a brain tumor. Yet, as Jung found in case after case, such illness is really healed only as the person relates to the realm of spirit and gains a religious outlook on life.

By investigating this world of spirit, Jung has shown that we are affected not only by a physically empirical reality, but also by a religious one. There are penalties for ignoring, for remaining unconscious of these realities that seek expression in us. Today's problems of psychic illness, of drugs and violence, suggest that ministers, if they can become aware of the need to deal with spiritual reality, are called back to a function that has become crucial in our social economy. In a letter written in 1945 to P.W. Martin, Jung wrote: "The main interest of my work is not concerned with the approach to the numinous. But the fact is that the approach to the numinous is the real therapy and inasmuch as you attain to the numinous experiences you are released from the curse of pathology."[2]

WHICH VIEW?

In a world that takes nonmaterial reality seriously and considers this realm very real, there is no doubt that ministers have an important function. They are to know this part of reality, and then mediate it to others. But when we do not seriously believe in the existence of such a sector of reality, where do we leave the priesthood? Being a priest in a universe where the nonmaterial does not exist is like trying to run a water wheel in a dry steam bed. It is more like working in a magnificent Rotarian fellowship, or sometimes an existentialist Browning Society, than in a church.

Unfortunately, we live in a time when most people seriously doubt the existence of any reality beyond that of the material world, or the validity of any knowledge without "objective" verification. Rational materialism has become dogma, not only in Marxism, but, unofficially, on Main Street, U.S.A. This belief is so prevalent that it provides the very intellectual air we breathe. Even the existentialists end by incorporating this very belief, which they set out to refute. In fact, it is almost pitiful when people finally realize that some of us do believe in another realm. They come timidly forward to tell of experiences of the nonphysical that they have had, but were afraid to share for fear of being considered off their rocker.

This timidity is understandable. If there is no nonmaterial reality, or if there exists no way of contact with it, then how can our religion be anything but illusion or a sickness? The psychiatrists who believe only in the rational and material aspect of reality, if they are consistent, are forced to look upon religion in this way. Ministers, holding the same belief, come to deal with ideas about spiritual reality rather than the reality itself, with theology instead of religion, and so they facilitate little transformation. One transmits ideas; the other mediates reality itself. The ideas are ours, and generally influence only those who already agree with us. The spiritual realities are God's, and have the carrying power that comes from and transmits convictions.

Dr. Jung called my attention in a personal conversation to the meaning of the word *conviction*. It comes from the verb "conquer" and means to be conquered by. We cannot argue ourselves into conviction; ideas seldom convince. Instead, we must be brought into the presence of something that conquers us—something of reality, which alone gives true conviction. If the job of the priest is to help people find religious conviction, then this has to come from some reality that can touch individuals. Unless ministers have come to know the reality with which religion is concerned, how can they expect others to take it seriously, let alone be convinced by it themselves?

Jung offers a way by which it is possible for people today to come into contact with such a reality. He gives us moderns a method of confronting and genuinely believing in the realm of spiritual reality, a method that can help us understand the spiritual leaders of other times. Jung's own experience convinced him that these people, far from being deceived or sick, were in fact dealing with a deeper level of reality than ordinary people. It is not the really religious people who are sick, he saw, but the nonreligious, and those whose religion is neurotic and rigid. They are the ones who are out of touch with reality. Jung offers us a way of approaching reality that can help avert much of the neurosis and sickness of modern men and women. It is not important how, as ministers, we learn of this spiritual world, whether by analysis or spiritual direction or overwhelming experience. What is important is that we come to know it, deal with it, and, as mediators, help others to do the same.

Thus the priest and the therapist will both work in this same realm, if they are trying to approach the whole person, but in different ways. Therapists will deal with this area of the unconscious in sick people, using special techniques to improve their relation to it. They cannot avoid the religious dimension if they bring genuine healing. But the same realities also move through the unconscious in more or less healthy people, and the important thing is to find our relation to them in health. The task of priests, then, is to mediate this reality for these more or less healthy people, through word and action, in pastoral contact, sacrament and ritual, and through spiritual direction.[3] In counseling the concern will also be to help the individual recover a healthy contact with spiritual reality when this has been disrupted. And finally, they will be sure enough of their own standpoint to work with doctors and psychologists and support them in their efforts to rid patients of specific psychological and physical ailments.

A knowledge of psychotherapy is a help in the priestly role. It offers ways that enable us to reach people, to evaluate their situations, and also to make more intelligent referrals of the problems that fall outside our function. It is essential in any real spiritual direction. It is valuable to understand the special techniques of the therapist, and to use many of them. But if the priest is to speak with authority of those realities which are the concern of religion, he can hardly take on the role of the permissive and nonvaluing psychological healer as well. Instead of priests who try to do so, or psychologists who try to become religious experts, each profession needs to understand and work with the other.

As priests, however, we need to be quite certain of the difference between being authoritative mediators and being authoritarian or judgmental. There is a big difference between definitely standing up for something and judging, which nearly always has an element of hostility and animosity in it. The clergy can stand for a great deal and still seldom judge.

Indeed, so far as we genuinely know the spiritual realm, just so far can we be secure and accepting of others, free of the need to judge and reject the person who falls short. The clergy who know something real will know also that only by an understanding and accepting attitude can they open other people to this realm. From the psychological professions they can learn much about caring and accepting in concrete practice. The psychologist can help the clergy obey the command of Jesus that we love one another as he has loved us. Still, we cannot pretend that our spiritual realities make no claim upon the individual, or that this realm does not set standards from which a person can fall short.

We have in the New Testament, as one analyst has reminded me, the best handbook on integration or psychological maturity ever written. Taken seriously as it is, and not picked apart, the New Testament is a description of the spiritual world and the encounter with it. The task of dealing with this realm is hard work; it demands the total person. It is also dangerous work; we can be sucked under by this realm of being. Yet this is the task to which the minister is called, the religious task of meeting and drawing life for others from these realities of which Jesus spoke. There is no higher calling, none more needed.[4]

NOTES

1. C.G. Jung, *Collected Works,* Vol. 11 (New York: Pantheon Books, 1958), p. 334. Dr. Jung did not change his view on this subject, as was impressed on me some years after he wrote this, when I had a chance to talk with him and exchange a letter or two.

2. C.G. Jung, *Letters,* Edited by G. Adler, Vol. 1 (Princeton: Princeton University Press, 1973), p. 377.

3. In spiritual direction the clergy will need to work with dreams, visions, and other such experiences, and this is quite possible without becoming analysts. It is a matter of using the same materials for different purposes, much as the builder puts together a house out of the same materials that a chemist might subject to analysis. See my book *Dreams: The Dark Speech of the Spirit* (Garden City, New York: Doubleday & Com-

pany, 1968); also Maria F. Mahoney, *The Meaning in Dreams and Dreaming* (New York: The Citadel Press, 1970). I am planning a longer book on the art of spiritual direction in the near future.

4. John Sanford, in *The Kingdom Within* (Philadelphia and New York: Lippin-cott, 1970) has shown this clearly by underlining the sayings of Jesus on this topic.

Also a short bibliography will be helpful for the interested reader; these books give a background for understanding the religious point of view of Dr. Jung and they should be read in this order.

C.G. Jung, et al., *Man and His Symbols* (Garden City, New York: Doubleday and Company, Inc., 1964); also Dell Publishing Company.

_____, *Analytical Psychology, Its Theory and Practice* (New York: Random House, 1970).

_____, *Memories, Dreams, Reflections,* recorded and edited by Aniela Jaffe (New York: Pantheon Books, 1963).

_____, *Modern Man in Search of a Soul* (New York: Harcourt, Brace & World, 1933).

_____, *Two Essays on Analytical Psychology* (Cleveland: The World Publishing Company, 1936).

_____, *Psychology and Religion: West and East* (Princeton, N.J.: Princeton University Press, 1969).

Chapter 2

JUNG AS PHILOSOPHER AND THEOLOGIAN*

THE contribution of C.G. Jung to medicine, psychology, and anthropology, as well as to our present ability to understand ourselves in depth, is well known. Concepts of his are part of the common vocabulary now used to describe human functioning. There is a growing appreciation of his importance that cuts across academic lines. Yet few people recognize that in still another area Jung made a contribution that may prove equally significant as the twentieth century draws to a close. Jung's thought in the fields of philosophy and theology may well provide these two disciplines a way out of the sterile desert in which they have both been stranded for more than two centuries.

Philosophy and theology are closely linked, despite the thinking of some theologians who keep looking through the wrong end of the binoculars. When philosophy provides human beings with some basis for a relationship with transpersonal meaning (or the "divine"), then the task of theology is within the realm of possibility: it then has the plausible task of exploring and elaborating our relation with that meaning. When philosophy provides no such basis, theology may whistle in the dark or concoct all sorts of intellectual ideas about meaning, but practically no one is taken in, except those who seek authority because of their insecurity. Jung has offered such a basis, and also a method for exploration.

Just how unique is Jung's contribution in this area? To see this in relief, let us review the main developments of modern philosophy, presumptuous as this seems, in a few sentences. (I have described these in

---

*This chapter is a highly technical treatment of theology and philosophy. The reader with no training or interest in these fields can go on to the next chapter, which is more practical in nature.

greater length in my book *Encounter With God*.) Starting with the skeptical certainty of Descartes, backed up by the Enlightenment, philosophers gradually came to place great confidence in our reason and in our knowledge of the world around us. By the nineteenth century this point of view had solidified into dogma, a dogma that the material alone was real and that it developed through rational and mechanical laws that would eventually be understood *in toto*. We were prisoners in this closed and unalterable system, since our psyche was merely an epiphenomenal by-product, "nothing but" the result of this material process.

Since then most philosophy has been an attempt to support or attack this dogma. Popular thinkers, from Comte to Marx and Skinner, developed the implications of this point of view. Hegel, on the other hand, tried to support the autonomy of "mind" and the "idea" by viewing the entire experienced world as a manifestation of mind. But with no place for the individual, Hegel's "ideal" system left us as much prisoners of an unvarying order as we had been in the materialistic system.

Kierkegaard and the existentialists who followed him reacted violently. Realizing that our unique individuality was lost in Hegel's magnificent dialectic, they turned attention to the individual, but without questioning the idea that the human being was caught in a closed, physical system. Since they saw no way for extraneous meaning to break through, all they could offer was a blind jump of faith in the tension of dread and anxiety. The lead of Hegel was picked up again by Edmund Husserl in the effort to base a whole philosophy (phenomenology) on the logical presuppositions of the conscious intentional act. Husserl saw no way by which we could reach meaning except through intellectual analysis.

Meanwhile, philosophers in Britain took a different tack. Building on the genius of Wittgenstein, Russell, and Whitehead, they developed a school of empiricism in which logic was seen as tautological. It could bring no new knowledge; rather, they saw all knowledge as derived from empirical observations. Since one never knows with logical certainty what new experience will bring, all knowledge is only probable and hypothetical. They did not deny that we might have other levels of experience than sense experience. But by pushing aside any other possibilities, they wrote off moral theory, metaphysics, and theology with a stroke of the pen.[1]

All of these major schools of philosophy deny that we have any significant immediate relationship with a meaningful reality that transcends this rational space-time world. Therefore, theology is hard put to justify itself, and intelligent modern men and women look in vain to find any substantial meaning in their lives. It is at this point that Jung enters the picture.

Jung did not become interested in philosophical questions out of theoretical curiosity, but for a very practical reason. Intelligent people came to him who were sick for no apparent reason, and yet were unable to reason themselves out of the sickness. They were suffering from psychological distress, as well as a host of physical symptoms that resulted at least in part from this distress. As we have mentioned before, Jung discovered that loss of meaning could itself result in exactly this kind of sickness. Being a committed physician, he set about to heal this neurotic illness by finding some meaning that could fill the gap that the absence of traditional religion left in these lives.

In this task Jung was singularly successful. He was particularly well qualified for it; he had been trained in the most rigorous scientific method, he had a competence in historical philosophy shared by few psychologists and scientists, and he had a wealth of empirical data about human beings and meaning. He also enjoyed the practical undertaking, and in it he laid the foundations for a new philosophical and theological understanding. At the same time he was participating in the growth of a new attitude within the scientific community itself.

Early in the twentieth century, awareness was growing that the outlook of nineteenth-century rational materialism was too narrow to take in the data becoming known about our world. Through the work of Becquerel and the Curies, of Planck, Heisenberg and others, the substantial atom exploded into an increasing number of particles that could not be understood on the basis of Newtonian mechanics. Einstein, in one of the greatest intuitions of this age, came to the conclusion that space might not be Euclidian in nature, and his studies of the speed of light brought a new concept of time. The whole conception of time and matter and scientific truth were going through a traumatic change. The scientific method had not produced final and certain truths after all, but hypotheses that could be overturned by new research and replaced with new understanding. Scientific "laws" could no longer be seen as ultimate truths; they were like maps, increasingly accurate, but still only maps of a territory that could never be fully known.

In biology and paleontology it was found that the idea of survival of the fittest does not always fit the facts, and that the relation between genetic factors and what Darwin observed appears to be directed in too complex a way to express without some idea of purpose. Thus, through thinking about evolution, the idea of teleology was reintroduced into the study of human beings. Pierre Teilhard de Chardin has drawn this point of view with brilliance and clarity in his many books.

From a medical standpoint, it has become increasingly clear that we can no longer be treated as a passive assortment of physical parts, operating in a purely material environment. Our hopes and fears, even hopes and fears about transcendental things, can well alter the whole course of an illness. This thesis was first suggested by Dr. Flanders Dunbar in her scholarly study, *Emotions and Bodily Changes,* and then by Dr. Jerome Frank in his equally well documented *Persuasion and Healing,* and recently by James Lynch in *The Broken Heart.*

This thinking has not taken hold generally, however. It has begun to make a deep impression on the philosophy of science, but the idea that these new conceptions may have a relation to our own lives, and to our finding meaning in this universe, has not occurred to many philosophers. Jung stands nearly alone in his effort to demonstrate that our experiences actually do bridge this gap.

JUNG AND MODERN THOUGHT

One great contribution of analytical psychology to modern thought is that it finds a direct, inner verification of the findings of the other natural sciences. Jung has described from direct encounter the processes that Teilhard de Chardin and others described from the outside. Building quite consciously on the work of Janet, Charcot, and Freud, Jung began to record the contents of an unconscious stratum of personality that was disclosed through neurotic disturbances, human error, intuitions, and most significantly, through the dream. He carefully sketched out an empirical framework in which purely psychic, unconscious experiences were given the same *value* as experiences of the physical world.

A second contribution of Jung was his realization that theories of the unconscious were as difficult to accept from a nineteenth-century worldview, as difficult to understand, as theories of quantum mechanics. In fact, Jung often drew attention to the analogy between quantum mechanics and depth psychology. He realized that in taking the unconscious seriously as an operative part of the human personality, he was breaking with both Western philosophy and the popular psychological tradition of Wundt, in which the psyche was viewed only from the standpoint of consciousness. He was prepared to support his position.

While he did not write a great deal about his methods or philosophical presuppositions, he was well aware of them, and they were clearly formulated. In various places in his writings he spoke of the relation of historical and current philosophy to his approach. His findings were presented within a careful and critical philosophical framework, which is seldom found among empirical scientists today. In addition, he had the knowledge and the interest to do an adequate job.

To begin with, Jung quite frankly accepted a philosophical realism, the organic realism of modern science with its empirical emphasis. He anticipated the work of Wittgenstein, Ayer, Carnap, and Popper, who have come to understand that human reason alone can bring no new knowledge, but only possibilities, which must be verified in experience.

But Jung did not limit his empiricism to sense experience alone — to that which can be objectively verified in a physical sense. In studying personal encounters with the autonomous unconscious, he applied basically the same test as the physical sciences: How does it work? What is the result in the individual? Does it recur? Father Hostie has described this empiricism at some length in *Religion and the Psychology of Jung*, defining Jung's method as "nonexperimental empiricism." Jung was fond of remarking that in scientific experiments the scientist asks the question, while in clinical practice the patient and nature ask it, and that it is not hard to see which asks the more difficult questions. Scientific experiment gives carefully defined data about a small area of nature. Jung's method gives less defined data about the nature of the human being, data we need for survival.[2]

Jung also accepted quite consciously Kant's basic idea that we have contact with two kinds of phenomenal experience, one related to the objective, external world, the other to the subjective or psychic world. To Kant, however, the subjective was exhausted by consciousness, while Jung dealt with the phenomena of an expanded subjective world, which included unconscious contents and processes. And this large component — perhaps the major component — was made up of contents that were not always as personally subjective as they might appear. They were experienced subjectively—as, after all, our experiences of the physical world are experienced—but they often seemed to come into the personal psyche from outside itself.

Thus Jung maintained that we have contact with an objectively real physical world, which of necessity is experienced subjectively, and an equally real world of autonomous psychic contents, which are experienced directly, inwardly, and subjectively. Both of these experiences give only phenomenal knowledge. Neither kind gives final, apodictic (or logically certain) knowledge of the "thing-in-itself," but only what can become known through its reaction with the subject. But this phenomenal knowledge can be made more certain as more attention is directed to the phenomena themselves. Either the physical object or the objective psychic contents that Jung described can become known through experience. What Jung wrote to me in 1958 summarizes his understanding as well as any of his writings; in this letter he said:

The real nature of the objects of human experience is still shrouded in darkness. The scientists cannot concede a higher intelligence to Theology than to any other branch of human cognition. We know as little of a Supreme Being as of Matter. But there is as little doubt of the existence of a Supreme Being as of Matter. The world beyond is a reality, an experiential fact. We only don't understand it.[3]

The failure of most people to realize that he was talking about the experience of contents that influence the psyche, not merely subjective ideas, exasperated Jung. When I was visiting him, a proof copy of a book titled *Jung and St. Paul* lay on his coffee table, and I asked him what he thought of it. His only reply was that the author had failed to grasp this most elementary point. As a practical matter, it is impossible to understand Jung merely by reading him, but only by dealing directly with the realities of which he has written.

In fact, one of Jung's important statements was that "Natural science is not a science of words and ideas, but of facts."[4] Let us look for a moment at how physical scientists handle these facts. They do not question the fact that they are "only" empirical observations, the experiences someone has had with matter. They ask what they mean, and then by induction or analogy, or often intuitive insight, they make an educated guess—the hypothesis that they proceed to test. In this way they formulate a theory that takes all the facts into relationship. Each new experience that does not fit requires an expanded or often an entirely new theory. One inconsistent fact, small enough to be overlooked by most observers, may even require whole new worldview. It is at this point that imagination is most needed. A new vision is required that must be tested through logic and pure mathematics. This may require a change in one's hypothesis (one's vision) and then more testing with logic and mathematics.

Changes in hypothetical construction are probably easiest to see by looking at a nutshell outline of our growing understanding of matter. From experiences of distinct atomic properties came the idea of hard little balls of matter. At the same time, as a result of the observations of Copernicus and Kepler, the same laws were seen to govern matter in the microcosm as among the planets, according to Newtonian mechanics. Then came the developments we have spoken of, which began in 1896 when Becquerel was looking for light-induced radiation and instead found his sealed photographic plates mysteriously exposed by a substance that had not even seen the light. This was followed by the experiments of the Curies, Rutherford, and others, and the work of Planck, Einstein, Bohr, Meitner, Fermi . . . and the blast. It was brought home to most people that matter does not always conform to the laws of Newtonian mechanics. A new hypothesis was needed.

Jung, who began his work a few years later, came upon his evidence almost as unexpectedly as Becquerel. He listened to the people who came to him for healing, and found that unconscious contents were pushing towards the threshold of consciousness. Many of these people were practical scientists who had neglected the whole area of feeling and unconscious experience. As they encountered these unconscious contents and dealt with them consciously, they not only found healing, but their experiences often involved strange elements of mythology and extrasensory perception. In many instances it was through experiences of this nature that a patient began to find meaning and new energy. Thus Jung was led to make careful studies of mythology and dream symbols, synchronicity, and other such experiences.

This new and detailed knowledge of the unconscious — coming from the most complex pieces of matter, human beings — showed that a new hypothesis was needed to understand both consciousness and the unconscious, and their relation to the material world. The older theories were no longer adequate, and Jung suggested a new hypothesis that stepped beyond the deterministic naturalism of the nineteenth century. The implications of his theory were both philosophical and theological.

Jung's direction had the support of a strong pragmatic bent in his thinking. He believed that electing a course of action that results in permanent healing, in human wholeness, comes closest to living with reality as it is. Jung was much influenced by James' pragmatism; he knew James' writings well and often quoted him. In pragmatism there is a further hypothesis, which Jung accepted, that life is more than just a chance and meaningless epiphenomenon. If there is ultimate meaning in the universe, and if our life expresses a high level or stage of that meaning, then what furthers and develops human life is likely to correspond to the meaning of the universe. Living life as fully and completely as possible is then likely to express something true about the world in which we live. Jung offered the theory that nature is meaningful in itself, and then adduced volumes of evidence from the inner life of human beings to corroborate this thesis.

His approach was also reinforced by experiences of unconscious contents that were not merely primitive and atavistic. The unconscious offers understandings that can be superior to those produced by consciousness, although they are usually expressed in images rather than abstract concepts. In the introduction to *Symbols of Transformation*, Jung carefully differentiated the two kinds of thinking of which we are capable — the directed, conceptual thinking characteristic of most logic, scientific demonstrations, mathematics, and philosophy, and the intuitive, symbolic and right brain "thinking" that comes from the unconscious. It is by this thinking in images that we convey our deepest meanings, particularly our emotional meaning. Art, drama, liturgy, folktales, mythology, all use archetypal images, and each night the dream also presents its meaning in symbols and pictures. Most of us, however, have lost touch with the capacity to think symbolically, and so we fail to understand either our myths or our dreams.

MAPPING A NEW UNDERSTANDING

If Jung's evidence for the unconscious is taken seriously, then we clearly have need for a new understanding of the total world of experience and of our place within that world. The hypothesis that Jung offers is very different from the materialistic rationalism that has swept the house bare for most of us. Instead, it finds us faced with an

experiential dualism. From this point of view, we are not only confronted with the objective reality of a physical world, but we are also
given experience which relates to the objective, autonomous reality of
a psychic world, and we ourselves are bridges between these two worlds
of experience. He also finds a nonconscious organizing function at
work within the unconscious, in addition to rational consciousness.

Through these unconscious contents and meanings, Jung found, we
are presented with a vast psychic world, as objectively real, as
meaningful and experienceable as the material and physical world,
and not reducible to the physical. In this view he came very close to
Plato's understanding of "the ideas," which Jung saw not as eternal
concepts, however, but rather as the philosophical version of his
"psychically concrete" archetypes.[5] He further agreed in principle
with Plato that we do not come to know and experience the realm of
"the ideas" through the exercise of reason, but only through irrational
means like those Plato described as prophecy, dreams, healing, art,
and love. Indeed, in "Psychology of the Transference,"[6] and in the last
pages of *Memories, Dreams, Reflections,* Jung expressed his appreciation of the cognitive value of love in a way very similar to Plato's
understanding.

This point of view can be shown in a model or schema like this:

A MODEL OR SCHEMA

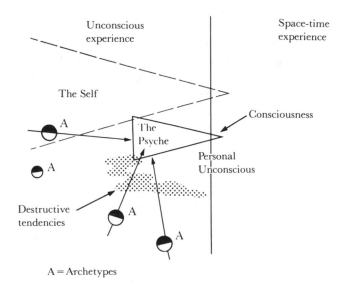

A = Archetypes

The two realms both present us with valid *phenomenal* experience. Either one can be understood better and better as we open ourselves to more and more significant experiences, and then let our rational and analytical capacities play upon them. Both are worlds of great complexity. The human psyche itself is based in the unconscious realm. "The self" (dotted lines, open-ended) represents those creative and suprapersonal contents that are so meaningful for human development. The destructive tendencies (shaded) are those described, for instance, in Jung's account of his encounter with the unconscious in Chapter VI of *Memories, Dreams, Reflections*. A few of the possible archetypes are shown, presenting both creative and destructive aspects. All of these realities impinge upon the psyche, with consciousness usually directed towards the outer physical world.

Such a diagram obviously has as many faults as a word-picture of a theory. It is oversimplified and maps the territory about as adequately as an oil engineer's map of Colorado shows what the Rocky Mountains are like. But it does try to represent the most developed points of Jung's philosophical thinking in a form that shows where to look for significant data. With some supplemental designations, it also suggests quite clearly the implications of Jung's thinking for philosophy and theology.

If Jung has mapped the territory correctly, then we are indeed in touch with complex realities that we cannot handle physically, which can only be known as we have the courage to encounter this other realm and try to understand and be understood by it. In fact, Jung's thinking can provide a philosophical basis for a modern, experiential theology, just as Plato's worldview provided such a framework for the Church fathers to express their Christian experiences. This Platonic base lasted for the first twelve centuries in the West and is still the basis of Eastern Orthodox thinking.

Religious people in all ages and among all peoples have spoken of a "spiritual world" apart from the physical world. As one of the greatest modern physicists, Werner Heisenberg, has reminded us, words like these, which come from the natural language, may well express a more direct connection with reality than the most precise abstractions of science.[7] Since Jung's evidence also shows that there is such a realm in which human beings have come into contact with a meaning superior to human consciousness, it appears that the idea of God is not metaphysical speculation, but rather the name which religious people

have applied to their experience of such a reality. In Jung's worldview
the religious undertaking and the religious object are not only po-
tentially meaningful, but necessary if we are to survive. Jung has laid
the foundation, and empirical theologians can build upon that base.

Two of Jung's own statements, late in his work, clearly point out
what we have sketched. In the first he wrote:

> I have, therefore, even hazarded the postulate that the phenomenon of
> archetypal configurations — which are psychic events *par excellence* — may be
> founded upon a *psychoid* base, that is, upon an only partially psychic and
> possibly altogether different form of being. For lack of empirical data I have
> neither knowledge nor understanding of such forms of being, which are com-
> monly called spiritual. From the point of view of science, it is immaterial what
> I may *believe* on that score, and I must accept my ignorance. . . . Neverthe-
> less, we have good reason to suppose that behind this veil there exists the un-
> comprehended absolute object which affects and influences us — and to
> suppose it even, or particularly, in the case of psychic phenomena about
> which no verifiable statements can be made.[8]

The second, the remark Jung made in his British Broadcasting
Company interview, is almost too well known to be repeated, but it
crystallizes all the other ways he tried to express this: "Suddenly I
understood that God was, for me at least, one of the most certain and
immediate experiences . . . I do not believe; I know. I *know.*" Philosophically Jung presents a consistent pragmatic realism built on a phenomenological base that can deal with religious experience.

Jung also suggested that empirical theologians take the problem of
evil more seriously. His experience made him balk at the Aristotelian
position that evil is only the absence or deprivation of good — the
privatio boni — with good naturally belonging to man, and so he had
to meet this problem directly. He dealt with it as creatively as any one
in our time, and set the stage for further theological encounter.

He would have agreed with the author of Ephesians: "For our fight
is not against human foes, but . . . against the superhuman forces of
evil in the heavens."[9] We have to wrestle with our darkness to find out
its nature, and then either integrate or reject it. Jung believed that the
doctrine of the *privatio boni,* first laid down for the Church by Augustine, and later developed by Aquinas, crippled us in this struggle. It
deceived us about the seriousness of this struggle. "The growing
awareness of the inferior part of the personality," Jung wrote, "should
not be twisted into an intellectual activity, for it has far more the

meaning of a suffering and a passion that implicate the whole man."[10] Dealing with unconscious contents or with God can be a painful process, a *via crucis* that most will avoid at any cost. This emphasis on the reality of evil and creative suffering has much in common with the teaching of Jesus of Nazareth. We shall deal with this further in the next chapter.

There is another very important element, if anything, the crucial element. This process of dealing with the unconscious or the spiritual world is not a process characterized by detachment and lack of personal involvement. One does not get far by detached objectivity. Nor does one need worry about God's being reduced in stature by familiarity. Furthermore, this encounter is seldom possible outside of a deep concern for another person involved in the same encounter.

In one of the concluding paragraphs of his autobiography, Jung all but stated outright that only as we give in to love can we know the way of wholeness, and thus the reality of the self, or of God. Love for Jung was as much the powerful, revealing daemon as it was for Plato. For most people the process of coming to creative relationship with the unconscious involves the whole person in contact with another human being. The process of integration requires and results in deepened human relationships. John put it well in his first letter in the New Testament when he said that none of us could love God who did not love the sister or the brother. Allowing ourselves to have this kind of relationship is a costly experience. Often, if we are capable of it, we will find ourselves deluged, because we all hunger for this kind of reality. We will also find more material for theological reflection than we can integrate and develop in less than a lifetime. The time is ripe for philosophers and theologians to take up the task that Jung has made possible and has shown is necessary for modern men and women.

We also need people, lay and clergy, who have made this encounter and have come to an *understanding* of it. These can be priests and ministers, spiritual directors who can accompany others on the spiritual quest. There is no greater need in the Church today than for people with this kind of experience and understanding.

NOTES

1. See A.J. Ayer, *Language, Truth and Logic* (New York: Dover Publications, 1952), for a brilliant exposition of this theory.

2. See Raymond Hostie, *Religion and the Psychology of Jung* (New York: Sheed & Ward, 1957), pp. 9 ff.

3. The full text of this letter is found in *C.G. Jung: Letters*, Vol. 2, 1951–1961, ed. by G. Adler and A. Jaffe (Princeton, N.J.: Princeton University Press, 1974), pp. 434 ff.

4. C.G. Jung, *Collected Works*, Vol. 16, p. 317; see also p. 303.

5. C.G. Jung, *Collected Works*, Vol. 8, p. 191.

6. C.G. Jung, *Collected Works*, Part II of Vol. 16.

7. Werner Heisenberg, *Physics and Philosophy: The Revolution in Modern Science* (New York: Harper & Row, 1958), pp. 200 ff.

8. C.G. Jung, *Memories, Dreams, Reflections*, recorded and edited by Aniela Jaffe (New York, Pantheon Books, 1963), pp. 351 f.

9. *The New English Bible*, Ephesians 6:12.

10. C.G. Jung, *Collected Works*, Vol. 8, p. 208.

Chapter 3

JUNG AND THE THEOLOGICAL DILEMMA

Some of us whose memories go back a ways have wondered how Carl Gustav Jung, with the education he received, could have become the kind of doctor and thinker he actually became. Medical training in the German and Swiss schools was excellent, but dominated by the attitudes of positivism. Not much was really important in people but the material facts, which could be handled with scientific objectivity. The religions of humankind represented only a primitive stage in development, long since replaced by metaphysical beliefs. And now that these were being relinquished for the certainty of science (the nineteenth-century brand) we were tasting the ultimate goal of intellectual development. This framework did not leave much room for ideas like Jung's about the individual, let alone individual commitment and growth in religious life.

When I asked Jung how he had escaped being taken over by this point of view, he told me that he had indeed been infected by it. But then he was "bitten" by the experience of the schizophrenic patient that we described in the first chapter—an experience of knowledge coming seemingly without access to it—and this made him realize that there are facts for which a rigid scientific naturalism does not allow. The very methods of science at that time excluded certain essential data, and he had to formulate a more hypothetical view of science, one quite similar to the one so well stated by Stephen Toulmin in his book *The Philosophy of Science*.

For as long as he could remember, Jung had been interested in religious ideas and experiences, as his autobiography reveals. His doctoral thesis was concerned with religious phenomena. The break with Freud was caused largely by their disagreement over Freud's refusal to consider religious data. As Jung's own practice grew, he realized more and more the importance of these factors.

Jung was consulted by people from all over the world. He summarized the importance of meaning to them in these words, which have been more widely quoted than anything else he ever wrote:

> Among all my patients in the second half of life — that is to say, over thirty-five — there has not been one whose problem in the last resort was not that of finding a religious outlook on life. It is safe to say that every one of them fell ill because he had lost that which the living religions of every age have given to their followers, and none of them has been really healed who did not regain his religious outlook.[1]

If Jung were writing now rather than forty years ago, he would also speak of the people in their early twenties who are caught in the same bind. Much of the neurotic distress that I see among college students is the result of having lost religious faith. Their neurosis is often a religious experience in reverse. The traditional faith no longer speaks to these students, and no one offers anything else. This group — a large and significant one — is ready to work with counselors who can bring our religious tradition into focus with reality. They sometimes wonder why so few have shown an interest in their need.

After World War II, Jung spoke out again, even more clearly:

> Everything now depends on man: immense power of destruction is given into his hand, and the question is whether he can resist the will to use it, and can temper his will with the spirit of love and wisdom. He will hardly be capable of doing so on his own unaided resources. He needs the help of an "advocate" in heaven, that is, of the child who was caught up to God and who brings the "healing" and making whole of the hitherto fragmentary man.[2]

It is not only those who must avoid neurosis who need meaning. There are men and women everywhere who need the same meaning, if we are to control our destructive aggressiveness and survive at all.

In his last twenty years, after a near brush with death and an overpowering vision that followed, his primary interest was in studying those human experiences that are called religious. During this period his goal was to present the data about religion in such a way that it could reach and touch educated men and women in the Western world, particularly those in the medical and scientific professions.

Certainly religion was a central interest of this medical man, who had one of the great minds of all time. For nearly thirty-five years I have worked with Jung's thought and his method, and for longer than that I have been delving into religious questions, particularly the Christian ones. Dr. Jung's thought and practice did something for me that no other approach had accomplished. It let down a barrier that had kept me from exploring the treasure house of my own Christian heritage, and over the years I have found that it did the same for many others who were boxed in by their single-track education. In fact, I have seen the "faith" that most Christians only talk about awakened in my own and other lives.

But at the same time I have been forced to struggle with the fact that this fresh outlook is not shared by many theologians today. Instead, Christian thinkers often find that Jung turns them off. So, let us first look at this reaction, and at certain of Jung's own shortcomings that may provoke it. We shall then consider his specific contributions to religious thought and practice, and how they can be presented to educated people today. Jung's thinking has much to offer higher education in religion, as well as providing guidelines for training pastoral counselors and spiritual directors.

JUNG AND CHRISTIAN DOCTRINE

Almost at the outset Jung's writings began to attract the interest of Christian thinkers. But it was a divided interest. Even though it was easy to see how different his ideas were from those of Freud and behaviorism, they often attracted as much hostility as interest, and sometimes even more. Many professional religionists reacted as though Jung were trespassing in their private park. At the same time, Jung did have a place for religion, and some thinkers found in him the answer to the religious dilemma. Finally, there were others who simply acknowledged that they found his ideas too difficult to follow. James Heisig, formerly at Notre Dame and now at Cambridge, reviewed more than four hundred discussions of Jung's religious thought. He concluded that the "scholarship on the borderlands between theology and archetypal psychology has grown tired." This study is now published as a book, *Imago Dei*.

What is it that makes Jung difficult for Christian theologians to understand? There are at least three significant reasons for this. First of all, Jung was not systematic. He seldom summarized his thinking, or gathered everything he wrote on a topic together. This is particularly true of his religious thought, which is scattered throughout his autobiography and the twenty volumes of his collected works. In addition, one has to know something of the development of his thought to be sure which statements represent his mature thinking. He rarely corrected an earlier point of view once he had moved beyond it, and so the casual reader can be completely misled. Raymond Hostie's book *Religion and the Psychology of Jung* does a real service by sketching his development.

Most theologians, on the other hand, attempt to be systematic. It is small wonder that they sometimes find Jung's writings almost a morass of unconnected ideas. For a theology that sees itself as merely a systematic and rational organization of religious concepts (and this is a great deal of modern theology) Jung has little to offer, because his most valuable suggestions have to do with religion as an actual encounter with religious realities. He may have even felt that these experiences do not lend themselves to systematizing.

Another difficulty lies with Jung's theological reflections. Sometimes he states them carefully, as a scientist presenting a hypothetical point of view, and then he suddenly steps out with an almost dogmatic set of pronouncements. When he writes about religious experience, he usually avoids this problem, but in writing philosophically and theologically about Christian doctrine, his lack of finesse becomes apparent. Or again, sometimes a poetic outburst of active imagination like his *Answer to Job* is seen as theological reflection. David Burrell has commented astutely on this problem in the last chapter of his book *Exercises in Religious Understanding*.

So Jung comes in for much deserved theological criticism. The tragedy is that many Christian thinkers seize on this failure of Jung and fail to consider the significance of the data he presents, or his evaluation of it.

The most important reason for the misunderstanding, however, is not *Jung's* problem; it is the theologians' almost complete failure to grasp the point of view from which he speaks. As I pointed out in the first two chapters, most theology is still caught in the framework of nineteenth-century science. It is still operating from a naturalistic view of humanity and the world—a view that has lasted from the Enlightenment almost to the present—and is still reacting to the atheism of that time. For this reason, most theologians cannot conceive of religious experience as valuable and significant data for shaping a worldview. What Jung says about these experiences goes into the same old kettle of theological stew, and is interpreted in a context in which it has little meaning.

Thus many of these men and women who are very much involved in seminaries and higher education today, particularly in shaping our ideas about religion, fail entirely to see his real significance. They do not see that he offers the young person in the university or the educated adult living in today's world an understanding of religion that can bring meaning to his or her own life and experiences, both individually and within the Christian framework. What Jung offers is a way of springing the trapdoor into real Christian experience and faith. And those who work with today's students and adults in midlife crisis can hardly avoid the fact that this is needed.

JUNG'S CONTRIBUTION TO RELIGIOUS THOUGHT

Advanced education in religion has certainly had little to offer in recent years. If forecasting has been called the dismal science, higher education in religion might be called the vacuous or absent science. It was just in this area—of understanding religion—that Jung made some of his most valuable and most needed contributions. He fills a gap that most thinkers have avoided. First of all, he provided a philosophical framework in which religious data can be entertained and discussed. Jung was one of the most sophisticated thinkers in modern psychology. He was also well acquainted with many of the physical scientists who brought about the new revolution in modern scientific thought.

Thus he was not taken by surprise as the realization grew that all scientific knowledge is hypothetical and lacking in certainty. Instead, it was clear that facts could not be eliminated simply because they were rarely seen or obscure. If physics was forced to consider the exploding atoms of Becquerel and Mme. Curie, then the data even closer to us human beings also had to be taken into account. And these religious facts required a new hypothesis about the nature of the universe; they strongly suggested that we are not confined to a space-time box.

Students, who are far from naive, can begin to understand religion from this point of view—even, or particularly, those trained in the rigorous disciplines of science. Discussing religious data in this way makes sense to them when Thomistic or existential or process theology formulations fail to get much response. For my own part, when I finally understood Jung's method of study, I could see the importance of the rare but significant religious experiences that I encountered in myself and others (and those who have used psychedelic drugs do not need a diploma to have such experiences). I could also understand the New Testament and the Platonic Christianity of the early Church. Jung's hypothetical framework makes possible an experimental and experiential theology, which can reach men and women educated in today's thought.

The same thing is true of his concept of the *self*. He maintains that a purpose other than that of the human ego is observable in one's experiences of the psychoid world. Although Jung's discussions of the *self* have been much misunderstood, this is probably the most significant concept he offered to religious thought. After examining his own inner experiences and those of thousands of his patients, Jung concluded that we can observe a reality coming into the psyche and organizing its experiences, meshing them creatively with human life. This reality, which he later suggested is very probably the same teleological force that organizes the universe, appears in the psyche as an archetypal image. Therefore it can be observed empirically in our inner experience. As Jung insisted, it is there in the psyche, to be seen by anyone who takes the trouble, just as all observers could have seen the moons revolving around Jupiter if they had been willing to look through Galileo's telescope. But only a careful analysis of Jung's statements about the *self* reveals that he is referring to an outer, objective reality, *as well as* to an inner, psychic one.

Thus Jung maintains that we can experience the central reality of which all the living religions of humankind speak. Most of Jung's later books were written to give the best available evidence for this conclusion; *Psychology and Alchemy*, *Aion*, and *The Mysterium Coniunctionis* deal mainly with it. If this conclusion is correct, then the reality known to Christian thought as the Holy Spirit can be experienced and observed. From the Christian point of view, this reality became incarnate in Jesus Christ, and so a study of his life gives a picture of the nature of this reality. While some Christian thinkers fear that considering God so objectively will put him on the dissecting table, I find that perceptive students and inquiring adults recognize that it is God who analyzes and dissects in these experiences—not the other way around. Even so, they welcome some way of knowing this reality. I have found few others who offer the opportunity.

There is another important area in which I find many modern seekers appreciate Jung's work. He dealt directly with the problem of evil as few modern thinkers have done. Besides the fact that a psychotherapist can hardly avoid this problem, Jung searched his own psyche and found that it revealed a terrifying confrontation with evil and destructiveness, as well as with creative purposefulness. He met the same reality again and again in his patients and, in a sense, struggled with this reality in them. Finally, he observed two world wars in which evil ran rampant around the mountain island of Switzerland. From these experiences he concluded that we are subject not only to personal and collective evil, which we can often assimilate; but there is also an archetypal or cosmic evil that invades us and can only be resisted.

Jung saw our destructive aggressiveness largely as a failure to deal with evil, particularly metaphysical evil, so that it is projected out in hatred upon other people and countries. According to him we wrestle with a metaphysical evil, which can be dealt with only if we can summon a power greater than the human ego to our aid. Jung's language is very much like that of Jesus, Paul, and the early Church. Thus he gives practical, psychological meaning to the classical doctrine of salvation. As we shall soon see, he also provides methods of invoking this saving power.

He also attacked the doctrine of the *privatio boni*—the idea that evil is only the absence of good—concluding that when we do not take evil seriously, we usually fail to deal with it. And this failure puts Western civilization in jeopardy unless we are willing to face both our own shadows and the cosmic evil that, it seems, wishes to possess us. Recent theology has had little place for evil as a reality; within a rationalistic system, evil is simply untruth, because it does not make sense rationally. Still, as Jung asks, how can Dachau and Buchenwald be considered an accidental lack of perfection? Many highly intelligent people who were undergoing difficulties have been grateful to Jung because his understanding *does* make some sense of their harrowing experience, and this often paves the way to a Christian understanding of salvation. Jung offers real experience in a way that is com-

municable and intellectually stimulating. However, in dealing with
the problem of evil Jung is most confusing, and many different statements can be found in his works. John Sanford's book *Evil, The
Shadow Side of Reality* deals with Jung's inconsistencies at length.
Nonetheless, sophisticated theologians like David Burrell and John
Dunne have found Jung suggestive, and those faced with loss of meaning in every age group are touched by him when they run into a blank
wall in most traditional theology.

JUNG'S CONTRIBUTIONS TO RELIGIOUS PRACTICE

Besides these contributions, Jung also searched for ways of encountering and dealing with the realities found in the psyche, and in
the process he rediscovered ways of praying and meditating that had
once been central religious practices. He came to believe, like the
fathers of the Church, that at times the dream could present an experience of the world beyond human consciousness, the spiritual
world, which Jung called the objective psyche or psychoid world.

Indeed, it was because of the suggestions offered by Jung that I began to take these Christian practices seriously. Using quiet, silence,
imagination, and dream analysis not only helped me out of the intellectual and emotional box in which I had found myself, but these
practices gave me intimations of a whole realm of reality about which
I had had little instruction in the seminary. I found his suggested use
of a journal of immeasurable help, as so many devotional masters have
suggested. These efforts led me to write *The Other Side of Silence*, a
book on Christian meditation, and *Adventure Inward*, a book on
Christian journal keeping. Others have taken his advice to paint or
model in clay, with equally satisfying results. Walter Wink's book
Transforming Bible Study puts all these suggestions into a useful and
workable method for Bible study. There is no better handbook for the
teacher of transforming Christianity.

Through my own use of these practices, prayer and meditation became real and important to me. And I have seen this happen often
enough in other lives to be sure that many people have similar needs,
particularly today's students and seekers. Many modern men and
women are reacting against the materialism of their parents, and
Jung's methods, used in the way he spoke of them, provide a way of
finding meaning that even the most sophisticated can and will use.

Certainly they are safer and have more creative results than the indiscriminate use of drugs. The dream provides a trip that is as engaging as and more creative than drugs.

Jung contributed something else to Christian practice that can temper, and help to sustain, the enthusiasm of the practicer. This is the realism of his insistence that dealing with the depth of the psyche is not something that everyone can, or necessarily should, undertake. It is like opening Pandora's box, and there are costs to be paid, as Baron von Hugel used to say. For the person who must hold to the inner way, and deal with the depths of psychoid reality, the toll has to be paid in creative suffering. Jesus said again and again that we have to lose our lives in order to gain them, and that those who would follow his way must pick up their crosses and follow him. So seldom do we ask enough of those who would go the inner way.

This emphasis is not on suffering for the sake of suffering, however. It is a process of transformation, which can only come through death and resurrection, a way of individuation which is steep and narrow simply because that is the fact. Indeed, Jung, for one, complained angrily to God about this difficulty in the *Answer to Job*. Realistically, how can we help questioning a good God who allows destructive evil in our world? I have dealt with this question in my book *Discernment*.

Christianity has often erred by making the Christian way either too hard or too easy. Certainly an intellectual faith, which demands only the application of thought, does not lead to the kind of reality with which Jacob wrestled at the brook of Jabbok, where the angel both wounded and blessed him. Jung's approach is to offer wise counsel, both about the goal, and also about the difficulties, the pitfalls, and dangers of the inner way. This hits home to those who are going through a difficult time themselves. And students suffer more than most educators realize, as do those faced with loss of meaning at forty-five.

Jung has also made a significant contribution on the subject of life after death. Not many thinkers since Plato have had as much to say about this subject, or been as positive about its reality, as Jung. In fact, little has been written about it in Christian circles since Copernicus upset the worldview of the Middle Ages—that view that Dante enshrined so magnificently in the *Divine Comedy*. Among many priests and religious thinkers there is even real doubt about life after death.

From Jung's basic philosophical point of view — which recognizes a realm of the spirit as well as physical reality — there is certainly no reason to deny life after death out of hand. Various data are available for examination, once one is open to consider them. Jung concludes that, although he cannot describe the nature of such life in any detail, he is convinced that it exists, and that we will live out the basic pattern we establish by our actions on earth. There is a remarkable correspondence between the view of Jesus and those of Jung, Dante, psychical research, and Eastern thought, about life after death. Those who discover this background of serious thought, and know their own pressing problems of belief, can scarcely fail to deal with this subject again. Why is it so important? The fact is that we are more consistent than we usually think, and few people can achieve their full development believing that all their efforts end in death. If, as Jung finds, there is good reason to believe in our continued existence, then we had better take this possibility into account. We shall deal with the problem of facing death in a later chapter.

In the last pages of his autobiography, Jung notes that there is a whole area, alongside of human reflection, of which he has said very little. This is the area of human emotion, which he then opens wide in a paean on love comparable to Paul's words in I Corinthians 13. While Jung had not written much on this subject, love was one of the chief characteristics of his life and practice, as Aniela Jaffe shows in her little book *From the Life and Work of C.G. Jung*. Only in his difficult and profound essay "Psychology of the Transference" did he show how important human emotion, particularly love, was to his essential thinking. Then, in this final description, he concluded: "Man can try to name love, showering upon it all the names at his command, and still he will involve himself in endless self-deceptions. If he possesses a grain of wisdom, he will lay down his arms and name the unknown by the more unknown, *ignotum per ignotius* — that is, by the name of God. That is a confession of his subjection, his imperfection, and his dependence; but at the same time a testimony to his freedom to choose between truth and error."[3] All of us can use as much genuine concern and love as we can get. I have examined Jung's contribution in this area at some length in my book *Caring*.

I often wish that these words had been written by a Christian theologian instead of a psychiatrist. They do, after all, express the essence of what was taught and lived by Jesus of Nazareth, and also by his followers when they followed his spirit. But I am grateful that they *were* written, and that they came from this man who was trying to provide us with a basis for living this message. The men and women I have come to know are looking for the reality that is expressed here, and they ask for more than words. Are there ways for us in the Church and in higher education to meet their challenge? And what may this mean for the future?

Jung's practice itself suggests a good beginning—through direct human relationships in counseling. He even remarked on the similarity of his approach to the best of spiritual direction. He told me that his practice was more like the classical direction of conscience in France in the nineteenth century than any other school of psychotherapy. With study and some training, most clergy and educators can make good use of many of his methods, and certainly his general point of view and his understanding of human beings. From this basis, both church and school can reach out to their people, especially those with a worldly and critical educational background.

In my own parish ministry, I was involved for many years in a church-sponsored counseling group—in fact, a clinic that operated from Jung's psychological point of view. Although Jung laughed and asked me how I got away with it, there were actually few problems. The parishioners who became most active and central to the church's life were the ones who had experienced some healing either in the clinic or through the educational program that also used Jung's thought as a model. I described this program in my book *Can Christians Be Educated?* Through it we discovered that genuine education and healing are not separable, but go hand in hand. A little understanding of the unconscious can have a very healing effect. Certainly most of us would be ready to accept such a program, and much of the loneliness and sterility of modern life would be transformed.

Many students come from environments rather different from the sophisticated, intellectual one at which the university aims. They often experience shock and chaos when they meet this new climate. Most of them do not become sick in the classic sense, but they do need integration and reorientation. It would seem that the university, which in a sense creates this problem, has a responsibility to offer an understanding of this orientation and the possibility to participate in this healing, now that it is available. Both Jung and others have found that his method is successful with scientists caught in much the same dilemma, and I have seen his thought and practice at work among members of my parish. I see no reason why this understanding and healing could not be offered to more people, young and old, helping them to find the wholeness that is so much needed by our world.

As for the future, we often forget that it is not we alone who have responsibility for tomorrow's ideas and understanding. With the knowledge provided by Jung of the realities that play into the psyche and how they affect our lives, and with a new appreciation of the importance of Christianity in dealing with them, all of us might well become new apostles. We might well find churches, universities, even our own lives, more vital and whole. I have great faith in modern searching people (and with good reason) once they are presented with the realities of the psyche as Jung described it.

NOTES

1. C. G. Jung, *Modern Man in Search of a Soul* (New York: Harcourt, Brace & World, 1933), p. 229.

2. _____, *Collected Works*, Vol. II, *Psychology and Religion: West and East* (Princeton: Princeton University Press, 1970), p. 459.

3. _____, *Memories, Dreams, Reflections*, recorded and edited by Aniela Jaffe (New York: Pantheon Books, 1963), p. 354.

Chapter 4

FAITH AND THE HEALING MINISTRY

From earliest times healing and faith have been interrelated. Whenever an individual was sick, he or she sought out either the temple with its priesthood and sacrifices or the religious experts, the shamans, who used their many rites and ceremonies to facilitate health. Indeed, to early Western observers shamans were so similar to physicians that they were often called medicine men or witchdoctors. Only later did anthropologists recognize that shamans were often women. One of the reasons for the ancient Hebrew rejection of medicine was that most healers or physicians were associated in some way with the pagan religions of Canaan and were thus contaminated.

This ancient connection between religion, faith, and healing would be little more than an interesting piece of historical data were it not for the recent recognition on the part of many physicians that faith is still a crucial factor in the healing process. When treating the whole person, one becomes more and more aware that the basic attitudes of the individual toward the doctor, the treatment, and the world in general will influence the course of the sickness. However, this basic faith is seldom treated directly in medical education, in professional discussions with the medical community, in seminaries, or in church periodicals.

In order to understand this somewhat elusive subject, let us first of all look at some recent statements by physicians concerning the place of faith in the healing process. Then let us analyze the word *faith* so that we can grasp the nature of this quality of life. A quick look at the history of faith and healing will help us understand the strange separation that has taken place between them in Western culture from the twelfth century until recent times. We will conclude by looking at the emotions that seem most antagonistic to faith and then we make some suggestions for avoiding these obstacles to the healing creativity of faith.

FAITH, DOCTORS, AND SCIENCE

It was, of course, the work of Flanders Dunbar that broke open the materialistic medical point of view which reigned supreme in the nineteenth and early twentieth centuries. In the 1930s Dr. Dunbar began to study the relationship of emotional disturbances to physical illnesses. Collecting all the scholarly references she could find, she went on to study patients in one ward after another of the New York hospital where she taught. Her book *Emotions and Bodily Changes* offered monumental evidence of the interaction between the body and the psyche which results in disabling illness. In pointing out the inadequacy of the medical point of view, she quoted a bit of satire written by the British physician F. G. Crookshank. This parody of the medical attitude comes from an article he published.

I often wonder that some hardboiled and orthodox clinician does not describe emotional weeping as a "new disease," calling it paroxysmal lachrymation, and suggesting treatment by belladonna, astringent local applications, avoidance of sexual excess, tea, tobacco and alcohol, and a salt-free diet with the restriction of fluid intake, proceeding in the event of failure to early removal of the tear glands.[1]

The impact of Dr. Dunbar's work was enormous. She expressed the changing spirit of the times and did so with impeccable scholarship and sensitive understanding. Within four years the journal *Psychosomatic Medicine* was founded. Edward Weiss and O. Spurgeon English produced their textbook *Psychosomatic Medicine: The Clinical Application of Psychopathology to General Medical Problems*, which has since gone through many editions.[2] More and more, physicians have noted and recorded the importance of patients' attitudes. In my book *Healing and Christianity* I have discussed at some length the changing attitude toward medicine initiated by Dr. Dunbar.[3]

Once it was understood that emotions could affect the body, it was not long before faith was seen as important in maintaining health. One of the finest statements of the connection between healing and faith was written by the psychiatrist Jerome Frank in his provocative book *Persuasion and Healing*. He concluded his study with these words:

The question of how far a physician should go to meet a patient's expectations is a thorny one. Obviously he cannot use methods in which he himself does not believe. Moreover, reliance on the healing powers of faith, if it led to neglect of proper diagnostic or treatment procedures, would clearly be irresponsible. On the other hand, faith may be a specific antidote for certain emotions such as fear or discouragement, which may constitute the essence of a patient's illness. For such patients, the mobilization of expectant trust by whatever means may be as much an etiological remedy as penicillin for pneumonia.[4]

A recent and delightfully written discussion of faith and healing by British psychiatrist Dr. Alan McGlashan is *Gravity and Levity,* published in 1976. In a chapter entitled "Concerning Humbug," he writes:

It is in fact very difficult to cure anybody of anything by means of a remedy in which you yourself have no faith. The successful doctor, no less than the successful "quack," is the man who is really convinced he has got something. Every medical man has had experiences of achieving impressive results with a certain drug, so long as he believes in it himself. As soon as he has some failures and begins to doubt its remedial powers, the results on patients tail off, and in a few months the "wonder drug" is, as far as that practitioner is concerned, discarded and forgotten.

He goes on to say that the efficacy of the treatment applies not only to drugs,

but also more alarmingly, to surgical operations. It is within the memory of many of us that a child who had several attacks of sore throat would almost automatically have its tonsils and adenoids removed. Statistics and authoritative textbooks of the period "proved" how correct and beneficial this procedure was. Now when belief in this particular measure has dwindled, statistics and authoritative textbooks of today "prove" precisely the opposite. This is not due to deliberate manipulation of the statistics. The procedure is no longer believed in; so it no longer works. The thing which was officially approved of by one medical generation is then scornfully condemned by the next.[5]

McGlashan then speaks about some of the remedies that have had enthusiastic support in past generations, remedies such as usnea, shoe leather and urine.

One of the most dramatic uses of faith has been developed by Dr. Carl Simonton in Fort Worth. His description of the use of meditational practices in the treatment of cancer shows an amazing application of "faith" technique to a specific problem. (Carl and Stephanie Simonton's book *Getting Well Again* is an excellent summary of the data available.)[6]

The data on healing in which faith is evidently a constitutive element is increasing. One recent survey of the material is found in a 1972 symposium transcript, *The Dimensions of Healing.*[7] The research in the area of faith and healing has been well summarized by students of parapsychology, who see healing by faith as another example of human openness to a dimension of experience beyond that of ordinary sensory experience. Excellent books have been written from this point of view by Charles Panati, Lawrence LeShan, Lyall Watson, Stanley Krippner, and Claudio Naranjo.[8] Current research at Stanford and the University of California at San Francisco has shown that the body has natural pain killers and healing agents called endomorphins. Faith is connected with their release.

One could go on and on giving specific instances of healing by faith. A careful reading of the available materials leaves little doubt that health and healing are related to "faith." What is this quality of life that has so creative and powerful an effect upon human wellbeing?

THE ANATOMY OF FAITH

It is easier to tell what is not meant by faith than to describe it clearly and directly. For many people the word *faith* stands for "the faith," the accumulated propositions of a belief system. It is also understood by some as belief in that for which there is no evidence, as in the persistent belief in unicorns. Here faith depends simply upon authority. To believe by faith means to make a jump of cognition which cannot be examined critically and rationally. Still others use the word *faith* when it is not appropriate. Some would say that they use faith in believing in the existence of a nonphysical or spiritual world. However, this other dimension of reality is not a matter of faith so much as a matter of experience and hypothesis. It is useless to hold to things by faith when experience is available.

Faith is none of these, but rather it is the basic conviction that the world around one is kindly intentioned toward one. This probably springs most naturally from a childhood in which the child is valued, cared for, and loved. The child is ministered to in hurt and difficulty. Faith is the attitude that one's total environment is supportive and caring, that not only those close to one, but one's own body, the community, the physical world, and even spiritual reality can be counted on. What a difference it makes whether the child learns to suspect and doubt the concern and caring of those around him or her because of parental blunders and lack of consistency, or whether the child learns to expect concern and care. One's attitude acts as a filter, selecting and interpreting the data of life. When a child has learned that life is uncaring in the home and family, it takes either the careful attention of a trusted person or some breakthrough such as a dramatic religious experience to turn around his or her basic attitude toward life. Sometimes it takes both.

As the child's horizon expands, the attitudes acquired in childhood are widened to take in the whole encompassing world. The one with faith sees the universe as essentially friendly and caring, accepting the evidence to the contrary as one of the necessary problems of life. The one who finds it difficult to find reason for trust and confidence in the universe sees the difficulties and pains as normative and moments of caring as chance or coincidental occurrences. To such persons the universe is either essentially meaningless or hostile.

As we have already noted, those who have been solidly indoctrinated in the materialism of the nineteenth century see human beings as totally irrelevant, purely epiphenomenal chance products of a meaningless universe. There is nothing to have faith in. Reality is an inexorable, blind, mechanical process. If it goes wrong and one cannot right it mechanically, there is no changing it. For such people to have faith, they must be shown that the best modern scientists no longer think they know enough to believe in such mathematical materialism. If physicians, psychologists, or clergy are to facilitate the faith process in an individual, they must certainly have some alternative to that materialistic and mechanistic conviction. This can be learned and taught.[9]

There is also an attitude, which is found among many primitive peoples, that the universe is not just meaningless, but more accurately, hostile, with demonic and destructive tendencies. Either the universe is essentially capricious or else it is like a punitive and demanding parent, punishing us when we do not live up to its impossible standards. Since this is the way most parents do, in fact, treat their children, it is easy to see how they are readied for such an attitude. This point of view is even more difficult to turn around than the former one.

Faith, then, is an attitude that is a part of one's central frame of reference. It views the world and its inhabitants as essentially friendly and concerned. If there is a belief in a world beyond this, it is seen as equally well intentioned toward the individual and the physical world. In the last analysis, the realities and powers of the universe are supportive of the one who has faith; they can be reached out to and depended upon. People without faith are on their own.

This does not mean that there will be no fear or anger or striving for success in those with faith. To have faith does not mean that one is carried about in an eternal womb. However, the fear and anger will be appropriate to the individual situation in which the person finds himself or herself. The person with faith is convinced that life and reality can be managed and difficulties can be overcome because the core of reality is kindly disposed toward human beings. Psychosomatic medicine emphasizes the dangers of anger, fear, depression, and stressful ego-striving on the health of mind and body. These are the emotions that tend to predominate in the individual who has little faith. When one has no confidence in the close family world or in the less personal total environment, one tends to become either fearful or angry, depressed or pressured with stress. This is the natural psychological reaction to being an alien in a family, a community, or a universe.

RELIGION, FAITH, AND HEALING

From the time of prehistoric shamanism and the historical cults all over the world right up to Edgar Cayce, healing, medicine, and religion have been closely related. Mircea Eliade has provided the definitive study of the shaman in his carefully researched study *Shamanism*.[10] The basic task of shamans was to find their own healing and then share their secret with the sick and dying. Most often they were individuals who had been afflicted by some sickness seen as a visitation of evil spirits. As they struggled to free themselves from the domination of these evil forces, they came in contact with positive spiritual powers and were healed through this experience. They learned how to lead others to these healing forces and so to health. On this level it is impossible to separate religion, faith, and healing.

This kind of practice is far from dead, as seen by the renewed interest in the American Indian shaman. We have descriptions of modern practice from Hosteen Klah, Black Elk, Lame Deer, and David Villasenor, as well as from Carlos Castaneda's books.[11] The Department of Health, Education, and Welfare appropriated funds to support the training of Navajo shamans because it was evident that they were able to cure some diseases that ordinary medicine could not.[12]

The basic point of view of shamanism is found all over the world. In this worldview there are evil and destructive forces, forces of disharmony and division, and there are spirits and forces of wholeness, restoration, and healing. In many languages the words for salvation and healing are related. The religious task and the healing task are essentially the same: to release the individual from the destructive realities and bring him or her into relationship with the protecting, positive, healing realities. This is found in nearly all primitive religions around the world, even in the sophisticated cultures of China, India, and Persia.[13]

The same point of view was common in the Mediterranean world in which Western culture arose. This view of healing was stated philosophically by Plato, who erected a worldview that integrated the fundamental elements of shamanism. For Plato it was almost unthinkable to treat the body without treating the soul. He wrote in the *Charmides* a line that could have been written by Flanders Dunbar: "For this is the great error of our day in the treatment of the human body, that physicians separate the psyche from the body."[14]

With this pervasive history of connection between faith, religion, and healing, one wonders where the separation between them took place in Western culture. The development of rational materialism came too late to account for the division that took place. As one reads the documents of the New Testament, one is even more puzzled upon discovering that Jesus acted more in the role of shaman than moral teacher. He is frequently misunderstood because it so seldom occurs to modern interpreters to see him in the role of shaman. Jesus healed because he saw sickness as destructive in itself and caused on the whole by destructive, demonic forces, from which he came to rescue humankind. The same tradition was continued in early Christian history, as recorded in the book of Acts and records of the first five centuries of Christian life.[15]

What has happened? As Western society disintegrated with the incursions of the barbarians and the collapse of the social structures in the fifth century A.D., men and women lost hope and turned back to the religious ideas of the Old Testament, in which God is sometimes seen as the giver of illness and destruction as well as healing. He punished disobedience with all manner of illness and destruction, as described in Deuteronomy 28:22 ff. The Old Testament is one of the few religious books having few positive references to the physician. Indeed, the Old Testament implies that what God gave in sickness should not be taken away. Healing was associated with the pagan cults, and was thus all the more taboo. It is true that in order to be declared clean of certain diseases, it was still necessary to go to the priests, but healing usually came as a gift from God *after* moral change. It must be emphasized that this was not the later Jewish point of view, nor is it the current one. The Jews have found it necessary to interpret the Old Testament through the Talmud, the Mishnah, and other sacred books. The Christian fundamentalist is about the only person who takes the Old Testament literally.

In the Middle Ages and later the attitude that one is really not holy unless one is sick became quite common. The healing sacrament of anointing with oil was turned into *extreme unction*, intended to help one die in a holy way. In the English Book of Common Prayer, written in the sixteenth century, the authors went so far as to say that unless one was sick, one was a bastard (the exact word used), since one did not know the loving correction of the Father.[16] In lecturing all over the Western world, I have been amazed to discover how deeply this idea of sickness is imbedded in the unconscious attitudes of Western Christians, both Catholic and Protestant.

In the thirteenth century the Church developed a logical and invariant theological system, especially through Aquinas, based upon the thinking of Aristotle (who had a materialistic view of healing) and the Christian scriptures. When the thinking of Copernicus, Kepler, and Galileo questioned the geocentric cosmology of the Church, she withdrew into her fortified walls of dogma. Thus science and religion came to a tragic split; Christianity developed with almost no critical or scientific point of view, and science with little or no moral or religious orientation. Science (from which modern medicine grew) became almost entirely materialistic and rational. The body was treated as another material object, and so the point of view parodied by Dr. Crookshank developed. Such a split never occurred in Greek Orthodox or oriental religions. As we read the latest developments of modern science, it becomes quite clear that such a materialistic point of view is no longer tenable. Paradoxically, medical people are far more open to the relationship of faith and healing than the clergy, who are still largely caught in the nineteenth-century religion/science split. Thus it is difficult for the physician to have a dialogue with Christian clergy on the relationship between faith and healing, and there are few other religious experts available.

FACILITATING FAITH

Destructive emotions arise when an individual is faced with a meaningless or hostile world. In such cases there is usually a sense of helplessness, powerlessness, and threat, to which human beings react in four basically different ways. One can react to this threat with agitated fear, the flight response; the whole of life is covered with a pall of anxiety. The physiological and psychic damages resulting from this attitude are legion. On the other hand, one can react with the *fight* response, turning against the world and other people with anger, hostility, rage, and violence. Any human being under this kind of constant pressure will also sustain physical or psychological damage. Similar to the fight response is the egocentric approach, in which the individual becomes "God," and sees it as his or her responsibility to take care of the problems of the whole world. This is a heavy burden and results in unbearable stress, with all its psychological and physiological concomitants. The fourth response is simple collapse before the threat. There is neither fight nor flight, just hopelessness, depression, loss of meaning. The individual gives up, since there is no point in doing anything. Simple depression of this kind is the common cold of modern psychiatry: The physiological results of this kind of giving up are found in every doctor's office; the emotional ones are a pastoral problem in every church.

When any of these negative reactions is an element in disease, the symptoms can be ameliorated through drugs, but confidence in some helping, redeeming factor is necessary before health is restored. This is the function of faith. How can the physician or other helping professional facilitate this kind of attitude toward life?

In the first place, the healer's own basic attitude will most certainly be picked up by the patient. If the healer feels hopeless, without meaning, helpless and under stress, this attitude will be communicated to the patient. If, however, the healer truly sees the world as meaningful, valuable, sustaining and promoting human fulfillment (in spite of the realistic evidence to the contrary), then this attitude is likely to be conveyed to the patient. This is most obviously true in psychiatric and psychological counseling, but it is true of all long-range relationships with others. Jung once wrote that a psychiatrist is a physician whose only scalpel is his own personality. This influence extends beyond psychiatry to all the helping professions.

One of the most effective methods of demonstrating to another that this is a meaningful universe is to treat the other person with care and concern. It is difficult to believe that the universe is basically disposed in a kindly way toward one until one at least discovers a human being who treats one in this way.

And how does one show that one truly does care? How can one communicate that this caring is an instrument of a more universal caring? Seldom can we show care unless we can listen to another person. Few human beings feel truly cared for unless they are listened to. Then one can respond with positive and caring words. Such words strike deeply into the human psyche. The physician is in a unique place to provide actions of caring in healing treatment.[17] Human touch is also healing, as it demonstrates caring concern far below the verbal level. Perhaps this is why Dolores Kreiger's experiments with healing touch have been successful.[18]

There are some people who are so locked into a meaningless worldview that they also need cognitive input in order to help them find a way out of their intellectual, emotional, and physical dead-end street. The more intelligent the individual, the more likely his or her intellectual viewpoint of hopelessness will affect the mind and body. Jung discovered that he had to attack this problem with many patients himself, because so few of the clergy were competent to do this. It may be necessary to provide the "faithless" one with a worldview that offers some hope of meaning. If we have worked at developing our own attitude of faith, we will be better able to help another from meaninglessness to faith and health.[19] A later chapter will offer some suggestions on how this can be accomplished.

Surveying the history of religion and medicine, we see that there is a close relationship between an attitude of confident faith, a belief in the meaningfulness of the universe, and healing. Those interested in providing permanent healing will consider the worldview and the emotional state of the sick, and will try to provide the kind of atmosphere in which faith is facilitated in them. Real pastoral care will involve the total person of the minister interacting with the total person of the individual who is being visited—mind, emotions, spirit, and body. Adequate medical and psychological care will provide the same kind of attitude. All members of the healing professions are needed, each with their particular expertise, if the sick are to become well and stay healthy.

NOTES

1. Flanders Dunbar, *Emotions and Bodily Changes*, 4th ed. (New York: Columbia University Press, 1954), p. 83.

2. Edward Weiss and O. Spurgeon English, *Psychosomatic Medicine: The Clinical Application of Psychopathology to General Medical Problems* (Philadelphia: Saunders, 1943 [2nd ed., 1949, 3rd ed., 1957]).

3. Morton T. Kelsey, *Healing and Christianity* (New York: Harper and Row, 1973), particularly chapters 1, 2, 9, 10, 11, 13. Complete references are provided in these chapters.

4. Jerome Frank, *Persuasion and Healing* (New York: Schocken Books, 1969). Another excellent study of the interrelation of healing and emotions and faith is found in William Sargant, *Battle for the Mind* (Baltimore: Penguin Books, 1961).

5. Alan McGlashan, *Gravity and Levity* (Boston: Houghton Mifflin Company, 1976), pp. 37, 38 ff. Dr. McGlashan also mentions healing that seems to flow from the individual with no desire on the part of the healer, a kind of natural healer. In 1960 a British physician wrote a book entitled *The Nature of Healing*, anonymously, on this subject. Another such book was called to my attention by C. G. Jung—*The Reluctant Healer: A Remarkable Autobiography*, by William J. MacMillan (New York: Thomas Crowell Company, 1952).

6. O. Carl and Stephanie Simonton and James Creighton, *Getting Well Again* (Los Angeles: J.P. Tarcher, 1978).

7. *The Dimensions of Healing, A Symposium*, The Academy of Parapsychology and Medicine, 314 Second Street, Los Altos, Ca. 94022, 1973.

8. Charles Panati, *Supersenses: Our Potential for Parasensory Experience* (New York: Quadrangle/The New York Times Book Company, 1974).
Lawrence LeShan, *The Medium, the Mystic and the Physicist: Toward a General Theory of the Paranormal* (New York: Viking Press, 1974).
—————————, *Alternate Realities* (New York: Evans & Company, 1976).
Lyall Watson, *Supernature: A Natural History of the Supernatural* (New York: Bantam Books, 1974).
Stanley Krippner, *Song of the Siren: A Parapsychological Odyssey* (New York: Harper & Row, 1975).

Claudio Naranjo, *The Healing Journey, New Approaches to Consciousness* (New York: Pantheon Books, 1973).

9. One of the best recent discussions of alternative worldviews is found in Alan McGlashan's *Gravity and Levity*. Several other books have been helpful in freeing my students at Notre Dame from the grip of this faith-denying worldview:

Thomas S. Kuhn, *The Structure of Scientific Revolutions*, 2nd ed. (Chicago: The University of Chicago Press, 1970).

Bob Toben and Jack Sarfatti, *Space-Time and Beyond* (New York: Dutton, 1975).

Werner Heisenberg, *Physics and Philosophy: The Revolution in Modern Science* (New York: Harper and Brothers, 1958).

C. G. Jung, *Memories, Dreams, Reflections*, Recorded and edited by Aniela Jaffe (New York: Pantheon Books, 1963).

All of the above books break through common scientific prejudices and open many doors. Jung's *Memories, Dreams, Reflections* gives an alternative worldview that I have summarized and diagrammed in my own *Encounter With God* (Minneapolis: Bethany Fellowship, 1972).

10. Mircea Eliade, *Shamanism: Archaic Techniques of Ecstasy* (Princeton: Princeton University Press, 1970).

11. Franc Johnson Newcomb, *Hosteen Klah: Navaho Medicine Man and Sand Painter* (Norman: University of Oklahoma Press, 1964).

John G. Neihardt, *Black Elk Speaks: Being the Life Story of a Holy Man of the Oglala Sioux* (Lincoln: University of Nebraska Press, 1961).

Lame Deer and Richard Erdoes, *Lame Deer: Seeker of Visions* (New York: Simon and Schuster, 1972).

David Villasenor, *Tapestries in Sand: The Spirit of Indian Sandpainting* (Healdsburg, California, Naturegraph Company, 1966).

Carlos Castaneda, *The Teachings of Don Juan: A Yaqui Way of Knowledge* (Berkeley: University of California Press, 1968).

_____, *A Separate Reality: Further Conversations with Don Juan* (New York: Simon and Schuster, 1971).

_____, *Journey to Ixtlan: The Lessons of Don Juan* (New York: Pocket Books, 1974).

_____, *Tales of Power* (New York: Simon and Schuster, 1974).

12. *The New York Times*, Friday, July 7, 1972, p. 33 has a full-page article on this subject.

13. For a survey of Persian thought, see *Healing and Christianity*, p. 38 ff. and my *Myth, History and Faith* (New York: Paulist Press, 1974), pp. 52 ff. For China, Japan and India, see *Half the World: The History and Culture of China and Japan* edited by Arnold Toynbee (New York: Holt, Rinehart and Winston, 1973), particularly Chapter IV, "The Path to Wisdom," pp. 95 ff.

14. Plato, *Dialogues*, translated by B. Jowett (New York: Random House, 1937). Further references to Platonic theory, which became the basis of Graeco-Roman thought and Christian theology are to be found in *Healing and Christianity*, p. 45 ff. There was little difference between this point of view and that of the healing shrines of Asclepius in which Greek medicine was born and grew.

15. A full account of this development is found in chapters 3 to 9 of *Healing and Christianity*. There is no other account of this data available.

16. See *Healing and Christianity*, p. 15 ff., for a full exposition of this point of view.

17. My book *Caring: How Can We Love One Another* (Ramsey, N.J.: Paulist Press, 1981), gives an extended discussion of the techniques and way in which we have developed a caring attitude.

18. Dolores Krieger, *The Therapeutic Touch* (Englewood Cliffs, N.J.: Prentice-Hall, 1979). This book by a nurse with a Ph.D. is an account of her work at New York University, in which this method is actually offered in the curriculum. See also, James Lynch, *The Broken Heart: The Medical Consequences of Loneliness* (New York: Basic Books, 1977).

19. Dr. J. Andrew Canale has written a paper expressing a similar point of view in an article published in the first issue in 1977 of the *Unitarian Universalist Review*. It is entitled "Dealing with Pain from the Perspective of Wholeness."

Chapter 5

THE HEALING MINISTRY WITHIN THE CHURCH

THERE are difficulties with presenting the Church's ministry of healing in capsule form. Although this ministry is being considered seriously today among a growing number of Christians, they are not exactly a majority in the Church. It is difficult for most modern Western Christians, clergy included, to see any particular relation between Christian practice and health of mind and body. Yet unless the clergy believe that, as clergy, they have something unique and valuable to offer to the sick, they will not become deeply involved in ministering to them. Instead, they leave it in the hands of others, or else they tend to become secular healers in their own right. This is certainly in contrast to the belief, in the early life of the Church, that Christians were given both the power and the direction to heal, as well as to teach and preach.

In order to see the rationale for healing in the Church, we will first consider this negative attitude and what lies behind it, in contrast to the basis for a different understanding. Touching next on the opposition between them, we will sketch some of the facts about healing in the Church's history. We then point out what leaders in both medicine and psychology have come to believe about the importance of religious life to bodily and emotional health. We will conclude with some suggestions as to what the Church can do, and what we in one particular church have done.

It took some thinking to reject completely a Christian ministry of healing. This ministry bulked large in the practice of Jesus and the early Church, so large that it was necessary to justify its absence in later times. Thus the idea gradually developed that Christians had neither the ability nor the right to heal the minds and bodies of men and women. It was the *soul* that Christianity should heal. It came to be believed that the suffering caused by illness had a real value in developing good Christian character. According to this belief, some illness (if not all of it) is sent by God for a reason, and one of the great Christian virtues is the courageous bearing of such sickness. Obviously, what God has sent for our good the Church should not presume to take away. By some quirk of logic, it was legitimate for suffering Christians to go to the doctor for relief; it was even good for the Church to build hospitals to minister to the sick. But neither the individual Christian nor the Church was to bring the direct power of God to bear upon getting rid of the sickness. The Deuteronomic editor of the Old Testament was more consistent.

As mentioned in the previous chapter, the English Book of Common Prayer states quite clearly that God sends most illness upon us as punishment for sin. Healthy people, since they have not received God's fatherly correction in the form of sickness, cannot be real sons and daughters because, as anyone can see, God chastens those whom he loves with divine chastisements like physical illness. Modern Protestantism has taken little official action to countermand this basic idea, and it still represents pretty well the popular, unconscious attitude, although we moderns are not quite so frank as they were in the 1600s. It is hardly a basis on which to build enthusiasm for any kind of healing ministry, or a spirit of cooperation with medical practice.

In addition, many of those who would revitalize a belief in religious healing by practicing it have been discredited by persons finding fault with their character and theology. Of course, there are things to question about Little David, Aimee Semple McPherson, Phineas Quimby, Mary Baker Eddy, and others, but how often must we remind ourselves that something does not become silly just because silly people may be doing it? Healing through the agency of the spirit either is a reality or it is not, and no *ad hominem* arguments are likely to change the fact.

In the end, the healing movement is rejected on the ground that it receives no support from the academic side of Christianity. The subject is simply not considered in most seminaries, and the excellent new works on healing are often not even found in their libraries. But this is not surprising; healing is first and last a practical matter, and this is not the modern theologian's forte. In 1962 the United Lutheran

Church, for instance, concluded a detailed, theological study of spiritual healing with a report that avoided the issue of belief from every angle and put the kibosh on any kind of sacramental healing practice in that church. However, the United Church of Christ in annual conference recently commended the practice to its people. This resolution came largely through the efforts of one laywoman, Anne Hancock. It shows what one person can do when determined and informed.

There are theological reasons for this rejection, which is essentially a denial that God and the world of spirit can have any real effect, healing or otherwise, on the minds and bodies of men and women. In brief, this point of view originates with Thomas Aquinas, who has had a far more pervasive influence upon both Catholic *and* Protestant thinking than most people realize. His theology is based on the philosophy of Aristotle, who allowed no room for a separate realm of spiritual reality. The belief in such an independent reality, with power to break in upon human beings and change their lives, offended Aristotle's idea of human freedom. Thus, from the time Aquinas' point of view was accepted, theology has had little room for the gifts of the Spirit that Paul enumerated in his first letter to the Corinthians.

But this is true only where Aristotelian philosophy has taken over. In the tradition of Eastern Orthodox Christianity, which was little subjected to the influence of Aristotle, there has been little question about the gift of healing and the power of God and the Church to heal bodies and minds, as well as souls. Eastern theology is based upon the thinking of Plato, which describes an objective realm of nonphysical reality that influences our lives and the world in which we live.

In the West, the philosophy of Aristotle has resulted in the modern materialistic attitude toward life that maintains that only the material realm is truly real. The spiritual, if it has any reality, is merely an aspect of the material world, tagging along without any significant effect upon matter. Thus the idea of the healing ministry is absurd before it can ever be investigated; who has ever "seen" spirit apart from matter? It cannot exist. This is basically the idea of modern existentialism from Kierkegaard to Sartre, and also of the theology of Bultmann, Barth, Bonhoeffer, and the Honest-to-God Bishop Robinson, who have all followed along to be tailored in the same shop. And unless one believes in a very real spiritual reality, which exists apart from the material world and interpenetrates and influences it, sacramental healing *is* a logical absurdity.

Once one does believe in such a realm — which was the belief of Plato, of Jesus, of the fathers of the Church, of the entire Eastern tradition, and also of depth psychology — then the healing ministry becomes entirely plausible. Then one can actually look at the facts about religious healing with understanding, facts that are available for those who will look. Healing is one of the ways the spirit makes its direct impact upon us. There are four other ways spoken of in the New Testament by which spirit makes contact — through dreams and visions, through the angelic and demonic, by ESP, and through prophecy and tongue-speaking. Together these five experiences touch about half the verses of the New Testament. Yet how little modern Christians wonder about these things! Our point of view about life and reality determines which facts we seriously entertain and which ones we do not see at all. If we are to consider the facts, we must take off our philosophical blinders and keep them off.

If our worldview makes this much difference, actually regulating what data get into consciousness, then it is well to ask what philosophical point of view is possible for thinking people today. Are we limited to the naturalism that was the point of view of science at the beginning of this century, or the existentialism that was the rage in continental academic circles a few years ago? Naturalistic philosophy sees no reality other than the material world; it is the basic outlook of behaviorism and materialistic thinkers like Bertrand Russell and others, who simply eliminate the spirit and the psyche, maintaining that anything not physical is unreal or nonexistent. The current existentialist holds that existence is all of one piece, and that there is no basic distinction between subject and object. This thinking has its roots in the nineteenth-century philosophic idealism of Hegel, who had the world pretty well worked out — except that it doesn't stay that way.

It is perfectly possible, however, to hold a worldview that sees us humans with access to two kinds of reality, which, as we begin to know from experience, are quite different from each other. We certainly have real, though imperfect, knowledge of the physical world, and science in the past sixty years has extended and deepened this knowledge in an amazing way. In a different way, we have just as real, though imperfect, knowledge of mind and consciousness, and also of the unconscious, which we come to know in dreams and similar phenomena. It is in this area that psychology and religion should give us increasing depth of knowledge and experience. If, indeed, there are two such separable realities that can be known, then human beings are the bridge between them, and both the nonphysical and the physical have their effect upon us. In this view a healing ministry is anything but absurd. This is the worldview I have outlined briefly in my book on the phenomenon of tongue-speaking, have supported in my book on dreams, and have detailed in *Encounter with God.*

IN THE CROSSFIRE

My own introduction to the healing ministry was an adventure in taking the blinders off. I started out with good reason to be suspicious of people who become involved in the healing ministry; there had been an unpleasant brush in my own family with one of the healing sects. Then, after I was through school and in a church, I came into contact again with the healing ministry. Searching for a vital religious life, and for some good competitive procedure for my own church, I turned to a serious study of devotional literature and to the use of a healing service based on the two prayers for healing found in the 1928 Episcopal Prayer Book. Of course, there was a whole story here, but in short, because of the influence of Agnes Sanford's book *The Healing Light,*[1] I shared in several remarkable experiences of mental and physical healing through sacramental means.

About the same time, I became very much interested in depth psychology, and when I found that both Jung and Freud had seen physical healings take place as the unconscious psyche was untangled, it became less absurd to me that God could influence the human body as well as the human unconscious. In my job one does not doubt that God can influence the psyche or soul of a human being. Once I realized how greatly the psyche influences the body, the seeming gulf between God and physical healing was bridged, intellectually as well as in fact.

When I was asked to do a series of lectures on the healing ministry, I began to study the subject in earnest. Three books came my way — Evelyn Frost's *Christian Healing,*[2] Percy Dearmer's *Body and Soul,*[3] and an excellent little pamphlet put out by the Liturgical Commission of the Episcopal Church, *Prayer Book Studies: The Order for the Ministration to the Sick.* I also carefully read Ethel Banks's booklet *The Great Physician Calling,*[4] which simply tells all the stories of healing in the Gospels in the order suggested by Percy Dearmer. I was amazed to find how pervasive the ministry of healing had been in the practice of Jesus, and not only in his ministry, but in the apostolic period and in the later Church. Either these authors spoke facts or they were gravely deluded — they were dupes or liars. Both of these possibilities cast grave doubts upon the entire value and authenticity of New Testament religion.

What had happened to the power to heal? The Church had abandoned its early teaching and practice, for reasons that are not very inspiring. In the New Testament, the power to heal was considered a gift of the Holy Spirit. As the Church became less and less moved by the Holy Spirit, and more directed by human authority and political considerations, the gift of healing began to disappear. What the Church was no longer able to do soon became seen as something the Church *ought not* to be able to do. At the same time, as the Western Empire was overrun, barbarian pagans were being taken into the Church faster than their ideas could be Christianized. In particular, the pagan idea that God punishes naughty people with sickness took hold in the Church, even though this was in fundamental opposition to the teaching of Christ. Finally, within scholastic thinking, healing became no longer intellectually respectable because theology had no place for it. The Church even began to take digs at medicine, going so far as to forbid physicians to treat a seriously ill patient until the priest had been called and had confessed him or her. This particular law remained in force in France until well into the eighteenth century.

The medical profession, of course, did rather well without religious help; it made such strides in healing by purely physical means that it seemed the human body was taken care of. By the first part of this century, most of us considered that, given time, medicine would solve all our physical ills, and do it by treating us just about as it would any other piece of matter.

The Church has not been conspicuous for protesting this nineteenth-century medical attitude; it has accepted as axiomatic that the physical is the only factor that contributes to physical healing. In the meantime, however, the medical profession has changed its attitude. Spiritual healing is no longer out of the question; it is simply advocated today by medical men and women for scientific reasons, rather than by the clergy for religious reasons.

THE CHURCH'S HERITAGE

Let us take a brief look at the Church's heritage in this matter. To begin with, nearly one-fifth of the Gospel narrative is concerned with healings or with discourses occasioned by them. This includes seventy-two accounts of healing that can be reduced to forty-one distinct instances when the Gospels are compared. This evidence was even supported by the opponents of Jesus, who accused him of healing through the wrong kind of power. And Jesus specifically sent his followers out to practice such a ministry, directing them to expect healings to occur as a part of being his followers. They were to teach, preach, and heal.

He was not merely continuing a Hebrew or a Hellenistic tradition in regard to healing. Instead, Jesus actively opposed both of these traditions. The Jews at the time looked on sickness as a visitation of God, a punishment, and the Greeks held much the same attitude; they viewed the sick as tainted and unlucky souls in disfavor with the gods. In most places, the sick were shunned and avoided; probably only in the temples of Asclepius were they welcomed. As Dr. J.W. Provonsha has traced so clearly, the passion for healing, which we so often credit to Hippocrates and his Greek heritage, is due instead to the influence of Jesus of Nazareth.[5] The teachings and practice of Jesus, from which modern medicine takes its cue, stood directly against the contemporary climate of thought and religious action of his time.

How do Christians manage to avoid these facts? Not many take the trouble to look, and most of them either reject the validity of these Gospel passages as later additions or misunderstandings, or they suggest that God gave this ministry only temporarily, to get the Church established, and that he then withdrew it. This latter view is known as dispensationalism; it offers an opportunist rather than a living, loving God. But in the main, people simply ignore the passages in which healing is discussed. In *The Interpreter's Bible*, for instance, there are 150 pages about the ministry of Jesus; one and one-half of them are devoted to this aspect of it, instead of the thirty or so that the Gospel stories would seem to require.

If we examine these stories of healing, we find a certain pattern of understanding. It was believed that Jesus had power to heal both physical and mental illness and that he did it, not by medical or psychological means, but by sacramental means. Somehow through the action and attitudes of Jesus the power of the Spirit of God made an effective contact with sick persons and they were healed.

The important consideration is: Why did Jesus heal? There are two basic reasons. In the first place, he saw that sickness had a destructive effect on human life, and he cared about human beings. God so loved the world that he gave; Jesus so loved that he healed. His healing sprang from his compassion for men and women, his feeling that he wanted to relieve them of their misery.

There is also a theological reason why Jesus healed. He was hostile to sickness and to that which made women and men sick. Most sickness was seen by Jesus, not as a chastening visitation of God, but as the work of the "evil one" and his minions; it was to be a battle to the death against this power that afflicted the children of God. The mentally ill were believed to be directly possessed by this evil power; they were under its control. The physically ill also seemed to be under the influence of an evil reality—call it demons, Satan, or simply something destructive and uncreative, the opposite of the Spirit and life of God. "Should not this woman be freed from Satan?" Jesus asked when he healed the woman who had been crippled for eighteen years (Luke 13:16).

I realize that few people have taken this theological idea seriously in recent years, but when we consider it in the dress of modern language, it does not appear that Jesus was as far off base as many modern Christians have feared. As the Catholic theologian Victor White has so competently demonstrated in *God and the Unconscious*,[6] the Satan and demons Jesus called by name were much the same reality as the autonomous complexes that the psychologist calls by the name he gives them. Jesus certainly thought—as some psychologists also seem to feel—that there is an evil force in the universe that he came to fight, and that sickness was one major result of the activity of this force. The crucifixion really makes sense only in terms of fighting against something—something that has been assiduously avoided by most modern Christians. But if Jesus was right, and the Church does have a problem of evil to face, particularly the evil of sickness, then the Church may well also be given the effective power to heal.

The apostolic Church continued the healing ministry just as Jesus had done. There are nineteen accounts of healings in Acts, healings brought about by Peter, John, Philip the deacon, Stephen, Ananias, Paul, Barnabas, and the apostles in general. In some ways the references in the Epistles are even more interesting. When Paul is mentioned, we usually remember that he had a thorn in the flesh—a good reason not to heal. But the fact is that, as Filson suggests,[7] the study of New Testament miracles should begin with II Corinthians 12:12, Romans 15:19, and Galatians 3:5, where Paul was writing to churches that would have challenged him if he had falsified the facts, and where he referred unhesitatingly to healings. He knew that even his enemies could not deny that mighty works like healings were happening around him, and the other apostles as well. Besides this, we find the classic New Testament passage in James 5:14 about anointing with oil for healing.

The fathers of the Church continued the same tradition. In nearly every one of the important Church fathers—Justin Martyr, Irenaeus, Tertullian, Cyprian, Origen—there is clear evidence of the belief in exorcism and the power of the Church to heal. The Church was *the* place in the ancient world to which to bring the demon-possessed, whether they were Christians or not, and these men make matter-of-fact reference to the healings that Christians performed as one demonstration of the truth they taught. Cyprian, at the end of the third century, complained that the Church was growing steadily more worldly, and so was performing fewer healings than in the days of its vitality.

The next age of the Church bears out this prediction, and at the same time gives renewed evidence of healings, now told about Christians, now called saints, who showed the devotion and sincerity of earlier days. Once the Church was no longer illegal, it soon became the official instrument of the state. Not only could anyone come into it, but suddenly the politic thing was to become Christian. This hardly made for the fervor of spirit around which healings generally occur. Even so, in writing the life of St. Antony in the fourth century, the great Athanasius simply assumed that Christians would heal, and only suggested they not get puffed up about it.

Many individual instances were told. Sulpicius Severus related the many healing miracles that made his friend St. Martin of Tours famous, and Jerome told the same stories about the hermits Paul and Hilarion. The Church historians of the post-Nicene era—Sozomen, Socrates, Theodoret—all told of similar instances. It was clear that orthodox Christians were distinguished from Arians by their power to heal, which Arians did not have. Fascinating stories of healing were told about two of the great Church leaders of the fourth century, Gregory of Nazianzen and St. Ambrose, and down through the centuries they were also told about St. Bernard, St. Francis of Assisi, St.

Francis Xavier, and St. Philip Neri, to mention only a few. In fact, in the Roman communion several miracles, usually healing, must be confirmed before sainthood is declared. Although healing has not continued to occur among all Christians, whenever a person has become truly kindled with apostolic fervor, we find one who is called a saint, and almost invariably healings have been recorded.

Thus one would expect a rebirth of healing among the Protestant reformers, and in the outburst of life and energy during the Reformation healings did occur. The story of Luther's healing of Melanchthon belongs to history, and expresses Luther's belief in healing. Both Wesley and George Fox wrote in their journals about the healings that took place through them. Finally, in this period the Huguenots, the Waldenses, the early Covenanters, and the Moravians all bore witness to the reality of the same ministry and the same power.

As a matter of fact, the ordinary practice of sacramental healing as a regular service of the Church did not die out in the West until the tenth century, when the sacrament of unction for healing was transformed into a sacrament for dying, or *extreme unction*. In the Eastern Orthodox Church, of which most Westerners are sadly ignorant, no such change in the healing sacrament took place; here the same services that began with the Church fathers have remained in continuous use.

Yet in the West the practice of spiritual healing did not entirely disappear with the loss of a sacrament for healing. It simply continued in less official ways, in the shrines and through the use of relics as healing media. In England, however, where shrines, relics, and monasteries were all banned in one fell swoop — and where the Reformation was hardly associated with the fervor that was apparent on the continent — the Church not only disavowed its belief in spiritual healing, but even turned its back on sickness and misery.

In our own time, among modern Catholic scholars and in the Second Vatican Council, we find a return to a healing sacrament. An actual move toward such return was made by the Anglican communion in 1930, when the Assembly of Bishops heard the report of the church's commission on healing and passed its recommendations without a dissenting vote. Whatever else the pronouncement of 300 Anglican bishops meeting in solemn conclave may mean, it scarcely represents the opinion of a left-wing or radical group theologically. In substance, the resolutions left no doubt about the importance of the healing ministry and the fact that it belongs to Christians and ought to be exercised. By continuing its function of healing, the Church is simply fulfilling its job as the body of Christ.

Evidence of healing power also continues in the ministries of people like Dorothea Trudel in Switzerland, Pastor Blumhardt in Germany, and Agnes Sanford in our own country. There is no point in multiplying this evidence; it tells the same story. Whenever the Church has been imbued with the Spirit of Jesus Christ, it has profoundly influenced the bodies and minds of men and women through spiritual means. The power of the Spirit is a real healing force, or else the evidence of Christians for centuries has been a distortion of vision and a poor hoax. There is no real alternative.

ANOTHER SIDE OF THE PICTURE

There is no doubt about the facts presented by Christian history in the matter of healing. We simply have to realize that modern science and medicine present another side of the picture—one that is often more exciting to modern Christians than their Christian heritage or the words of Jesus. But here the picture is changing. The day of scientific belief in a self-contained and rational universe composed of comprehensible particles of matter is long past. Matter no longer appears simple and easy to understand, and the distinction between matter in the ordinary sense and energy is becoming more and more difficult to maintain. As far as healing is concerned, the physical scientists in the healing professions are the ones who are stressing the interplay of body and emotions, of the physical and the nonphysical.

Medicine as a physical science has accomplished incredible feats in the past sixty years. It has added about twenty years to the average American life; it has eliminated most of the major bacterial killers, as well as some of the viral plagues; it has made having babies quite safe, not to mention the almost fantastic repair jobs being tried. But as people escape these ills, does it follow that they live out completely healthy lives? Far from it. Statistics demonstrate that more people are going to doctors' offices today than ever before, and not only in old age. Medicine has come to realize that a great percentage of diseases have an emotional component. Once it is realized that religious experience and vitality have a strong and determining effect upon emotional health, we shall be able to trace a direct relationship from religion to bodily health.

At a meeting several years ago sponsored by the Department of Religion and Health of Good Samaritan Hospital in Los Angeles, Dr. George Griffith, one of the country's leading cardiologists, spoke to a group of physicians and clergy about the alarming increase in atherosclerosis. This disease of the blood vessels has reached almost epidemic proportions in this country. In enumerating the various factors that contribute to it. Dr. Griffith emphasized the tension under which the modern person lives—a factor, he admitted, that is beyond the competence of the physician. Even the psychiatrist finds it difficult to deal with today's death-dealing tension. And this becomes the business of the Church.

Ultimately, we will remain tense until we see our lives in the context of a transpersonal meaning, until we have had experiences that bring conviction that such meaning does indeed exist. Neither a meaningless life nor a purely rational idea of meaning can save one from tension and its perils. It appears that lack of vital religious experience and confidence is as much a disease, a spiritual disease, as atherosclerosis is a disease of the body. But the answer does not lie just in religious ideas; they can neither take the place of religious experience nor provide faith. Because the spiritual disease of lostness and rootlessness has somatic as well as psychic effects, there is a big job for real religion in providing experience that gives meaning, and thus reduces tension.

We have already presented evidence that maturity of emotional life has a very positive effect on the body. There is evidence that emotions can affect nearly every organ of the body, and that persistent functional disturbances can, and often do, end up as structural disorders. More recent work has shown the effect of improved emotional health on such disturbed organs as the heart, stomach, and kidneys. Not even the teeth are immune, it now appears.

The most important mechanism of the body through which emotions play upon bodily health is the autonomic nervous system. This system is not controlled by the cortex, but by a part of the brain as old as the history of animal life. Thus it can be stimulated by fears, by anxieties, angers, or resentments lying far beneath the surface of conscious life, which may trigger reactions without our even being aware of them. The autonomic system has a close relation to heart action, blood clotting time, blood pressure, breathing, digestion, immunity to disease, and other physiological functions. Through this system continuing fears, resentments, or angers, even unconscious ones, can destroy the body as effectively as can an invasion of bacteria or a dose of poison.

The religious and the scientific belief that emotions have a profound influence on bodily health is borne out by all depth psychology. In fact, the principal work of this branch of psychiatry originated with patients who suffered from physical as well as mental disturbances, and whose reactions were often so complex that their mechanism is scarcely understood. Jung showed more clearly than anyone else that the religious conviction of the patient has a great deal to do with emotional health, and so with physical wellbeing. Thus both medicine and psychiatry show that there is a clear and direct bridge—one even the most materially-minded people can see, once they believe in it—by which the realm of the spirit directly influences the bodies of men and women for health or illness. Perhaps, then, the Church has not been quite so ridiculous as many people have imagined when it stressed the possibility that spirit can have a creative and upbuilding influence upon the body.

WHAT CAN THE CHURCH DO ABOUT HEALING?

How can the Church mediate the kind of spiritual influence that leads to healing? We offer five suggestions for how Christian ministers of today can participate in the healing ministry.

1. First, they must believe that there is some reality other than material reality that can effect a creative change in the bodies, souls, and minds of men and women. They must have a theology in which the Spirit, with the gift of healing, has an essential place. If this is accomplished before anything else, then the healing ministry becomes a natural part of our religious activity and function rather than an isolated, overweighted goal.

There is no conflict between the legitimate healing ministry of the Church and medical practice. The clergy's job is to provide one essential part of the condition of healing, the spiritual soil in which it can occur. To accomplish this, cooperation with the physician is essential. Once ministers believe that they have something to offer in the healing process and value their role, this cooperation is possible, instead of the either/or isolation in which both professions have worked for so long.

It is then up to ministers to provide some intelligible formulations for the doctor, whose training is not in this field, and to help construct a basis for dialogue between medical professionals and clergy.

As part of this undertaking, it is necessary for the clergy to reexamine the Gospels and study the healings and other nonrational experiences that occur in the New Testament. We have to come to terms with these stories in relation to the present. It is very helpful to preach on these events and to introduce the people of a church to this essential Christian tradition. Ministers who have not done so may be in for some surprises as their congregations see correlations with their own experience and needs.

2. A second task of the Church is to provide a place where there can be discussion of the issues involved. Groups for lay people are needed in which the basic ideas and experiences of Christianity can be discussed and understood. There is no better method for this than small group discussions. At the church of which I was rector we had nearly 100 adults engaged at a college level in weekly discussions of basic religious issues. It took the half-time work of one professional person to plan and direct these groups. This takes money, of course, but how else can Christianity and its basic message touch either professional or lay people who are enmeshed in the world and its point of view? The question is simply: How important *is* the message of the Church for the community?

In addition, a semimonthly luncheon with a psychiatrist kept me abreast of latest medical developments, gave me a place to refer people with problems, and enabled me to share something of my researches in meaning and the significance of philosophical and religious ideas. Every member of the clergy needs this kind of fellowship with some physician if the minister and the Church are to be most effective.

3. A third task of the Church is to provide sharing groups where people can let down their defenses and get to know and care about one another. They can pray with each other about their concerns. This kind of small group sharing was the genius of early Methodism. It heals.

4. Once this kind of background has been created, the clergy can move quite naturally into a healing ministry. It is best to begin quietly, without making a "federal case" about what is being done. The clergy are simply following obediently Jesus's commands to a

threefold ministry of preaching, teaching, and healing. As I have suggested, healing in this sense is no usurpation of medical function, but rather is another dimension of the whole process.

Where results are concerned, obedience is far more important than belief. For instance, at the hospital the minister can lay hands upon a sick person quite naturally while praying. Later it may seem wise to have a healing mission by some well-known leader in the field or, after the proper teaching, to institute a regular service at which the laying on of hands is available to any who wish it. This service should *never* take the place of or be part of the regular Sunday morning worship. In our own church we used all four of these methods, and offered at least three services during the week at which those who wished could participate and receive the healing sacrament.

5. Through the counseling ministry the clergy can, in still another way, bring the full impact of the Christian personality to bear upon other individuals in spiritual or psychological need. The counseling ministry is at least as old as St. Antony; it was described as one of his great gifts by his biographer, St. Athanasius. This kind of Christian healing is desperately needed in these days of myriad emotional and physical problems. The minister can help many people simply because of the archetype they project upon him. My medical friends often refer people to me for this very reason.

As the clergy find that they cannot meet the needs of all those who seek counsel, they probably will find it necessary to turn to others in the counseling professions for help in bearing the load. They soon discover how many people are seeking the roots of their own meaning, and how many are confused by doubts, problems, and meaninglessness, which lead to physical as well as emotional illnesses. In my own church we had several people trained in counseling who assisted the clergy; most of them were busy for all the time they had to give. There is a great need for counseling with a dimension of meaning, which can have both physical and emotional effects.

In these ways healing comes to be seen in a new light. As we have seen, this is a understanding, a context that is both old and new. In brief, it is this: that healing is a living process, and as such it is a mystery, in the end known only to the cells and psyches that are involved. Thus it is one about which we cannot know very much. In the end, healing is given by the creative center of things, who is not only living, but needs all the help we can give.

In particular, healing occurs when the conditions are right. There are the physical conditions, which only the physician is qualified to know and treat. There are psychological conditions that aid the healing process, which those skilled in the human psyche know and facilitate best. Healing also requires conditions of a spiritual nature, which can best be seen and helped along by one trained and practiced in our religious traditions. Together they make a team, one of which God has need.[9]

NOTES

1. Agnes Sanford, *The Healing Light* (St. Paul: Macalaster Park, 1947).

2. Evelyn Frost, *Christian Healing* (London: Mowbray, 1954).

3. Percy Dearmer, *Body and Soul* (London: G. Bell & Sons, 1899).

4. Ethel Banks, *The Great Physician Calling* (Notre Dame, Ind.: St. Luke's Press).

5. J.W. Provonsha, See editorial, "The Healing Christ," *Current Medical Digest,* December, 1959.

6. Victor White, *God and the Unconscious* (Chicago: Regnery, 1953).

7. *The Interpreter's Bible*, Vol. 10 (Nashville, Tenn: Abingdon Press, 1953), p. 411.

8. *Healing and Christianity,* which I wrote over a twenty-year period, is still the only careful study of healing within the Church that deals with all three components of the healing process.

Chapter 6

PASTORAL COUNSELING AND
THE SPIRITUAL QUEST

There are at least six quite different ministries within the Christian Church. All of them are legitimate and needed. The problem is that most lay people at least unconsciously expect their pastor to be an expert in all of them. Without the gift and ministry of administration the organization of the Church would cease to be. Without the teaching ministry the basic message of the Church would not be communicated. The prophetic ministry involves us in the areas of life that have not been touched by our Christian outreach. Quite different from these is the ministry of liturgy, which orchestrates a group into meaningful worship. And then there is the pastoral ministry, which ministers to the tensions and hurts that all of us bear. Finally there is the ministry of spiritual guidance, in which the pastor tries to help the individual in his or her spiritual quest. This requires additional training, and an expertise different from that required for ordinary counseling. It is a much needed and a little provided ministry in the Christian Church today.

In order to see the relationship between pastoral counseling and spiritual guidance, let us first of all look at the expressed need for spiritual direction among modern Americans. Then let us examine the problems posed by recent non-experiential theology. We will then offer a worldview that has a place for religious experience and altered states of consciousness, pointing out the difference between much of Western meditation and Eastern, non-Christian meditation. We will conclude with a description of meditation through imagery.

INTEREST IN THE SPIRITUAL QUEST

There is a growing appreciation of the need for spiritual guides who are also trained as pastoral counselors, and therefore know the methods of dealing with individuals and groups in a meaningful way. The California Institute of Transpersonal Psychology in Menlo Park, California is trying to approach this need from the secular side. The Committee on Priestly Life of the United States Catholic Bishops presented a paper on the need for spiritual counselors to the Catholic Bishops meeting in November 1976. The document was published by *Crux* in their November 15, 1976 newsletter. The Benedictine Abbey in Pecos, New Mexico has begun a training program for spiritual directors. Five times as many people, lay and clerical, applied for this program as could be accepted. Wainwright House in Rye, New York has implemented a program for training spiritual guides. The San Francisco Theological Seminary inaugurated a program in spiritual disciplines in September of 1981.

The purpose of spiritual direction is to bring men and women into touch with the central meaning of the universe and to enable them to relate all aspects of their lives to this meaning. There was a time when people could be given a rational view of the universe that they could accept and integrate. For many generations the Church believed that most people would accept a view of the universe on the authority of the Church and live according to the dictates of authority. As long as most people still had faith in reason and authority the task of spiritual direction was relatively simple, except for those who made a special vocation of the life of prayer and contemplation.

However, many modern men and women have lost their faith in both reason and authority as sufficient explanations of life and reality. This is particularly noticeable among intelligent college students. Twenty years ago one could speak dogmatically to students at Notre Dame and they would listen. Today such a presentation of the Christian faith would not even be considered. Dr. Alan McGlashan suggests that "the current conflicts of youth against age and authority are in essence a revolt against *smugness,* against the closed, superior attitude of mind which assumes that somewhere there is always a final truth to be found, if only reason is followed patiently to its conclusion. Youth in some unconscious or intuitive way has tuned in to the physicists' discovery that there is no final truth to be found anywhere, that reality in the last resort is ambiguous, open-ended, a recurring balance of contraries."[1] The modern person, of whom the modern youth is a harbinger, demands *experience*, as well as reason and authority. Reason and authority are taken seriously only when experiences can be provided to offer verification.

Thus the person who would provide meaning for the questing modern person must be able to provide methods to attain transpersonal experience that supports the worldview suggested. In addition, they need to be able, like any pastoral counselor, to relate to people in a way that engages the whole person and helps the individual through conflicts and depersonalizing emotional problems. Behind ordinary problems of sexuality and authority (which everyone has) one often finds a spiritual void that has intensified the problems.

THEOLOGY AND THE SPIRITUAL QUEST

At this point we run into a very serious problem. Few theological works in the last two hundred years have any place for Christian experience. John Macquarrie's *Twentieth Century Religious Thought* carefully critiques one hundred and sixty theological thinkers from 1900 to 1960.[2] Only two of these, Baron von Hügel and C.G. Jung, stress the importance of experience in the religious journey. Thus spiritual directors must be able to put together a theological framework of their own that has a place for religious experience. Skill in philosophical or theological formulation is not often found in conjunction with pastoral skill. On one side there are the psychologies (and sometimes even pastoral psychologies) that have nothing to say about transpersonal experience; on the other side there are the spiritual directors who know Christian mysticism, but know little about the complexity of human nature or how to distinguish between neurotic and spiritual problems. For nearly thirty years my personal interest and work have been directed toward bridging these two areas.

It is amazing to see how Christian theologians have ignored people's religious experiences, the experiences that involve perception of something different from the space-time continuum. In the middle 1970s Andrew Greeley received a grant from the Henry Luce Foundation to add a group of questions on mysticism to a national random sample questionnaire of some sixteen hundred respondents. The results were quite surprising, even to this priest sociologist. Some 39% replied that they had had mystical experiences. The experience had been carefully defined using the four characteristics proposed by William James in *The Varieties of Religious Experience.*

In a post-test recheck the investigators discovered that half of these people had never told anyone of their experiences prior to the survey. This was because they feared ridicule from the secular world. Greeley also found that the last person they would tell about their experiences would be professional religious people. The respondents felt that these people didn't believe in such things anymore! Also built into the questionnaire was a scale to test psychological maturity. Far from indicating that these people were regressive personalities, the study showed that people having many mystical experiences had a very high correlation with emotional maturity. A similar study in Great Britain by David Hay and Ann Morisy, working out of Manchester College, Oxford and the School of Education at the University of Nottingham, provides comparable results. It is interesting to note that these figures are similar even though only one-third the number of people attend church in Great Britain as in the United States. A similar study has been done in West Germany.

The modern human being is far less secular than many thinkers have believed. I have some statistics about the use of hallucinogenic drugs among people under twenty-five. My experience at Notre Dame led me to believe that somewhere between two-thirds and three-fourths of this group have used marijuana. Half of these have used something stronger.[3] According to Andrew Weil, in his book *The Natural Mind,* the present-day drug culture is an attempt to provide altered states of consciousness that religious institutions no longer believe in or provide.[4] My students agreed with Dr. Weil's basic thesis.

Meditative attempts to secure transpersonal experience have become so common that a Gallup poll was taken on this subject in 1976. Some twelve million Americans had tried Transcendental Meditation or some other form of Eastern religious practice. Some five million had been involved in some form of Yoga. Three million Americans had been involved with the Charismatic Renewal, and another three million in some other form of "mysticism." Nearly 10% of the American populace have been searching for some experience that our religious institutions do not seem to provide. And yet I heard the head of one of the leading Catholic seminaries, when presented with the

Greeley data, remark, "I do not see what mysticism has to to with training seminarians."

There is a development in psychology that takes account of this kind of experience. Robert Ornstein's *The Psychology of Consciousness* is one example of this trend, which shows an interest in studies of the bicameral brain and other data of transpersonal experience.[5] The paper of Eugene d'Aquili and Charles Laughlin, Jr. in the March 1975 issue of *Zygon* takes these factors into consideration in the study of religious ritual. Their paper is entitled "The Biopsychological Determinants of Religious Ritual Behavior."

ANOTHER VIEW OF REALITY

It was Aldous Huxley who provided the first popular framework for understanding the importance of hallucinogenic drugs. After taking mescaline, he reflected upon his experience and wrote these words:

"Each person is at each moment capable of remembering all that has ever happened to him and of perceiving everything that is happening everywhere in the universe. The function of the brain and nervous system is to protect us from being overwhelmed and confused by this mass of largely useless and irrelevant knowledge, by shutting out most of what we should otherwise perceive or remember at any moment, and leaving only that very small and special selection which is likely to be practically useful." . . . Most people, most of the time, know only what comes through the reducing valve and is consecrated as genuinely real by the local language. Certain persons, however, seem to be born with a kind of by-pass that circumvents the reducing valve. In others temporary by-passes may be acquired either spontaneously, or as the result of deliberate "spiritual exercises," or through hypnosis, or by means of drugs. Through these permanent or temporary by-passes there flows, not indeed the perception "of everything that is happening everywhere in the universe" (for the by-pass does not abolish the reducing valve, which still excludes the total content of Mind at Large), but something more than, and above all something different from, the carefully selected utilitarian material which our narrowed, individual minds regard as a complete, or at least sufficient, picture of reality.[6]

It is very difficult to perceive what we do not expect to see. Bruner and Postman's study "On the Perception of Incongruity: A Paradigm" points out that anomalous playing cards like a red six of spades are not easily recognized. If this is true of ordinary sensation, how much more true it would be of reports of altered states of consciousness that do not fit into one's worldview or paradigm.[7]

One reason why the data of parapsychology have not been taken more seriously is that they do not fit into the ordinary paradigm of the Western world, which we have already described. Most pastoral counselors are unaware of these data.

In 1955 J. Robert Oppenheimer was asked to address the American Psychological Association. His address, entitled "Analogy in Science," pointed out that psychologists were unreasonable to base their psychology on a model of physics that physics had abandoned. Twentieth-century science has become less and less certain about the ultimate nature of matter, and far less sure that there are not other dimensions of experience. There is no longer universal certainty about all experience being essentially reducible to material reality. The new uncertainty is traced by T.S. Kuhn in *The Structure of Scientific Revolutions*.[8] Even in mathematics "Gödel's Proof" has put an end to universal certainty about mathematical truth. The scientific community is entering a new era of far less materialistic dogmatism and far more openness to talk about other dimensions of experience.

As I have already pointed out repeatedly, for several centuries the Western intelligentsia believed that the material world alone was real, and the spiritual-psychological-nonphysical world was illusion. Our fellows in the East held largely the opposite point of view: The physical world was illusion and the spiritual world alone was real. *The Tibetan Book of the Dead* and many other Eastern texts assume this point of view. It is my suggestion that both dimensions are real, and that the task of the spiritual guide is to deal with both of them.

In order to present this material clearly, let us show it diagrammatically in the chart on page 74. *A* represents the premodern Western viewpoint, where only the space-time-energy-mass world is real. *B* represents the point of view of the East, in which only the spiritual world is real. Our contention is that both realms of experience are real and that the human psyche has legitimate access to both modes of experience. This is represented by paradigm *C*.

It may seem that we have belabored the theoretical aspect of the spiritual quest. It needs to be emphasized once again that human beings are more consistent in the long run than we ordinarily believe. Unless, however, one provides a paradigm that gives meaning to one's actions within a total context, it is difficult to help another person with

A. THE UNKNOWN VOID

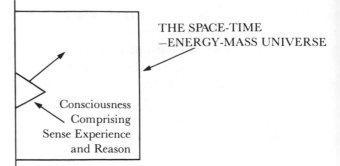

THE SPACE-TIME
—ENERGY-MASS UNIVERSE

Consciousness
Comprising
Sense Experience
and Reason

B. THE NONPHYSICAL OR PSYCHOID WORLD

THE ILLUSORY WORLD

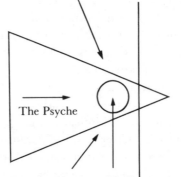

The Psyche

Vague Awareness of Self
or Undifferentiated Consciousness,
With no separation
from the Unconsciousness

C. THE NONPHYSICAL OR PSYCHOID WORLD

THE PHYSICAL WORLD
OF SPACE AND TIME,
ENERGY AND MASS

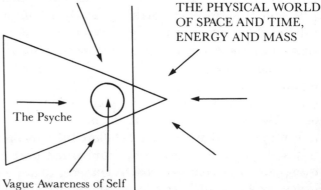

The Psyche

Vague Awareness of Self
or Undifferentiated Consciousness,
With no separation
from the Unconsciousness

74

an independent investigation of spiritual reality. Once one can provide such a paradigm, one can also direct one's critical capacity toward an understanding of altered states of consciousness or nonsensory data. Obviously, if there are legitimate experiences relating to another dimension of experience, the spiritual guide should have experience in this realm, or his or her guidance is a case of the blind leading the blind. Such practice would be as if a chemist who had never stepped into a laboratory were to try to teach organic chemistry.

Plato, in the fourth century B.C., laid out a philosophical framework for the worldview we are describing. He pointed out that, in addition to sense perception and reason, humankind was endowed with mathematical intuition, and also with four forms of "divine madness." This was madness in the sense that it is unreasonable and similar in its givenness to sense experience. The forms of it were: the prophetic perception, the healing or cathartic intuition or perception, the artistic understanding, and, maddest of all, the perception given to the one in love. Poets and artists of all ages have pointed out that their inward perception was of a reality beyond their making. No one has expressed this more clearly than William Blake as he struggled against the tendencies toward rational materialism in the early days of the Enlightenment. I have come up with thirty additional ways that the spiritual world breaks through into our lives.

Religion has usually been an attempt to bring the individual into a creative relationship with ultimate meanings, which are experienced in altered states of consciousness as well as through ordinary sensory channels. Men and women have spontaneous religious experiences, as Greeley and others so carefully report. These experiences originate in the right hemisphere of the brain where pictures, images, intuitive insights, and even stories are formed. Our perceptions of nonphysical reality come from this side of the brain, in contrast to the left half, which deals largely with the outer, physical world, concepts about it, mathematical relationships, language, etc. Religious ritual is another way of using the right side of the brain, and so involving the individual in image-thinking and a different kind of perception, as Eugene d'Aquili and Charles Laughlin, Jr. have pointed out. Meditation is still another method by which the individual attempts to deal in an active and creative way with the realm of nonphysical reality. The spiritual guide needs knowledge of both kinds of experience — "physical" and "nonphysical."

THE DIFFERENCE BETWEEN EAST AND WEST

Essentially there are two kinds of meditation, one characterized by Eastern mystics and by many Western spiritual writers, the other by the general stream of Western spirituality, both Catholic and Orthodox. The Eastern method involves quietness and detachment, and seeks to come to imagelessness. It is typified by TM, Zen, and certain other practices of Hinduism and Buddhism. The other form understands the image as a form of psychoid reality that cannot be superseded. Indeed, ultimate religious experience can be expressed by images in the same sort of inadequate way that sensory experience and images describe the physical world. I described the differences between these two methods in *The Other Side of Silence.*[9]

Various systems of Western meditation attempt to help the individual relate to the nonphysical world and interact with it. *The Spiritual Exercises* of Ignatius Loyola provide one example of this kind of meditation. Loyola's genius consisted more in the form that he gave the exercises than in any original contribution. He was giving form to the general practice of the ten centuries before him.

If, indeed, there is another side of reality, it is important to know something of its nature. East and West view it quite differently. The East on the whole (and all generalizations are only partially true) sees ultimate reality as cosmic mind, with which one merges, losing one's ego identity. Christianity in its most characteristic practice perceives the core of the universe as love, with which one relates. The first path leads to imagelessness and to the loss of much of one's sense of individuality and separateness. (The ego relates the individual to an illusory world and partakes in its illusory character.) The second path never transcends the use of images in meditation; it leads to an enhanced sense of individuality achieved through an encounter with God. One's method of spiritual direction will depend upon one's view of ultimate reality.

Several modern schools of therapy have used the image method of meditation for psychological goals. Assagioli has provided the method of *psychosynthesis* and Jung has suggested the method of *active imagination.* Jung's method has been elaborated by Walter Wink in his excellent books *The Bible in Human Transformation* and *Transforming Bible Study,*[10] and by Elizabeth Howes and Sheila Moon in *Man, the Choicemaker.*[11] I have sketched out the same method in my book *The*

Other Side of Silence. The basic idea of this active imagination is that emotion expresses the depth of the psyche and can be dealt with creatively only as it is allowed to reveal the image hidden within it.

Both Eastern and Western methods suggest the importance of relaxation and silence, of detachment and the asceticism of quietness. Imageless detachment often becomes an end in itself in the East, while in the West one returns after silence to the image. The image is seen to lead the individual not only into the depth of the human psyche, but also into the spiritual world that impinges upon us human beings.

Jung described his method of active imagination in an answer to a question during a seminar he gave in England in 1935. This is reported in his book *Analytical Psychology, Its Theory and Practice*.[12] He was treating a young man, trying to lead him to use imagination therapeutically. The patient was an artist who gave his imagination free reign artistically, but could not for the life of him use it inwardly. He finally learned to direct it inward by looking at a poster and imagining himself in the poster among the cows on a hill in the Bernese Alps. Then he imagined he was passing over the brow of the hill and down the other side, over a stile at a hedge and around a rock, until he found a chapel. There on the altar was a statue of the mother of God, and in a flash he saw something with pointed ears disappear behind the altar. When he questioned his experience it disappeared, but he discovered that when he returned to this experience the same content repeated itself. The moment he went over the brow of the hill he encountered unconscious data. His imagination was expressing something real within, and perhaps even beyond himself. So he learned to use his imagination for psychological purposes. This method, of course, embodies the same principle utilized in the Rorschach and TAT tests.

FIVE METHODS OF MEDITATION

I have found five different ways in which this form of meditational activity can be used with people who are seeking spiritual guidance. Sometimes they are helpful with college students who, because of involvement in the drug culture, have been precipitated into contact with this reality at an early age. These methods are important psychological and pastoral tools. I have given examples of each of them in the last chapter of *The Other Side of Silence*. I shall show in a later chapter how they could be explored in a class on meditation.

The first method is that of entering into the mythological story. I use myth in the way that C.S. Lewis and Charles Williams have described it — as a pattern of reality that can be revealed either in imagination or in history or in both. By stepping into a biblical or mythological story imaginatively one can share in its transformative power. One of the great values of liturgy is that it is an acting-out of a mythological pattern. It is religious play in which the participants step into the very reality of that pattern. One of the reasons that many people get little value from reading the Bible and other religious literature is that they read with their heads rather than imaginatively stepping into the story. One can imagine oneself going with Mary from Nazareth to Bethlehem and realize how hard it is to have the Christ child born in oneself, an arduous task, with rejection all along the way, and then even a flight into Egypt. Coming into the religious way is not easy. Or in deep depression over loss one can imagine oneself in the garden of resurrection with the other Mary, and share with her the experience of joy and victory as she met the Risen Christ. One can step into the story of the Samaritan and the man who fell among the thieves, or any other parable. Since the biblical stories all point toward victory, stepping into them can facilitate the possibility of victory within the individual's life.

A second way of using the imagination meditatively and therapeutically is by the inner dialogue. Many schools of psychotherapeutic thought have suggested dialogues with dream symbols to allow these symbols to reveal their meaning and affective value. Progoff stresses this in his writing on the intensive journal. Gestalt therapy uses the same method. It is only a step from this to the religious colloquy of Ignatius Loyola, in which one dialogues with the Risen Christ, the Virgin, or some other religious figure. One can dialogue with one's favorite saint, or with any religious figure in any religious tradition. This can open up a level of meaning that can hardly be reached in any other way. Such an exercise may even bring one to a relationship with a highly creative level of the objective psyche external to one's own personal psyche.

When Jung was passing through his own dark night of the soul following his break with Freud he discovered that as he allowed his emotions to be expressed in images he was able to deal with them in a creative way. The very problem of moods is that they are so amorphous and unconfrontable. James Hillman, in his profound study of human affect, *Emotion*, has shown how deeply related inner images are to emotions.[13] As one is able to allow the mood or emotion to express itself in an image, one can sometimes begin to deal with the emotional situation. One can gently lead a negative imaginary situation toward a positive solution. When this occurs the worst of the mood of anger, fear, or depression is often dissipated. One friend found that only as the novel he was writing could be brought to a nontragic solution did his own inner emotional situation begin to heal and mend. One can seldom become what one has not first of all conceived imaginatively.

Dante's *Divine Comedy* is a magnificent example of such imagination written in superb poetry. Dante moves from the dark wood of his inner fears to the white rose of paradise, as Helen Luke shows in her study *Dark Wood to White Rose*.[14] Bunyan's *Pilgrim's Progress* is another example of imaginative working through of one's inner psychological and religious problems. The "Stanzas of the Soul" of St. John of the Cross is another example of such creative imaging. Many people find this method of dealing with their inner reality incredibly creative and transforming.

Dreaming is a natural altered state of consciousness. Paying attention to the dream is a fourth method of meditational practice. The dream often reveals the depth of one's self through images, pictures, and stories. One does not have to have expertise in dream analysis to find meaning in one's dreams. One student recounted to me a series of dreams that charted the way for him through a time of crisis and transformation.[15] He never had an hour of analysis. In his book *The Savage and the Beautiful Country* Dr. McGlashan asks the question: "Who is the dreamer within who provides a picture of one's inner condition and the health of one's relationship with the outer as well as the inner world?"[16] Understanding the dream can become a kind of imaginative play in which one finds one's inner direction. One can also start with a negative dream, imagine and nudge it in a more positive direction, and actually change the quality of the human psyche and its relationship to the world around it.

And finally, there is the method of becoming quiet and coming to observe the flow of one's inner life. Both by sensory deprivation and through concentration on a symbol or mantra one can step out of ordinary experience and observe the flow of images that is ordinarily found in dreaming. Since one is more conscious during meditation, one can more easily alter the flow of images while in this state. It is also possible to bring the image of a healing and transforming figure or power into one's meditative situation. This can change the direction of the inner imagery, and thus the general direction of the personality. It is nearly impossible to bring a person to religious creativity until that person has first imagined the possibility and expressed it imaginatively.

This process can be experienced not only in writing, but in drawing, modeling clay, weaving, dance, and sculpture. Through this method one can come in touch with deep and often hidden aspects of the personality and integrate them into a creative solution for one's life.

Guiding others on the spiritual quest should certainly be one area of expertise for some pastoral counselors. Since modern theology offers little help in providing a framework for such practice, pastoral counselors are faced with the difficulty of forging their own synthesis. Likewise, they need to learn of meditational techniques that have been all but forgotten, not only in Protestant but in Catholic practice as well. One cannot ethically guide another in such an understanding where one has no experience oneself. The field is wide open and there is a great need. Guiding people on the spiritual quest would appear to be one of the most important and distinctive areas in pastoral counseling in the decades to come. How do we go about it?

NOTES

1. Alan McGlashan, *Gravity and Levity* (Boston: Houghton Mifflin, 1976), p. 11.

2. John Macquarrie, *Twentieth Century Religious Thought* (New York: Harper and Row, 1963).

3. An article in a recent *Newsweek* quoted a government study that supported this observation.

4. Andrew Weil, *The Natural Mind* (Boston: Houghton Mifflin, 1972).

5. Robert Ornstein, *The Psychology of Consciousness* (San Francisco: W.H. Freeman, 1973).

6. Aldous Huxley, *Doors of Perception* (New York: Harper and Row, 1970), pp. 22ff.

7. *Journal of Personality*, 1949, 18, 206–223.

8. T.S. Kuhn, *The Structure of Scientific Revolutions* (Chicago: University of Chicago Press, 1970).

9. Morton Kelsey, *The Other Side of Silence* (New York: Paulist Press, 1976).

10. Walter Wink, *The Bible in Human Transformation* (Philadelphia: Fortress Press, 1973), and *Transforming Bible Study* (Nashville: Abingdon Press, 1980).

11. Elizabeth Howes and Sheila Moon, *Man, the Choicemaker* (Philadelphia: Westminster Press, 1973).

12. C.G. Jung, *Analytical Psychology, Its Theory and Practice* (London: Routledge and K. Paul, 1968).

13. James Hillman, *Emotion* (Evanston: Northwestern University Press, 1961).

14. Helen Luke, *Dark Wood to White Rose,* (Pecos, NM: Dove Publications, 1975).

15. John Sanford has done a detailed analysis of these dreams in *Healing and Wholeness* (Ramsey, NJ: Paulist Press, 1977).

16. Alan McGlashan, *The Savage and the Beautiful Country* (Boston: Houghton Mifflin, 1967) p. 72.

Chapter 7

BECOMING A SPIRITUAL GUIDE

We can certainly agree—for openers—that most people come into the counseling situation with a problem. These people, in fact, have become a problem to themselves, or to those around them, and the counselor's task is to provide a situation in which they can see clearly what their difficulty is and begin to deal with it creatively. Over the past seventy years there have been great strides in developing methods for doing this—methods of creating the conditions through counseling so that people can approach and handle many of their pressing problems. In this way many have been able to resolve conflicts, to come through one crisis or another, to find new energy and wholeness.

It was natural that ministers became interested in the methods that secular counselors had developed for dealing with people who were troubled and came for help. In many communities the only person for miles around remotely connected with the helping professions was the minister. Training ministers in these techniques became a standard part of most seminary programs. Clinical Pastoral Education developed from the original inspiration of Anton Boisen, and most seminarians take at least one quarter of training under a supervisor in which they actually deal with patients in a hospital or other institution. Some ministers come to understand that their primary vocation is dealing with troubled people. In order to give some direction and professional standing to those engaged in this particular ministry, the American Association of Pastoral Counselors was formed. I became a member at its inception.

Seward Hiltner and Carroll Wise wrote two early and very influential books on pastoral counseling, and books on the subject have continued to be published to meet the interest on the part of clergy and counselors.[1] However, most of those writing these books insist that no reading or classroom education alone can train us for counseling. We learn to be counselors as we are counseled, and as we deal with actual human beings in trouble and are supervised in these encounters. In later chapters we shall give some examples of group interactions that can help people to understand themselves and others.

This is not the place to go into the subject of pastoral counseling in general. This would require more space than we have. But we do need to remind ourselves of some of the characteristics that make for good pastoral counseling before we go on to the subject of becoming facilitators for those on the spiritual quest.

1. Counselors need to be approachable. Only the approachable person will encourage self-disclosure, and without this there is little to counsel about.

2. There is an art to listening that is more than hearing. Listening can be learned. We will say more about this in a later chapter.

3. Few people will tell what is really on their minds if they think they are going to be judged. This does not mean that the counselor has no standards, but rather that counseling seldom goes to much depth when the one being counseled feels judged. Most people are judging themselves too harshly already.

4. The counselor needs to know something of the nature of human problems, of the difference between psychosis and neurosis, the nature of sexual problems, authority problems, and the more common neuroses. They should know something of the methods that have been helpful in their treatment. Seldom should pastoral counselors deal with the psychotic unless they are under the direction of a psychiatrist.

5. Human concern and caring have a healing effect. Few people have ever experienced this kind of treatment. I have discussed the subject in my book *Caring: How Can We Love One Another?* The healing power of genuine love is incalculable.

6. The task of pastoral counselors is to allow the individuals who come to them to develop and unfold according to their own pattern, and not according to the blueprint of the counselor.

All of these require considerable self-knowledge, understanding, and maturity on the part of the counselor, whether secular or pastoral. However, there is one human circumstance that leaves many well-trained counselors perplexed, feeling they lack either the expertise or

the understanding to work with it. This is the problem of meaninglessness — the failure to find meaning in life, or the loss of meaning. These
people are stopped, bottled up; they see no reason to step out into the
rough and tumble of life, or even to arouse themselves to the problem.
Yet this is a problem that shows up in the counselor's office, either
masked by some symptom or reflected by a feeling that they simply do
not know what can be the matter with them. Generally it is clear that
nothing quite makes sense. Among primitives this condition is known
as "loss of soul," and it is my experience that it occurs very frequently
among moderns, who do not know what to call it.

The person suffering from this basic illness — and illness it is — can
show a variety of symptoms. Loss of meaning can manifest itself as depression the so-called "simple" depression for which clinical psychology and psychiatry are able to do so little, as the statistics show. It may
surface as a floating anxiety, hanging like a gray cloud over people's
lives and robbing them of any sense of vitality or joy. Or, the anxiety
can be concretized as a specific phobia (or fetish), attached to an object or action in a way that even the individual affected may realize is
silly. The same anxiety, through a defensive reaction to the fear, may
be turned against either the outer world or oneself in hostility or rage.
In the one case, the feelings of fear and frustration are generally acted
out by hostility towards other people; in the other, they are turned
against the individuals themselves, keeping them from functioning as
they wish. In *Man Against Himself*, Karl Menninger spells out in
detail the many ways this self-hate can interfere disastrously with a
person's life. As we will suggest, some of common problems like alcoholism can be traced to this reaction, born out of a fear of finding
oneself in a meaningless universe. The recent play and movie *Equus*
portrayed this confusion dramatically.

In the counseling situation these reactions can be brought into the
open and understood. Once a good relationship has been established
with the counselor, so that those being counseled are more free to explore their real feelings, they are able to see which ones are based in
reality, and which ones do not fit their actual experience. As they survey their lives, they may realize that they have had few childhood
traumas, that they have successfully come through their identity crisis,
establishing at least an adequate self-image, that they have been able
to handle their sexual conflicts quite well, and have a good enough relationship with parents and others. These problems do not account for

the lostness and the depression these people feel. They seem to be adrift, without an adequate meaning to which they can moor their lives.

In my own counseling I have worked with quite a few people who found that their real difficulty was one of finding meaning, and when they became aware of this, the parts of the puzzle began to fall into place. My experience is that most people coming in to talk really do not know the nature of their difficulties. Some came thinking that their misery was largely psychological and secular, when it turned out in the end to be a question of finding meaning, a religious problem. Some came thinking they had religious difficulties, only to discover they had unresolved sexual or authority problems. Recently a young minister at a conference wanted to talk about his difficulties in prayer, and ended by airing his fears of his bisexuality. It is essential to be open to whatever people bring up and to follow their lead. For this reason, anyone who would guide another through meaning and on to the spiritual quest needs to be aware of the range of human problems covered in ordinary counseling.

FILLING THE VACUUM

Two of the major problems facing American society today suggest strongly the present need for meaning. These are drug abuse and alcoholism, problems which the counselor will meet again and again. Alcoholics Anonymous and Teen Challenge are among the few really successful attempts to deal with these problems, and both of them base their efforts on an attempt to fill the vacuum of meaning in the victims' lives. Most of us are familiar with A.A. Teen Challenge, as described by David Wilkerson in *The Cross and the Switchblade*, tries to release the drug addict by offering them the pervasive meaning of the Pentecostal group.

Studies of the American Indian also suggest clearly that an increase in alcoholism among Indians has occurred wherever the traditional religion has lost meaning and there has been no other to fill the gap.[2] On some reservations the rate of alcoholism is as high as 50%. Apparently both drug addiction and alcoholism today are symptoms of meaninglessness. Both represent an escape from life, which has lost value and purpose, and they are only the most striking examples of the current fear of life-without-meaning. This is also reflected by the increase in chronic and psychosomatic illness. Again this fact has been recognized among the Indians. The Department of Health, Education and Welfare has subsidized a school for shamans, or medicine men, among the Navajo, specifically because studies have shown that mental and physical illness among the Navajo can be healed by this means, which has religious meaning to them, when medical science has been powerless to help.[3] I have seen much the same thing confirmed in my own work, along with the fact that finding meaning and value in life usually, at the same time, brings resolution of the contrary emotions of hatred, anger, and hostility.

There seems to be little question that some situation is needed in which meaning may be found. And it is my suggestion that this situation can be provided through counseling, once ministers and other Christians realize that they have something to offer that most systems of modern thought do not allow for, and that is needed in many of the human situations they ordinarily deal with. These are the impasses that require faith, someone's faith in meaning and purpose beyond the individual, in order to be resolved. Counselors who cannot offer this kind of help when it is needed fail their clients.

If we are adequately equipped as counselors, we will be prepared to meet this need. This does not mean that we will simply try to impose our own value system or worldview on the client. Rather, it means that — when the situation suggests it — we are able to present the case for a meaningful universe both in *what we say* and *in what we are*. There is no basic difference between this and one's primary task as counselor, that of learning to listen to people who come, without judging them according to one's own value system. In offering meaning, one is trying to help others find their own way and their own values. So many do-gooders, particularly religious ones, have tried to push their moral or religious ideas onto those in need that we have let our fear of this hamper our work. We fail to see that there is a time and place to help others find meaning, not by imposing it, but by letting them share in what we have found. At the same time, counselors need to be thoroughly aware of their own values and religious beliefs, so that they will not find themselves imposing them upon other persons. It is as much an art to provide meaning when this is needed as it is to keep still when it is not.

We have already discussed at length the importance of faith, yet there is little suggestion in most modern schools of counseling that

confidence, trust, and meaning might be indispensable factors in resolving problems. On the contrary, orthodox Freudian psychotherapy
functions on the assumption that we are equipped with only *reason* to
hold our ground against the blind and inexorable forces of the universe. Freud's religious point of view is drawn out very clearly in *The
Future of an Illusion*. Individuals face a cold war, and must gird
themselves to keep these forces—the id, death wish, and superego—
balanced one against the other. Maturity means being satisfied in a
meaningless universe—which few people can endure.

Behaviorism offers the individual, particularly the conscious and
perceptive person, no more in the way of meaning or ultimate hope.
In this system, the human being is considered merely a complex configuration of conditioned responses, with little to look forward to or
have faith in, to be manipulated by other people through operant conditioning. This approach can often produce dramatic results with
problems that do not involve the person's system of values. But if the
problem is value and meaning itself, just what can this discipline
offer? Students, I find, steer clear of discussing their real problems
with behavioral psychologists, because they have no desire to be manipulated. And anyway, I doubt if one can be operantly conditioned
into a sense of meaning. The conditioned pigeons don't often ask what
it all means.

The existential and humanistic psychologists do consider us more
than things to be dealt with; they believe that meaning arises from the
depth of the individuals themselves in some peak experience. But if a
person looks deep within and finds no meaning, the humanistic counselor has little more to offer. In a world riddled with war, confusion,
and pain, there is not much to point to that will help a person who already lives with fear. If their peak experiences cannot be seen as
coming from any reality beyond human life, then they are not likely to
give them a reason for overcoming fear and stepping out into life with
courage.

On the other hand, what if there *is* some reality beyond the individual, something in which we can trust? Then counselors have a very important task. It is up to them, when a person is seeking, to facilitate a
relationship with that reality that can give meaning and hope. This is
certainly a viable hypothesis. It has been held by the majority of people in every age—even our own, outside the sphere of Western culture—and many of them have described experiences of that reality.

Just because our own religious faith has broken down under the impact of positivism is no reason to put religion on the shelf. Instead, it is time to examine the dogmas of naturalistic thought that deny that such experiences are possible, and this is just what Carl Gustav Jung has done. If counselors are to help people who have lost their meaning they need to have a secure and communicable meaning themselves.

THE NEED TODAY

For fifteen years I directed a clinic at St. Luke's Church in Monrovia, California, where again and again we were faced with problems of loss of meaning. Until we searched for ways of dealing with this problem, we were often unable to help those who were suffering. I did not find the situation appreciably different among the students at Notre Dame, or among the groups I meet while lecturing throughout the country. Some people have deep roots of faith and are not threatened by the disbelief of our age. Others find meaning through the Pentecostal experience, the Jesus movement, or Cursillo. But there are many who are not touched in any of these ways, and many of them seek solutions through counseling. Yet there are still relatively few religious counselors to whom these people can turn. The task, the people in need, are there, waiting for us:

The people who fear that they are alone, in the midst of a meaningless or hostile universe, who have never experienced a center of reality that has power and that cares. . . .

The ones who are angry because they stand defenseless against a purely neutral or destructive society and world, who do not suspect that there is a loving concern in the universe that reaches out to those who are helped to see and seek it. . . .

Those whose sexual confusion makes them feel alien and unwanted in the universe. . . .

The people who are chained to a lead weight of depression, who do not dream that life could be touched and changed by an experience of meaning and value. . . .

None of these experiences is easy to mediate, but the importance of helping people find the meaning they have lost is greater than we can even guess at. In addition, counselors who are able to lead the way receive several benefits themselves. Their own contact with the source of meaning and purpose is renewed, usually when this is most needed. They no longer have to rely on themselves alone as the transforming agents. Thus counselors come to see themselves more as removers of roadblocks than as healers who have ultimate responsibility. They find themselves acting only as catalysts, enabling other persons to seek their own healing. They become more free, then, to do their own part, and this brings growth for the counselor, as well as for the client.

Finally, one of the principal problems of the counseling situation becomes easier to resolve. This is transference, or the emotional dependence of client on counselor, which is difficult to resolve once it has been constellated. Where there are no gods to worship or to deal with, we are often picked to fill the role of God. This is particularly true of the understanding, nonjudgmental counselor. But when the therapist and client both realize that the healing and transformation come from beyond the counseling situation, then the transference/countertransference situation is put in proper perspective. As it is resolved, both of them, enriched by a new human relationship, share the meaning that is given to them and the reality they have found.

If, as so many have asserted, there is such a reality, which we can seek in relationship together, then it is important for the counselor to keep one eye peeled for problems of meaning. Usually only the trained counselor, after careful study, can determine whether the person's problem is an ordinary psychological one, or this deeper need. It may well be that problems of meaning require a specialty within the counseling profession. Religious experts who are competent to help with things of the soul are hard to find, and there is, of course, real difficulty about referring a person with whom a relationship has been established. For this reason, a counselors' counselor in these matters might offer a possible solution.

Where the problem *is* one of meaning and purpose, the principal task is to encourage the individual to search for the transpersonal reality that can fill the need. This can be sought first in the records of those who speak of this reality; then people can turn to their own experience. The counselors' experience will play a part in the confidence and trust they impart, but there are specific guidelines as to how the search can be directed. These have been described by many of the devotional masters, Baron von Hügel, for instance, as well as by Jung, and I have discussed them in *Encounter with God*.

In a sense, when we intervene with meaning, we are stepping into another person's universe in order to suggest ways of seeking. We are in the business of removing roadblocks. This may be the only way to help many people with the problems they have with themselves and others, and it may well offer the counselor benefits just as great. Next we need to ask how we can prepare ourselves to intervene with meaning.

FINDING MEANING

There is a real problem in relating to those who have lost their sense of meaning and purpose, who have been cut off from their religious roots. It does no good to say to them, "Now snap out of it! Have faith." This is exactly what they cannot do. They are no more able to have faith than neurotics are able to snap out of their phobias or projections. In fact, trying to argue or preach them into faith usually only increases their guilt and tension. People who are caught like this are in much the same spot as Christian Scientists who believe that sickness is the result of error, and then find themselves suffering with cancer. They are sick and guilty at the same time.

Many Christians have a strange attitude towards disbelief and disbelievers. They treat them as the worst of sinners and shun them as the ancients used to shun the sick and the poor. Yet if there *is* a meaningful reality that we can know and be touched by, and someone is unable to find it, the trouble is with their understanding, not their defective morals. Perhaps the reason for this attitude towards agnostics and atheists is the unconscious lack of belief on the part of many Christians in the last three or four hundred years. Condemning others may well be the Christians' reaction to their own unconscious doubt.

What can counselors do to prepare themselves to help the person who does not believe, who is suffering a neurosis of meaning? Before anything else, of course, they must be trained like any other counselors. But they need other qualifications as well—four others, as I see it: *one*, they need to recognize doubt as a real problem; *two*, they will have developed an intellectual framework in which meaning has a place; *three*, they will know and practice certain practices that lead towards meaning; and *four*, they will exemplify the meaning to which they direct their clients. Let us look at each of these qualifications.

THE WOUNDED HEALER

It is nearly impossible for counselors to help someone who has lost faith in a meaningful universe unless these counselors themselves have wrestled with the problem of meaning. Those who have never had any doubt are simply unable to comprehend what someone suffering an existential neurosis is enduring. In this situation there is almost nothing so annoying as a visit from others who are so full of joy and happiness that they cannot understand what on earth is the matter with their gloomy friend. I remember once, when I was going through some dark and difficult times, I had an assistant who had just had a tremendous religious experience and was bubbling over with joy. He came to me quite concerned because he wondered what was the matter with my faith that I did not show more joy. It is bad enough to be enduring darkness without this kind of judgment on top of it.

The idea of the wounded healer — the one who is able to heal because he or she has suffered and come through illness — is perhaps more useful in dealing with loss of meaning than in any other area. Those who have struggled through the problem can reach out a hand and offer a way. Belief, of course, is necessary; the counselor who has found no meaning, or who simply doubts that there is any, will obviously not be of much help. But belief without doubt behind it is something else again. Rigidity of belief is most often a defense mechanism to protect us from having to face our own uncertainties, and doubt that remains unconscious only reinforces the doubts of those who are seeking help. The person sitting opposite me often sees into my unconscious better than I do.

The wounded healers in this case, then, are those who have had the courage to look within and deal with their own inner doubts and uncertainties, and have found at least some answers. Or, if their doubts were less conscious, they may have penetrated into the unconscious depths to discover that doubt that is common to nearly all of us. It is our human condition, and by wrestling with it we find that there is a way, a reality in which to believe, and one we have confidence to impart. Any other confidence rests on very shaky grounds. Adolf Guggenbuhl-Craig's *Power in the Helping Professions* gives an excellent introduction to the reality of the wounded healer.

AN INTELLECTUAL FRAMEWORK

While the counseling process relies largely on affective and emotional skills and disciplines, there is a place, particularly in relation to meaning, for cognitive content as well — good, solid, cognitive content. It is not a matter of either affective skill *or* knowledge, but of both knowledge and affective skill. This is difficult for us human beings, who like to see things one side at a time. Yet if we want people to understand organic chemistry, we do not expect them to discover it on their own; we give them textbooks *and* laboratory experience. As teachers, we also know that a warm affective climate helps the learning process. Similarly, in today's confused and troubled world, where some of the keenest minds have doubted, we are wise not to expect people to discover belief on their own. They need both intellectual content and a warm, understanding climate in which to learn.

The most basic insight is to realize that we are dealing with denial, and that most denial systems are dogmatic. When people say that there is *no* spirit, no God, no meaning, they are saying quite a mouthful. From a logical point of view, a negative statement about something's existence is the most difficult one to support. They are saying that either they know *everything* about the world, or they know the *essential reality* of the world; either they have *seen* that the "thing" does not exist, or they have *proved* that it is impossible. Either one assumes a lot more knowledge than the most respected scientists are willing to grant. We simply do not know enough about the world to deny much of anything categorically. And in much the same way, the insistence that human beings are completely contained in a physical, space-time world is a backhanded denial of any other reality, a denial that cannot be supported.

We have already described how modern science has laid aside its claim to absolute certainty. As Heisenberg once remarked, science is now so skeptical that it has become skeptical of its own skepticism.

This attitude is grasped by students today. One paper turned in for a class in "The Theological Foundations of Religious Instruction" is typical of the attitude of many students who are searching for meaning. He wrote that the religion classes in high school had done little to convince him of the reality of the spiritual world or of the validity of religion in general. His paper went on:

I had received an excellent training in the sciences from grade school on, and I was operating on the assumption that science would inevitably discover everything that could be possibly known about reality. I was a positivist without knowing it.

Starting with this faith in materialistic science, he was then led by a physics teacher

. . . through Heisenberg's uncertainty principle, Einstein's theory of relativity, and in doing so the ultimate mysteriousness of reality, even physical reality, was revealed to me. It is significant that the intellectual experience that was probably the singly most important experience in allowing me to reconcile myself with my religion came not in a religion course, but in a physics course.

What was true of this student, to begin with, will also be true of the counselee caught in the nihilism and skepticism of the nineteenth century. Can the counselor deal with it? For this student, it took only a little training in modern science to open a new perspective.

The next question is: How can this point of view be facilitated in experience? And how can it be verified in experience? It is difficult to explain a whole way of life in a few pages, but let us try. To start with, it is important to realize that we Westerners are as underdeveloped in our understanding and differentiation of our inner life as Eastern peoples are in their perceptions of the outer, physical world.

Once people believe that they contain something beyond consciousness, then they can take the time to be still and look within. We can seldom discover much about the inner world until we do take the time to be silent and look within. We may be amazed by what we discover about the psyche.

Dreams have been called the royal road to understanding this inner being. From the earliest times the dream has been viewed as giving access to another dimension of reality. Dreams were once seen as the medium through which God and the spiritual powers spoke to us. As we recover from the brainwashing of dogmatic, materialistic science, we see more and more evidence in our dream life of things unknown. Dreams reveal not only forgotten parts of the individual—inherited and undiscovered dispositions within the psyche—but they even give access to the archetypal spiritual reality that surrounds us.

Through dreams we can find not only the destructive aspect of reality, but we can encounter, at times, the numinous, creative, caring reality as well. Learning to interpret a dream is like learning a foreign language. There is no easy Berlitz system, however; we have to watch for the connections, and observe again and again the varied and revealing symbols. They have meaning for ourselves; if we would be catalysts for others, we must know all that we can of myths and symbols, and then wait for meaning to emerge. Few exercises are more impressive to agnostic students than to watch carefully the dreams that arise every night within them. Some meaning from beyond their egos is working within them, and once this is experienced, disbelief begins to crumble. In *God, Dreams and Revelation* and *Dreams, a Way to Listen to God* I have described both the place of dreams in Christian history and a way of interpreting them.

There are other ways of tapping the unconscious through developing fantasy and imagination as we have already noted. The same depths can be made conscious through writing, painting, dance, or modeling in clay. In these ways we learn to look within, to see the bubbling inner life, and to bring the best of our conscious direction to the process. This is similar to the Christian practice of meditation, which I have described in *The Other Side of Silence*.

Jung has called active imagination the process by which moods and emotions are allowed to be transformed into images so that one then has a chance of dealing with them. There are almost unlimited uses for fantasy and imagination in counseling, especially in counseling those with a problem of meaning.

A record of our encounter with this inner world, a journal or spiritual log, is important. It will include our intuitions, our dreams and interpretations of them, sometimes poetry or stories, and our imaginings and reactions to both inner and outer occurrences. Few experiences are more convincing than reviewing a record of this kind. We realize that we are not as simple as some people would like us to believe. By looking back over our own experiences, we can see that we may well be in touch with another realm of reality, different from that of the senses and the physical world.

Any one of these suggestions could be expanded into a full chapter or a book, and yet this would not tell the story. To experience the depth within, and in this way to discover another level of reality, takes time and effort. We have to learn the way by trying. The Church once knew how to approach this other reality. But the Church was so overawed by the materialism of a bygone science that it not only rejected its own practice, but then forgot that we had any need to deal with the realm of spirit. It is clear that we have to start all over again, without this guidance, and counselors have to try out the way and know the experiences themselves. As with any matter of experience, we can lead no further than we have been ourselves.

There is one more requirement for anyone who is trying to lead another who has lost meaning back to it, and this is probably the most demanding and difficult part of the process. There is no way for counselors to convince a client that any source of creative power and concern actually exists unless they can show its effect on themselves. How does anyone realize that there is a loving God? Usually the first realization is given to the child through loving parents. And as we learn painfully in society, the child who is not given this love grows up severely crippled, and sometimes criminal. Baron von Hugel's penetrating biography of Sir Alfred Lyall in *Religion and Agnosticism* points out this truth clearly.

One can speak words *ad infinitum* about loving concern in the universe, but they will not be taken seriously by those who have lost faith until they are demonstrated in actions towards them. There are counselees who sometimes deliberately try to test counselors. They refuse to take counselors seriously until they see whether they can be jarred loose from their positions. Often the person's change begins once the counselor has passed such a test.

I was once on both the giving and receiving ends of this testing. It was a time when one of my children was having difficulty in school. I found myself sitting opposite a psychologist who informed me that this child's main problem was that he did not believe that I really cared for him. I complained that when I tried to show interest and concern, it was rejected. The psychologist replied, "Has it ever occurred to you that he is testing you to see just how much you do care?" I took him seriously and managed to show this child that I did care. The results were dramatic. How can one expect adults, with their full-grown suspicions, to be any less demanding than this eleven-year-old child?

James Hillman has spoken about the difficulty of dealing with depressed and suicidal patients in his sensitive little book *Suicide and the Soul*. Speaking of the potential suicide — and one must remember that this person has simply reached the logical conclusion of depression and meaninglessness — Hillman reminds counselors that in this situation their inner attitudes will be found out. We had better know our inner selves before the client discovers them. We need to submit to the rigorous training it takes to show care and concern for the person who is suffering real depression.

Most people who have enough problems to land in the counselor's office have at least some need for this kind of meaning. Somewhere along the line, they have been denied the effects of positive affection, of love. And this final ingredient is the most important one counselors can add to the pot. In part, it comes from conscious effort; in part, it is inseparable from their own being. And perhaps this is the reason we become, and go on acting as, counselors — we are forced to reconcile the parts of ourselves, and to care about them for dear life.

One may well ask: What is the difference between this kind of counseling and religious education? The answer is that there is little difference, except that in religious education we are trying to answer the questions before they have been asked. In the counseling situation, people are asking why they hurt, or why they cause concern to those around them. For those whose problem is essentially that of loss of meaning, the answers come most effectively from a counselor who has wrestled with the problem of doubt, who can provide meaning through a solid intellectual framework, who can open a door to meaning through dreams and imagination, and their own meditational practice, and finally from one who is trying to manifest the reality of loving concern of which we all speak, sometimes loosely.

There is probably no illness more pervasive in the Western world than loss of meaning, and no task which challenges the religious counselor more. Even the books which supposedly deal with spiritual direction seldom deal with the problem of meaning.[4] People are needed who are trained to deal with this problem of love and faith.

NOTES

1. Four books are representative of this literature:

Seward Hiltner, *Pastoral Counseling* (New York: Abingdon Press, 1949).

Carroll Wise, *Pastoral Counseling, Its Theory and Practice* (New York: Harper and Brothers, 1951).

Dana Farnsworth and Francis Braceland, *Psychiatry, The Clergy and Pastoral Counseling* (Collegeville, Minn: St. John's University Press, 1969).

Edgar Jackson, *Parish Counseling* (New York: Jason Aronson, 1975).

2. United States Department of Health, Education and Welfare, Office of the Assistant Secretary for Health and Scientific Affairs, "First Special Report to the U.S. Congress on Alcohol and Health," Health Services and Mental Health Administration/National Institute of Mental Health/National Institute on Alcohol Abuse and Alcoholism, December 1971.

3. *New York Times*, July 7, 1972, cover story, Section D.

4. Four recent books on spiritual direction do not deal with this subject. There is no attempt in them to deal with the problem of meaning or of integrating psychological counseling with pastoral counseling. These books are:

L. Patrick Carroll and Katherine Marie Dyckman, *Inviting the Mystic, Supporting the Prophet* (New York: Paulist Press, 1981).

Tilden Edwards, *Spiritual Friend: Reclaiming the Gift of Spiritual Direction* (New York: Paulist Press, 1980).

Kenneth Leech, *Soul Friend: The Practice of Christian Spirituality* (New York: Harper and Row, 1980).

Carolyn Gratton, *Guidelines for Spiritual Direction* (Denville, N.J.: Dimension Books, 1980).

A helpful survey of the thinking involved in the history of Christian spirituality is to be found in Urban T. Holmes, *A History of Christian Spirituality: An Analytical Introduction* (New York: Seabury Press, 1980).

Chapter 8

PASTORAL CARE AND MEDITATION

Courses in Christian meditation are not the usual thing in departments of religion and theology or in parishes. Educators in this country and Europe show little interest in the subject, for good reason. Within our present theological framework, where people's relationship with the divine is inferred almost entirely from sense data, meditation has very little meaning. At worst it is seen as a process of self-deception, and at best merely some kind of communication with oneself. It is difficult to devise a course of study that is meaningful within this framework. One can study the mystics and their insights and speculate about their source, but the academic and theological worlds consider it outside their province, if not beneath their dignity, to get into the practice of meditation.

A great many people seem to have a need to meditate, however, and since this need is ignored in the West by Protestant and Catholic churches alike, those versed in Eastern ways of meditation have stepped in to provide a rationale and a practice. We have schools of yoga, Zen, and Transcendental Meditation in every college town of any size, and it would be hard to guess how many students (and professors) have felt an impelling need to try out these methods. The suggestion even comes from Dr. Herbert Benson of Harvard that the business community replace their coffee breaks with a demystified form of TM. He proposes this practice as a way of making employees healthier and increasing productivity, and therefore profits.

On most college campuses the drug culture provides another method of reaching a meditative state. Dr. Andrew Weil, in his book *The Natural Mind*, investigates the reasons people use drugs. He believes that human beings have an instinctual need or desire for altered states of consciousness, and that their main reason for taking drugs is to reach a state similar to that in meditation. After several years of listening to drug users on a college campus, my conclusion is that in most cases Dr. Weil is quite correct.

My experience with immature users in my parish in California was different. Where drug taking is seen simply as an escape from reality, it becomes far more pathological. In academic circles, on the other hand, I find brilliant and sophisticated young people who know that in taking drugs they are searching for an expanded consciousness that modern religion and theology seldom provide. Many of them are aware of how dangerous it is to experiment in this way. But these young people are dissatisfied with the gray-flannel-suit culture of their parents and are determined to find experience of something more on their own. They are open to religious guidance if it can tell them about finding such experience. We might as well try to outlaw religion as to attempt to eliminate the use of these psychotropic drugs by legal means alone.

It was with factors such as these in mind that the Department of Graduate Studies in Education at Notre Dame asked me a few years ago to provide a class offering experiences in some of the better known meditative techniques. Since the purpose was to provide teachers of religion with the tools for working with students and church members who want to try ways of meditating, it was decided to start with two courses giving a basic approach to the subject and then to introduce the various practices of meditation.

In the following pages I will outline how we went about providing an approach to religious experience and a practicum in seeking such experience through meditation. These courses were intended to help pastors and religious education coordinators bring this material to the parish level. In my book *Can Christians Be Educated?* I show such courses in operation on a parish level.

AN APPROACH TO RELIGIOUS EXPERIENCE

The first course was called "Science and Spiritual Direction." The purpose was to show that the view of humankind that came out of the Enlightenment is outmoded, and to present an alternative to this idea that human beings are totally contained and can be completely understood within a space-time-energy-mass "box." Students were introduced to recent developments in physics, chemistry, mathematics, parapsychology, some branches of anthropology, medicine, and depth psychology, all of which show that it is no longer possible to comprehend ourselves and our world totally in terms of sense experience and reason. These developments were contrasted with the thinking of the few professionals—theologians, behavioral psychologists, sociologists, and engineers—who still maintain the obsolete worldview of the nineteenth century. The new understanding of human beings and the world was then put into a model or schema (which we presented in Chapter 2) in order to give the group a framework within which to test and analyze their own experiences. Some such hypothesis is essential for critical evaluation of our worldview and our experiences of the world. Readings for this class were taken mainly from my book *Encounter with God*, in which the basic point of view and most of the reference material are presented.[1]

The second course—The Phenomenology of Religious Experience—was largely academic. In order to reach an understanding of the experiences themselves, the group first studied Mircea Eliade's *Shamanism*, and then modern examples of shamanistic experience, including *Black Elk Speaks, Lame Deer: Seeker of Visions*, and some of the books by Carlos Castaneda. Three works were used as a basis for analyzing these experiences—Rudolf Otto's *The Idea of the Holy*, Baron Friedrich von Hügel's *The Mystical Element of Religion*, and C.G. Jung's *Psychology and Religion: West and East*. We then turned to the main unit of study, religious experience within the specifically Christian tradition. Healing, dreams and visions, tongue-speaking, extrasensory perception, and discernment of nonphysical elements were studied in some detail.

Once this conceptual framework was understood, there was little difficulty in introducing groups to the experiences themselves. They grasped the idea that there may well be valid experiences coming from beyond the space-time continuum, and that the only way to test this hypothesis is by practical experience. Without trying to experience the spiritual dimension the result would be somewhat like trying to learn football (which is fairly important on our campus) by diagramming plays in the locker room, without ever trying them out in scrimmage. One student suggested that working with the experiences was like a specialist examining samples of blood or listening to hundreds of hearts in order to learn what to expect in our bodies. There is no way, in fact, to discover what can touch the depth of our being except by experimenting with actual experiences.

As a general rule the "Practicum in Religious Experience" was limited to groups of fifteen students. Although there were always more applicants than could be accommodated, our effort was to provide an atmosphere in which interaction could take place freely between all the members, students and instructor alike. Most of the members had already taken the prerequisite courses, but those who had not were asked to read several books clarifying the schema that would be used as a basis for analyzing and criticizing the class experiences.

In addition, the groups were carefully screened. Not every student should be exposed to these experiences, and individuals with a rigid defense system, and those who were already dangerously close to the unconscious, were screened out. Since the groups met once a week for three-hour sessions, it was expected that a close bond would develop between them. Therefore the voluntary nature of their participation was stressed, as well as the fact that students and instructor were all seekers together. In any group where people are asked to share intimately, one individual who is hostile or angry at having to participate can destroy the rapport of the entire group. This is particularly true of sharing religious experiences, which are undoubtedly the most intimate of all our experiences.

In a group seeking this kind of openness to the inner world, individual problems often come to the surface. Thus it is important for the instructor to have some understanding of the dynamics of the human psyche and to be able to offer students help in individual conferences, or to have resource people available to deal with these problems. As group leader, one must also be thoroughly at home in one's own practice of meditation. Otherwise, it is simply a case of the blind trying to lead the blind. With this in mind, let us look at how we approached the experiences.

THE EXPERIENCES THEMSELVES

The group met in a quiet place, usually in a meditation room or a chapel. We kept the sessions informal, generally sitting on the floor in the chapel-like atmosphere, and there were rarely any absences. The first meeting was arranged mainly as an opportunity for the students to get acquainted with each other and to learn something of the backgrounds and interests of those with whom they would be sharing. The course requirements were then outlined.

The students were asked to read at least one book each week. This reading provided background material for the kind of meditative exercise in which the group would be participating. They were asked to keep a journal recording reactions to both the readings and the class experiences. It was also suggested that they use the journal to record their dreams, in order to learn about these natural states of altered consciousness and to find out what unconscious experiences and reactions were going on autonomously within their own psyches. Later they were asked to include a record of their meditations. While these records were entirely private, anything in them could be shared with the group if a student wished to do so. It was understood, however, that there would be no pressure to do this, and that the instructor would be available to discuss any experience too personal to talk about in the group setting. Finally, a written evaluation of the course and the individual experiences was required at mid-term and upon completion of the course at the end of the year.

After some further analysis of the possibility of experiences from beyond the physical world, the first experience — that of silence — was offered. In preparation for this experience the students had read *A Testament of Devotion*, by Thomas Kelly, and Edward Rice's *The Man in the Sycamore Tree*. When the class assembled, the plan for the three hours was explained. We would start with fifty minutes of absolute silence. During this time each person would try to cut off all sensory awareness and halt the "talking" to oneself that goes on within us most of the time. It was suggested that they try pinpointing their attention on some object, a cross, the corner of a table, an inner image, narrowing the focus until awareness came to a vanishing point. We would then take twenty or more minutes to record what was experienced, and use the rest of the period to describe what had happened and to discuss such experiences in general. The descriptions varied. Some of them simply told what they had done to stop their inner talking. Some described reaching a state of utter blankness. Others found that they were beginning to be flooded by images and sensations that could not have come from their physical surroundings. There were a number of experiences similar to the ones described by Dr. Woodburn Heron in his contribution to the book *Sensory Deprivation*.[2]

Nearly all of the students found this experience a valuable one.

Most of them had never before tried, deliberately and consciously, to become silent, or even to still their thoughts and ideas for this length of time. There were second- and third-year seminarians in the group who admitted that this was their first experience of real silence. As we discussed the effects and the power of silence, it became clear that the students wanted to know more about the kinds of images and experiences that could come to them when their attention was turned completely away from outer sensory experiences. This led directly to the subject of dreams and spontaneous visions, which are the clearest examples of how experiences like these seem to happen naturally to human beings as a normal function of the psyche.

For the next two sessions each student was asked to read two books out of a selection of four works that would give an understanding of the dreaming process. The four works were *Dreams: God's Forgotten Language* and *The Kingdom Within*, both by John Sanford; C.G. Jung's *Memories, Dreams, Reflections;* and my own book *God, Dreams, and Revelation.* Jung's book offers one of the most penetrating studies of dreams and their meaning ever produced, while the other three are studies of the dream in Christian history and in relation to present-day Christian life.

The next two classes began with brief interchanges about the results of attempting to become silent, and then several students reported dreams that they had not understood and asked the group for help in interpreting them. In many cases another individual with intuitive insight was able to grasp the meaning of the dream symbols, sometimes showing their direct relation to a current problem, or opening up some deep connection with the symbols and themes in Christian history, particularly the stories in the Bible and the parables and images used by Jesus of Nazareth. The group began to understand that since a dream is speaking to one's own *un*conscious, another person who has become conscious in exactly that area may quickly see the meaning that was entirely hidden from the dreamer. When such insights related to individual concerns, it was stressed that only the dreamer could tell whether they were correct or not.

It became more and more clear to the students that most of their dreams were dramas presented by the unconscious mind on the stage of the psyche in order to compensate for some lopsided conscious attitude. The possibility was then considered that this meaningful activity might even be directed by some reality with aspects that reach beyond the human psyche. They began to ask questions very much like the one posed by Dr. Alan McGlashan in *The Savage and the Beautiful Country*, to which we have already referred. Who is this dreamer, they wondered, who touches so unerringly on my deepest and most sensitive problems? Where do these solutions come from that are so often creative and useful in my life? Is there a guide within me who is concerned with my religious attitudes?

These efforts to understand dreams led the students to see that there might be an autonomous and purposeful realm of experience both within the psyche and surrounding it, perhaps on all sides. This opened the door to the possibility of working with meditation in the way it was practiced by Ignatius Loyola and by both the medieval and the early Church, from which Loyola drew his inspiration. They also learned to enter into dialogue with their dream images, and in these dialogues they often found contents emerging of which they had never been aware. They came to see that there could be a creative use for images in meditation.

MEDITATION IN PRACTICE

As preparation for understanding the process of using images in meditation, we used Ignatius Loyola's classic work, *Spiritual Exercises*, one modern example of secular meditation, *The Saviors of God*, by Nikos Kazantzakis, and certain chapters of my book *The Other Side of Silence*. To supplement this material, several other sources were recommended, including Roberto Assagioli's *Psychosynthesis*, the section on active imagination in C.G. Jung's *Analytical Psychology: Its Theory and Practice*,[3] Robert Johnson's *He!* and some parts of his book *She!*, John Sanford's *The Man Who Wrestled with God*, and Helen Luke's *Dark Wood to White Rose*.

The different ways of using images in meditation that were described in Chapter 6 were then suggested to the class to try. These are ways that can help the individual find an experience of God once he or she has crossed the threshold of silence and is open to the realm of autonomous images. The first and simplest of them is to step into some religious or biblical story imaginatively. This method is an adventure into the story in which one identifies with the characters and sees them as parts of one's self. For instance, there is one who is paralyzed in me and also parts of me that are somehow clever enough to let the paralyzed element down through the roof to be healed by the Christ. Or I can feel my own hopelessness and lostness vanish as I follow Mary from the empty tomb to confront her Lord; or something that has died and rotted within me may come to life as I experience the raising of Lazarus.[4] A number of students shared ventures like these with each of the classes.

Another very similar way of meditating is to allow the images of a work of poetry or other literature to come alive within oneself, letting the experiences of it unfold on their own. The last stanzas of T.S. Eliot's *Four Quartets* (Little Gidding, III, IV, and V) awaken this kind of experience as fully as any passage of poetry that I know. When these lines were read to students already in a quiet state, they loosed a torrent of images and religious ideas. Many of the group found that stories like those of Tolkien or the Narnia stories by C.S. Lewis opened them to much the same meditative experiences.

A third method is simply to turn inward in silence and let one's own images arise and present their story. Nearly everyone we worked with found in this process—which is described in the readings of Jung, Assagioli, and my book on meditation—the most important lesson of all for their religious development. Just as in dreams, a person's inner story can emerge in this way from the unconscious. But in sleep we have little power to direct or alter these unconscious elements, which so often rise up to make or break our lives. In meditation one can watch them develop, and if they take a course headed for disaster, one can introduce the Christ or some other savior figure into the story to change its direction. Almost any powerful religious symbol can usually have some effect upon these inner elements, even when a person only half believes in its value.

The trouble with modern religious practice is that so much of it is based on an acceptance of an existential point of view, which sees no possibility for this kind of creative change. Nihilistic existentialism writes imaginatively about the human condition, and then leaves the individual stuck in the same mud it describes, with no CB to call for help. Unless one can at least imagine the possibility of salvation, of being touched by some force that can push us towards a creative solution, there is not much hope of our moving under our own power toward wholeness and creativity. As psychological studies of great literature show, the writer can produce only that which is emerging into his or her consciousness. Yet the very fact of dealing consciously with these inner realities helps people to develop and grow. In the case of two of the world's great artists this has been demonstrated beyond question. Students who read James Kirsch's *Shakespeare's Royal Self* and Helen Luke's *Dark Wood to White Rose*[5] agreed that the writings of Shakespeare and Dante led these men towards wholeness. They also realized that by allowing one's own story to emerge out of the naked flow of one's unconscious, and then interjecting realities of meaning and transformation into the process, any individual can start on the way of transformation. For many persons this kind of inner work is the only way that such development can take place.

There were some students who found that when they turned inward, destructive emotions came up like a storm front from within and prevented them from becoming still at all. They were sometimes beset by fear or anger of tornado force, or sometimes engulfed in a depression that seemed like an inpenetrable fog. These individuals had to try another method of reaching a meditative state. By observing a mood and then picturing it in images, one can get a grasp on these emotions and begin to deal with them. One cannot work with a mood as long as it carries and absorbs one's whole being into it. Seeing it as a concrete image gives it some stability and the possibility of pinpointing its source. One can then bring a creative image between oneself and that destructive source in order to take action and relieve the negative pressure. By bringing the images to a positive resolution, the mood often begins to fade and one soon becomes free.

Such a resolution is not always permanent, however. This process may be necessary again and again, and meditations that allow one to deal with deeply destructive emotions and moods are often quite violent. Contact with someone who has been this way and can help one keep one's bearings is sometimes necessary. This process can then bring real growth. Examples of such meditations are found in the last chapter of *The Other Side of Silence*.[6]

Listening to one's own dreams and "befriending" them provides a fifth method of meditating that leads to development and growth on the inner way. The groups found that almost anyone can enter into a dream in the same way that one steps into a biblical event or a story of any kind, and that this is one way of dealing with one's inner life and directing it towards a more creative destiny.

Finally, if one can work with one's inner story and one's dreams in this way, it is certainly possible to bring the Risen Christ into our meditations in the same manner. This is the method described as a *colloquy* by Ignatius of Loyola. In these meditations one becomes quiet and then turns towards the Christ figure in whatever situation and symbolism that is most meaningful, asking questions and listening. At first this process often seems stilted and unreal, but gradually the inner images and voices begin to move on their own and one comes to depths of insight that are seldom found in any other way. Sometimes no words are spoken; one simply comes into the presence of the Christ and knows his transforming power. It was out of just such a meditation that St. John of the Cross wrote his *Stanzas of the Soul.* This great work of imaginative poetry concludes with these verses:

> *Oh, night that guided me,*
> *Oh, night more lovely than the dawn,*
> *Oh night that joined Beloved with lover,*
> *Lover transformed in the Beloved!*
>
> *Upon my flowery breast,*
> *Kept wholly for himself alone,*
> *There he stayed sleeping, and I caressed him.*
> *And the fanning of the cedars made a breeze.*
>
> *The breeze blew from the turret*
> *As I parted his locks;*
> *With his gentle hand he wounded my neck*
> *And caused all my senses to be suspended.*
>
> *I remained, lost in oblivion;*
> *My face I reclined on the Beloved.*
> *All ceased and I abandoned myself,*
> *Leaving my cares forgotten among the lilies.*

We discovered that quite ordinary beginners could step upon this way and that the very effort to use imagination helped their inner lives to grow and develop creatively. In some cases this effort was sparked and helped along by imaginative expressions like painting, modeling, sculpturing, or even dancing. Even these students, however, were asked to record as much as they could in their journals so they might look back and see the effect on their lives of coming into contact with the divine.

It would have been easy to spend the rest of our time working with these experiences, but our goal was more comprehensive than this, and so we moved on to other ways of approaching the inner life. The first two were experiences in the Christian tradition.

OTHER EXPERIENCES

To introduce the use of the Jesus prayer the class read *The Way of a Pilgrim* and a little book published anonymously in 1967 called *The Prayer of Jesus*. We then met and used the Jesus prayer for about fifty minutes, then recorded our reflections before sharing our experiences together. As expected, the main difference was that there were more individuals who described experiencing images than earlier in our work with meditation. For some this was a powerful, and even frightening experience, especially for one person who had been hiding from guilt.

We next invited a group of leaders of the Charismatic movement to come and present a Charismatic meeting, with tongue-speaking and other charismata that might emerge. The group found this a productive session, especially after the background reading of *A New Pentecost?* by Cardinal Suenens, or my book *Tongue Speaking*.

Then, in order to provide balance, we introduced several experiences from other traditions. Some members of a spiritualist church were invited to meet with us to offer an understanding of this Western kind of experience, particularly the positive thinking discussed by Claude Bristol in *The Magic of Believing*. The readings were selected from the vast literature of New Thought, Christian Science, and spiritualism. For these sophisticated students, both undergraduate and graduate, this material provided the least stimulation. Few of them had even known that many of these ideas existed.

Their interest in Eastern forms of meditation was much greater. They were asked to read part of the *I Ching* in Richard Wilhelm's edition, including the introduction by Jung. The use of the *I Ching* was then demonstrated to the class and compared with the use of tarot cards. Jess Stearn's *Yoga, Youth and Reincarnation* was read next, in preparation for a session in which a nun who is well trained in yoga explained and led the group through a series of yoga exercises. To prepare for an afternoon conducted by Hare Krishna chanters, we read *Be Here Now* by Baba Ram Dass. While it was not possible to find anyone trained in Zen, William Johnston's book *The Still Point* provided an understanding of this way of meditation. We then had a discussion of those aspects of TM that could be revealed without breaking confidence. This was led by a priest who had been trained in a special course in Transcendental Meditation for professional religious people.

We concluded our fourteen three-hour sessions with a Eucharist as a prime example of religious experiences, using the early liturgy of St. Hippolytus, with sections of my book *Myth, History and Faith* serving to emphasize the symbolic imagery and atmosphere of this experience.

REACTIONS AND REFLECTIONS

Most of the individuals who took part found this practicum of help in their own inward journey. They found that using a journal was a tremendous aid in clarifying and understanding their inner lives and the varieties of religious experience open to them. They realized that Eastern forms of meditation, although valuable and adding many insights, did not provide the content or the encounter and relationship with the divine that most of them were seeking.

Thus there was clearly a difference, they saw, between Eastern and Western meditation. In the Eastern forms there seemed to be a desire to merge into the cosmic mind, to come to imagelessness and be absorbed intellectually into an infinite Oneness. A number of students observed that the kind of Christian meditation which is based on the ideas of Plotinus and Proclus seemed to have more in common with the Eastern religions than with much Western Christianity. They realized that the traditional Christian way of meditating, which uses images with the goal of encountering the divine Lover, had more to offer them than the Eastern form, with its aim of losing individuality in the cosmic oneness. When they tried the two on for size, the traditional Christian way seemed more valuable and more useful to most of them.

As they analyzed their experiences in terms of the schema we had provided, they discovered that there were two reasons for this. Meditation that used images tended to bring the individual to psychic wholeness, because it took emotional problems into account. Thus this kind of meditation could bring healing that was impossible if one followed the Eastern route of "getting off the world" in order to avoid these problems. The second reason was that Christian meditation required both a vertical and a horizontal relationship, while the Eastern way was limited mainly to the vertical one. The Christian way had meaning. It led first to God, and then to reaching out with the love that had been found. One needed human fellowship, first in order to develop as this kind of meditation required, and then to express this love to others and help them to find it within themselves.

Religious educators and seminarians who had been threatened by Eastern and occult practices found that as they understood these practices and compared them with the best of Christian practices they had nothing to fear. And, as one student said, "This meditation gives a trip that I couldn't get on any drug!"

NOTES

1. The course outlines are found in the appendix at the end of this chapter.
2. These experiences are discussed by Charles Panati in his book *Supersenses*. (New York: Quadrangle/New York Times Book Co., 1974).
3. C.G. Jung, *Analytical Psychology: Its Theory and Practice* (New York: Random House, 1968), pp. 190-198. (Also in *Collected Works*, Vol. 18, *The Symbolic Life*.)
4. Several examples of this kind of meditation are given in M. Kelsey, *The Other Side of Silence* (New York: Paulist Press, 1976), pp. 239-67.
5. A study of the psychological meanings in Dante's *Divine Comedy*.
6. M. Kelsey, *The Other Side of Silence*, pp. 289-97 and 303-05.

APPENDIX

UNIVERSITY OF NOTRE DAME DEPARTMENT OF THEOLOGY

Course: Science and Spiritual Direction

The goal of the course is to present the implications of scientific thought for the spiritual direction of individuals living in the present scientific age. Materials from psychology, physics, the philosophy of science, and the history of philosophy will be presented.

Since it is difficult to help another in the crisis of belief caused by disparity between much Church dogma and scientific thought unless one has faced these issues oneself, the course will aim at bringing these differing attitudes to light within the class and working them through individually and with group discussions.

The student is to read the book assigned for the week *before* the class so that intelligent discussion of the material can develop. Six short papers of reaction to the materials will be required in addition to a longer paper in which one's own fundamentals of belief are discussed. The following books form the required reading list:

Week 1: *The Inner World of Childhood*, by Frances Wickes.
Week 2: *The Natural Mind*, by Andrew Weil. Also relevant: *The Greening of America*.
Week 3: *Encounter with God*, by Morton Kelsey.
Week 4: *On Death and Dying*, by Elisabeth Kübler-Ross.
Week 5: *Language, Truth and Logic*, by A.J. Ayer.

Week 6: *Physics and Philosophy*, by Werner Heisenberg or *The Philosophy of Science: An Introduction*, by Stephen Toulmin, and Chapter viii of *Gödel's Proof*, by Nagel and Newman; *The Structure of the Scientific Revolutions*, T.S. Kuhn.

Week 7: *The Future of an Illusion* and *Civilization and Its Discontents*, by Sigmund Freud.

Week 8: *Modern Man in Search of a Soul*, by C.G. Jung.

Week 9: *Analytical Psychology: Its Theory and Practice*, the Tavistock lectures, by C.G. Jung, or *Lectures on Jung's Typology*, by M.L. Von Franz and James Hillman. C.G. Jung's *Memories, Dreams, Reflections*.

Week 10: The Masculine and Feminine: *He*, by Robert Johnson, or *She*, by Robert Johnson, or one of the following: *Knowing Woman*, by Irene de Castillejo, *The Way of All Women*, by Esther Harding, *The Way of Woman: Ancient and Modern*, by Helen Luke.

Week 11: *Supersenses*, by Charles Panati; *The Christian and the Supernatural*, by M.T. Kelsey.

Week 12: *Plato*, by Paul Friedlander, Chapters 1-3; *The Symposium*, by Plato; *The Art of Christian Love*, *The Reality of the Spiritual World*, and *Finding Meaning: Guidelines for Counselors*, by Morton Kelsey; *The Meaning of the Creative Act*, by N. Berdyaev—chapters on creativity and sex and creativity and love.

Week 13: *Myth, History and Faith*, by Morton Kelsey; *Four Quartets*, by T.S. Eliot. Collateral reading: *After the Fall*, by Arthur Miller, and *Dark Wood to White Rose*, by Helen Luke.

UNIVERSITY OF NOTRE DAME DEPARTMENT OF THEOLOGY

Course: Phenomenology of Religious Experience

☐Orientation: The purpose of the course is to acquaint the individual brought up in the Western culture with the varieties of religious experience common in our day. This is essentially the cognitive side of the subject, while the Practicum in Religious Experience provides the more experiential dimension. The course is limited largely to Western experiences.

Requirements: 1. Complete required readings *before* the week in which the class occurs.
2. Complete informal report papers by the time due.
3. Complete graduate research paper two (2) weeks before close of semester.
4. Pass final examination.
5. Keep a journal.

Readings:

Week 1: Drugs and religious experience:
Carlos Castaneda, *The Teachings of Don Juan*; Andrew Weil, *The Natural Mind*.

Week 2: The dream and vision as examples of religious experience:
M.T. Kelsey, *God, Dreams and Revelation*; Report paper: The dream-vision and being stoned.

Weeks 3
& 4: The psychological study of religious experience:
       C.G. Jung, *Psychology and Religion, West and East* (Vol. 11, *Collected Works*) — sections 5,4,1,3,6. Report paper: Psychology and religions.
Weeks 5
& 6: Analysis of mystical experience:
       Selections from the two volumes of Baron Friedrich von Hügel, *The Mystical Element of Religion*; Report paper: Analysis of religious experience in von Hügel.
Week 7: A survey of the material:
         Morton Kelsey, *Encounter with God*.
Week 8: Religious experience — Shamanism:
         Mircea Eliade, *Shamanism*, pp. 259-511; Report: Shamanism and Christianity.
Week 9: The idea of religious experience:
         Rudolf Otto, *The Idea of the Holy*.
Week 10: Meditation as religious experience:
          Morton Kelsey, *The Other Side of Silence*.
Week 11: The Charismatic experience:
          Morton Kelsey, *Tongue Speaking*; Cardinal Suenens, *A New Pentecost?*; Report paper: The meaning of Charisma.
Week 12: Evil, demonism, and healing:
          Morton Kelsey, *Healing and Christianity*.
Week 13: Medicine, psychology and healing:
          Finish reading *Healing and Christianity*; Report paper: The significance of healing as a religious experience.
Week 14: Contemporary Shamanism:
          Carlos Castaneda, *Tales of Power*.

UNIVERSITY OF NOTRE DAME DEPARTMENT OF THEOLOGY

Course: Practicum in Religious Experience
   Orientation: The purpose of the course is to probe in an experimental way the meaning of the religious experience in the individual life. Religious experience only has meaning in an individual. Certain readings are offered to guide the individual into various kinds of experience.
   The important part of the course will be a sharing of experiences in an honest and open way. Since these are personal experiences, the group will be asked to keep these personal expressions within the group, unless the individual expressing the experience gives assent to telling it outside the group. It is hoped that the group's expression of experience will make us more sensitive to our own experiences and more able to express them.
   Another extremely important part of the course will be keeping a journal and recording dreams, religious experiences, experiences of *déjà vu*, etc.
   Thus the course has three aspects: cognitive, personal, and group experience.

Requirements: 1. Attendance at every class is of prime importance; if the individual will not be able to attend regularly then he or she should not take the course.

2. A careful evaluation of the course is due at mid-term and again at the conclusion of the course. Reflections on changes in one's own experience or new attitudes from reading, group, or personal experience will form the basis of these papers.
3. Reading the material appropriate to the area under discussion and exploration will be expected *before* the time of discussion.

Readings: The course will consider various forms of religious experience that are currently viable. Because of the immense variety, a selection had to be made.

Week 1: The prayer of quiet:
Edward Rice, *The Man in the Sycamore Tree;* Thomas Kelly, *A Testament of Devotion.*

Weeks 2
&3: The use of images in meditation:
Ignatius Loyola, *The Spiritual Exercises*; Nikos Kazantzakis, *The Saviors of God*; Morton Kelsey, *The Other Side of Silence.*

Weeks 4
&5: The dream and vision (read two of the four):
M.T. Kelsey, *God, Dreams, and Revelation*; John Sanford, *Dreams, God's Forgotten Language*; John Sanford, *The Kingdom Within*; C.G. Jung, *Memories, Dreams, Reflections.*

Week 6: The Jesus Prayer (read one):
R.M. French, *The Way of a Pilgrim and The Pilgrim Continues His Way; The Prayer of Jesus* (no author), Desclee, 1967.

Week 7: The Charismatic movement:
M.T. Kelsey, *Tongue Speaking*, or Cardinal Suenens, *A New Pentecost?*

Week 8: New thought, unity and positive thinking (read one):
Bristol, *The Magic of Believing*; N.V. Peale, *The Power of Positive Thinking*; The works of Joel Goldsmith, Christian Science, Science of Mind, etc.

Week 9: Psychic phenomena and mediums, etc.:
S.E. White, *The Unobstructed Universe*, or Morton Kelsey, *The Christian and the Supernatural.*

Week 10: The *I Ching:*
The best translation is that of Richard Wilhelm.

Week 11: Yoga:
Jess Stearn, *Yoga, Youth and Reincarnation.*

Week 12: Eclectic modern method:
Baba Ram Dass, *Be Here Now.*

Week 13: Zen and Christianity:
William Johnston, *The Still Point,* or William Johnston, *Silent Music.*

Week 14: Eucharist as religious experience:
Morton Kelsey, *Myth, History and Faith.*

Chapter 9

MINISTRY TO THE LONELY

There is little written specifically on the subject of loneliness. It is difficult to find the subject in an encyclopedia. There are several reasons for this lack of interest, and I will deal with some of the more significant ones at greater length later on. At this point let me simply note that the subject of loneliness does not interest sociologists simply because it is an inner feeling, and orthodox positivistic sociologists can no more deal with unmeasurable feelings than can a Skinnerian behaviorist. They can only deal with suicide (loneliness leading to depression and despair), divorce (one result of two people being lonely together), alcoholism and drug abuse (two ways to escape loneliness), crime (often the angry reaction of lonely people), poverty, and social disintegration. But loneliness is beyond their expertise.

Likewise, psychologists seldom have people entering their offices simply because they are lonely. Most of the lonely ones are more likely to join a lodge, Parents Without Partners, or a church group to alleviate loneliness, or they get married. Psychologists on the whole are interested in helping us to become more comfortable with our inner emotional states or enabling us to overcome inadequate social behavior. They use positive thinking, operant conditioning, reality therapy or analysis of intrapsychic factors. They try to release patients from neurosis, depression, and psychosis; loneliness is seldom the direct focus of their enquiry, and little is written by them about alienation.

The best study of loneliness known to me is that of James Lynch, *The Broken Heart*. Dr. Lynch is a clinical psychologist teaching psychiatry at the University of Maryland Medical School. His book discusses the medical consequences of loneliness, and then offers suggestions for avoiding the destructive human experience of being alone and without companionship.

We human beings are very complex, and so is our loneliness. In order to get at the subject I shall first look at the contribution of sociology to our understanding of human personality and the human need for others. Then I will examine the contributions of some recent psychologists who have dealt with the problem of human aloneness. After that I will deal with the mass of evidence brought forward by James Lynch, and then summarize the basic causes of the sense of alienation in human beings in their several stages of social and psychological development. I will conclude with some suggestions that the ministry of the Church can implement in order to alleviate some of the destructiveness of loneliness and alienation. We are not likely to be motivated until we know the facts.

SOCIOLOGY AND ALIENATION

Sociology as a scientific discipline is not yet one hundred years old. It is difficult to realize that a subject that is so much a part of the modern academic scene began with the work of Emile Durkheim in France in the late years of the nineteenth century. Durkheim is to sociology what Freud is to modern psychiatry. Durkheim believed that division of labor rendered workers more alien to one another and more dependent upon one another. One of his most important works treated the subject of suicide. He found suicide to be less common where human beings were deeply and genuinely integrated into the culture. He described three kinds of suicide, those required by society and social custom (such as the hara-kiri of the Japanese or the recent mass suicides in Guyana), egoistic suicide, where the individual has too few ties with his or her community, and anomic suicide, where crisis has shattered the individual's relationship with society. Durkheim believed that most Western suicides fell into the latter two categories, and were the result of inadequate integration into social groups. Subjectively this would be experienced as loneliness.

Human beings do not become human beings unless they are brought up with other human beings. Language and humanness are acquired in the socializing process. A dog or a cat is a dog or cat whether brought up by humans or ducks. Language is necessary for the development of human potential, and language is learned from some social group during certain crucial years of childhood. The individual is shaped in many ways by the customs and language of that group. Children lost from society and brought up by animals in the jungle are more animal than human. They will, however, quickly learn to be human if introduced into the human social environment early enough. Human beings never brought into contact with other human beings can hardly be called human at all.

It is easy to jump to the conclusion that humanness is totally and exclusively the product of the observable social structure. Many sociologists make that jump. They fail to give adequate emphasis to physical inheritance as one of the factors essential to the developed human being. And the great majority of sociologists reject out of hand the idea that humans might experience something beyond the physical environment.

An example of this positivism is given by Kalish and Reynolds in a paper printed in the *Journal for the Scientific Study of Religion.* They did a careful sociological study on what people believed about contact with the deceased after death. They discovered that 44% of their cross-cultural sample stated that they had had such experiences. Reviewing the literature, they found that no one had ever done a study on this subject. Within the sociological worldview it was simply impossible to ask about such experiences. Incidentally, their work has been replicated by other sociologists.

There is certainly no doubt that the social group contributes much to the development of human beings nurtured within it. A seed can develop into a normal tree, be dwarfed into a bonsai, or it can germinate and die. Among nonliterate people, individual self-consciousness is not highly developed. Within these societies social influences predominate, and banishment from the social group can result in death.

Taboo deaths are a fact. When individuals in a close-knit society break its taboos, they feel cut off from the group, even though physically present. Thus they can have no meaningful relationships with others. They feel outcast and valueless, and often retreat to a corner, curl up, and die. For many of these people, banishment is a fate as dismal as a death sentence. After three months alone in Switzerland some years ago, and after wrestling with the Swiss authorities over my passport, I remember the sense of relief upon putting my feet on American soil again, even though my stay in Switzerland had been voluntary.

Studies of those subjected to brainwashing techniques in Korean prisoner-of-war camps also show the value of a solid social embeddedness. The Turkish soldiers were unquestioning Muslims. They were firmly integrated into a collective pattern. They were largely untouched by brainwashing attempts. Those without such a background, Americans or New Zealanders, were much more easily influenced. The greater the acceptance of the social mores, the greater the stability of individuals under pressure. However, unquestioning adherence to a collective framework allows less flexibility to individuals and less opportunity for creative adaptation.

Being separated from other human beings and having little meaningful contact with them is the essence of loneliness, and can result in anything from suicide to mental breakdown, depression, alcoholism, divorce, or even physical illness. Suicide diminishes dramatically during wartime, when people are joined together in a common cause and effort. Few human beings can live meaningful lives apart from a social group. However, the stage of psychological development and the psychological structure and type of the individual determine how that person handles loneliness and what is done with it. And so we turn to the psychological understanding of our subject.

PSYCHOLOGY AND ALIENATION

There are many modern psychologies. The behaviorist claims that all human qualities are the result of the operant conditioning to which the individual is subjected. Social forces are but one aspect of that conditioning. In *Walden Two* Skinner sketches out his theory in novel form. He describes individuals who have been properly conditioned within his utopia, and they are perfectly happy. He would probably also suggest that individuals could be conditioned to seek and endure loneliness. From this point of view the human being is a complex piece of matter, which can be manipulated in nearly any desired direction.

Once the individual is seen as a psychological entity, as well as a physical one, psychological study really begins. This psychic reality consists of the well-known conscious aspects of personality and the deeper unconscious determinants of our lives. We have already indicated that the person is shaped to a large extent by the love and concern that person received as a child in the family. If loved and genuinely cared for, that child will develop normally and become an adult having an adequate self-image, able to relate to other human beings in a meaningful way. Indeed, as von Hügel suggests, God created the human family just so we might learn human love and so be able to respond to Divine Love. Children who have been wisely loved will feel alien neither among other human beings nor in the larger spiritual dimension.

Children who do not receive this kind of tender, loving care are lonely to begin with. They often project their own problems upon others, and seldom can relate adequately to other human beings. They continue to be alien and lonely because they are unable to relate to human beings or be open to the love that is available from a divine encounter. Only as they undergo a reorganization and reliving of their early lives, through interaction with a truly caring person, through psychological analysis, or by religious experience and spiritual direction, will this personality set be altered. The autistic person is one who, for reasons we do not understand, is unable to relate to anyone else. The neurotic has scrambled and inappropriate inner reactions, and often cannot develop meaningful relationships no matter how hard he or she tries. The psychotic lives within a private, inner world, unrelated to outer social norms or the feelings and attitudes of other human beings. Psychosis and autism are the nadir of unproductive loneliness.

Adler and his school of thought emphasize social factors in the development of the human being. They teach that lack of social relatedness tends to destroy any sense of purpose and leads to a death wish, or even suicide. They believe that separation from the social group, loneliness, can hardly be tolerated by human beings.

Freud in his later years added a most pessimistic element to his concept of the human psyche, the death wish. Not only are human beings in inner conflict, but deep within the unconscious is a desire to return to the inorganic state, to death. According to Freud, if human beings don't project this instinct out upon other human beings in conflict, race prejudice, hatred, and war, they are likely to turn it in upon themselves and commit suicide! In both *Beyond the Pleasure Principle* and *Civilization and Its Discontents,* Freud's view of human nature makes alienation among human beings almost inevitable. According to Freud, even sexuality is tinged with violence. Alienation is thus the natural state of human beings.

Jung contributes two major new insights to the understanding of loneliness. In his study of psychological types he distinguishes between introverts, who are primarily interested in their own inner psychic worlds, and extraverts, who prefer to deal with the outer physical world and the people in it. What the extravert would consider lonely, the introvert might find a pleasant or desirable situation. Some people die on the vine without many social contacts, while others can be tormented by them. Some countries, like Switzerland, are predominantly introverted. The Swiss find it difficult to understand extraverted Americans.

In *Modern Man in Search of a Soul* Jung describes the conditions necessary for individuals to be truly accepting and supportive of other human beings. In order to come to this point individuals must be able to accept all of themselves, and this is a heroic task. It can be frightening to come to know the idiot and murderer within ourselves. To reach out and accept another in a real way, we must be able to accept all of ourselves. When we do not know and accept ourselves we often project our faults and weaknesses onto others. Acceptance of the dark side of our intrapsychic contents is a prerequisite for reaching out to the loneliness of other people and for freeing us from our own isolation. Jung goes on to show that intellectual doubt that keeps us from a real relation with a real God can lead to existential loneliness and despair.

Sexuality is usually viewed as an expression of intimacy and closeness. Rollo May in *Love and Will* and Masters and Johnson in *The Pleasure Bond* stress the fact that sexuality does not necessarily lead to intimacy. It is the other way around: Among somewhat conscious people adequate sexuality is the result of dialogue and relationship. Sex between alienated people is not a satisfying experience, but contributes further to the loneliness of the individuals involved.

LYNCH'S STUDY OF LONELINESS

The most provocative study of loneliness and its devastating effects is by James Lynch. It shows that loneliness increases the death rate from most diseases. Physicians have been in the habit of looking only for physical causes of illness. In the much publicized Framingham study of causative factors in heart disease, the files kept on individuals do not even have a place for the marital status of the individual. Dr. Lynch marshals evidence to show that in every age group deaths from coronary heart disease are significantly higher among divorced, widowed, and single people than for married people. The death rate for the nonmarried is 20% to 300% higher than for married people. The following chart of death rates per 100,000 population shows the

difference between the married and the divorced white male, ages
15-64, in the United States, 1959-61. (The following chart appears in
James Lynch, *The Broken Heart,* page 43.)

	Married	*Divorced*
Heart disease	176	362
Motor vehicle accidents	35	128
Cancer — respiratory	28	65
Cancer — digestive system	27	48
Stroke	24	58
Suicide	17	73
Cirrhosis of liver	11	79
Hypertension	8	20
Pneumonia	6	44
Homicide	4	30
Tuberculosis	3	30

One of the most interesting studies on the effect of human companionship and touch was done in an intensive care unit in which the heart is monitored continuously. Dr. Lynch discovered that the simple touch of the nurse taking the pulse had a tendency to stabilize the heart of patients seriously sick with heart disease. Dr. Lynch's studies demonstrated that this occurred even when no other change in the heart was observed for three minutes before or after this simple touch.

Studies of dogs show that in a strange environment they will exhibit a wildly beating heart. The presence of a human being will quiet the dog's heart. If the person goes into the room and pets the dog, the heart goes into a rhythm of complete relaxation.

Some of the most dramatic studies of the effect of loneliness upon health relate to children. Dr. Rene Spitz first described the disease of *marasmus,* the gradual wasting away of infants. It was discovered in foundling homes in the United States and Canada. Ninety-one children in these homes were carefully studied. Even though the children received "meticulous medical care," 34 of the 91 died. At Bellevue Hospital in New York systematic fondling or mothering was introduced by aides in pediatric wards. After several years of this practice the mortality rates for infants under one year of age fell from almost 35% to less than 10%.

Dr. Lynch states that interaction with other human beings, both verbal and nonverbal, is the only way to avoid the lethal effects of loneliness. A bad marriage is better than no marriage, as the people involved at least have some kind of interaction. (My wife tells me that I could never afford to divorce her, as she is such good health insurance!)

Ashley Montagu, in his book *Touching: The Human Significance of the Skin,* writes that touching is an important biological need—as basic as breathing, eating, or resting. Monkeys brought up with a terrycloth surrogate mother do not develop natural sexual instincts. Without interaction from other living beings like themselves, the monkeys are emotionally crippled. Studies have shown adult schizophrenics are four times more likely to have lost a parent before the age of fifteen by death or divorce than ordinary adults. Loneliness destroys the very fabric of life itself.

Interesting pictures have been made of the laying on of hands for healing using Kirlian photography. Before the laying on of hands, the healer's fingers show a full nimbus or halo of light, and those of the sick person show only a faint one. After the laying on of hands the situation is reversed. Something has taken place. In all creative relationships we impart a real life force to one another. The lonely person is cut off from this. Lonely people do not have the same will to fight disease and they do not have the same will to live as those with satisfying social relationships.

Carl and Stephanie Simonton, in their book *Getting Well Again,* show that most cancer occurs within six to eighteen months after some major stress crisis, usually related to a disruption of meaningful relationships. They find that deeply hidden in most of their cancer patients is an unconscious wish to get out of a meaningless life situation. Most of them cannot fight off their disease until they deal with their meaninglessness, which is often caused by a sense of isolation and alienation.

THE CAUSES OF LONELINESS

Surveying all this material, it becomes apparent that loneliness is a feeling that can arise from a number of causes.

1. Disruption of one's social ties and separation from the social matrix create a sense of alienation and loneliness. For those living largely within the collective frame of reference, this can spell death itself. Since most religious meaning is mediated through the social group in largely collective societies, those cut off from the group are also cut off from religious meaning and experience an existential lone-

liness as well as a human one. Indeed, among primitive, preliterate
people human and religious values are not clearly distinguished.
Human beings share in a common worldview and a common set of
experiences, which Levy-Bruhl calls *participation mystique*. It is
important to realize that each of us carries some remnants of this level
of human development within us. My first parish was in a railroad
town. The men often began working on the railroad when they were
teenagers. Often they would not live more than a few months, or even
weeks, upon retiring after fifty years of service. Cut off from their ordinary life and social contacts, they just died. Several years ago I went on
sabbatical leave and left a very busy life for an almost entirely isolated
one. Even though my wife was with me and life was pleasant, I experienced a sense of deep loneliness and depression. I had looked forward
to this time of retreat. People should prepare for retirement in which
they are taken out of the ordinary social situation.

2. As individuals become more aware of their own individuality and
their own uniqueness, they tend to break away from the social group
and its mores. They often develop small and very intensely intimate
groups. This can be observed as societies move out of the more collective framework. We can trace this development clearly in ancient
Greece, and in many cultures at present. The same process is at work
among adolescents in our society. This is a difficult time, as we have
no initiation rites to help the individuals through this crisis. David
Riesman addresses this problem in *The Lonely Crowd*. Loneliness
seems to be a natural stage in societies, as well as in individuals, as they
move toward greater consciousness.

3. Individuals who find it difficult to give total allegiance to any
social group or worldview have an increased need to find intimate
relationships. They wish to meet some others in complete and honest
sharing. Because of the depth and complexity of the human psyche,
this is very difficult. This means accepting not only the parts of ourselves which are like an idiot and a murderer, but also accepting these
parts in the other person. This is a real exercise in consciousness, char-
ity, and true religion.

4. There is a fascinating footnote in James Lynch's *The Broken
Heart*. He suggests that one of the reasons that our society does not
value human relationships is because it has swallowed the objective,
scientific-medical attitude that has had no place for the healing effect
of human relationships and human touch. He states that even the
Church has accepted this way of thinking, and has therefore aban-

doned its very significant and valuable healing ministry. This footnote was a whole chapter in the original book. The publisher excised it as not relevant to the subject. Lynch writes, "Lonely people who began to develop physical symptoms were sent by other human beings to drug-stores to buy aspirins, tranquilizers or antidepressants. They were denied the only effective healing agent — human contact — that could possibly have cured loneliness, because no one any longer believed it to be very effective."[1]

5. Everyone faces death and the death of those one loves. Some people without the courage to bear the inevitable pain of life form no deep relationships, for fear of losing those they might love. If there is no reality beyond death, then one must learn to endure it. If, however, there is some continued existence, then learning to deal with the reality of a life that continues into another dimension is an important part of dealing with loneliness.

Many people find that no other one human being totally satisfies the human need for intimacy and relationship. God alone satisfies this need. Human beings plunged into confrontation with a nonphysical dimension of reality may find themselves in existential loneliness that only an encounter with God can satisfy in any ultimate way. Celia, in T.S. Eliot's *Cocktail Party*, typifies this experience. Indeed, sometimes it is only through this experience of divine love that relationships with other human beings are put in proper perspective. Those having a continuing, fulfilling encounter with the divine can offer more genuine relationship to others, and can often lead them on to a similar encounter themselves.

THE TASK OF THE CHURCH AND ITS MINISTRY

If the Church is to deal with the problem of human loneliness it must realize that different human beings have different needs, and none of these are to be scorned.

1. First of all, the Church needs to provide meaningful rituals, rituals of action and silence in which people can be brought together and can share in common significant actions. Churchgoers actually have far fewer coronary attacks than nonchurchgoers. This kind of group activity satisfies a deep human need.

2. Fellowship groups, in which five to twenty people meet to cook dinner or sew quilts, also offer some people needed group contacts. Such groups are not to be scorned.

3. For others, dialogue groups are valuable. In them the nature and depth of human beings and their varied interests can be explored. Such groups are not encounter groups, but study groups, within which individuals may search together for deeper meaning and fellowship at the same time. Jesus had a group of twelve. The vitality of early Methodism was due in large part to the small groups of believers who met together to share their inner lives and support one another in following their religious method. Alcoholics Anonymous provides similar group support for this group of lonely people.

4. Human beings in trouble need real pastoring. In death, sickness, and loneliness they need to be called upon, ministered to, and treated with love and concern. *In our modern society only clergy among helping professionals have a right to initiate calls on lonely human beings.* The early Church grew and prospered at least in part because it offered such care. Pagans looked at Christians and said, "Look how they love one aother. We would like to share in such a community of love."

Each church needs lay people as well as clergy to minister to the lonely. Such activity must be organized if it is to reach the increasing need of our fragmented society.

5. Some human beings find that they have been called to deal with the spiritual world and find their own way towards God. The Church needs to provide those people with spiritual direction. The spiritual world is at least as complex and dangerous as the physical one. People can get lost in it. This can result in a sense of loneliness and alienation that is just as difficult to bear as the loss of loved ones or banishment from one's social group.

When the Church is not ministering to human loneliness on all levels it is failing in its task. This is an awesome responsibility. It is missing the mark as much as, or even more than, when it fails to feed the hungry or clothe the naked. Loneliness is social, psychological, and spiritual starvation. If the Church is to live up to its prophetic role and task, it cannot let the lonely slip through the cracks of its activities.

NOTES

1. James J. Lynch, *The Broken Heart* (New York: Basic Books, 1977), p. 186.

Chapter 10

MINISTRY TO THE HOMOSEXUAL

Nearly twenty years ago, on one of the Los Angeles television stations, a panel discussion was held on the subject of homosexuality. I was asked to participate as a clergyman who had done considerable counseling with homosexuals. A judge, a lawyer, and a psychiatrist were the other members of the panel. We went on the air quietly after a heated preview discussion, and moments later the judge was stricken with a cerebral accident. The program was suspended, and he was taken to a hospital, where he later died. The tragedy was certainly symbolic of the violence of attitude that still surrounds this subject.

Thus interrupted, the program did not have the continuity it might have had, but I will never forget one question asked me by the moderator: "What is the Church's moral attitude toward homosexuality?" For a moment I was speechless, because I had never viewed the subject from the point of view of morality. I made some feeble response. Later I told a psychiatrist friend of mine of my failure to give an adequate answer to the question. He replied, "Of course you would have had difficulty giving an answer to the question. Homosexuality is no more a matter of morals than is the peptic ulcer." And I realized that this was precisely my own attitude, as it has been to this day.

More recently, when I was asked to give a paper on the subject of religion and homosexuality, I began once again to read the literature and to ponder the reactions of the Christian Church. As I tried to fit homosexuality into the total Christian worldview, I found that first of all I was appalled at the "Christian" attitude, and then overwhelmed by the complexity of the subject of homosexuality itself. I discovered a morass of different ideas on the subject coming from many different sources. First there is the popular attitude, and next the legal and social viewpoint, which is closely allied to the popular attitude. Then

125

there is the viewpoint of physical medicine. Psychology presents several other points of view of the subject. In addition, many different attitudes toward homosexuality are discovered in the study of comparative religion and in the history of philosophy. Still another view of the subject can be found in the expressions emanating from the "gay" world.

If we are to see some order in the confusion, we had better begin by defining what we are talking about, and then consider some actual facts. I propose to describe the various medical and psychological attitudes and to try to see historically how the current ideas about homosexuality came into being. This will necessitate a discussion of the Church's thinking about sexuality in general, and this expression of it in particular. Then we will discuss the Church's overall attitude toward sickness and psychological variation, and see how it applies to the homosexual. This will bring us to the question of the Christian valuation of love and relationship. We will conclude with our observations by trying to see what the Church's attitude and action ought to be on the basis of the teaching and practice of Jesus. Our consideration will be mainly directed to male homosexuality, since female homosexuality does not seem to present problems of the same magnitude to our society or in the Church.

What is homosexuality? It is the sexual desire on the part of an individual for a member of the same sex. Sexuality is here viewed in the full range of its physical and emotional expression. Homosexuality is empowered with the full energy of the reproductive instinct, and therefore falls into the same category in regard to its potency as the drive for food and self-preservation. It has deep unconscious roots and takes heroic strength to control. This desire can be expressed in action and in acts of bodily contact. There are as many variations of physical gratification of the homosexual urge as there are of heterosexual desire. The more common ones are mutual masturbation in various ways, fellatio, and sodomy. This desire, on the other hand, may be latent, but consciously known and suppressed and sublimated. The desire may also be unconscious and repressed, and so expressed in some neurosis because of the unconscious conflict within the personality. Some of the rebellious teenagers of our society who are involved in violence are overcompensating for their unconscious homosexual feelings. There is also probably a relation between unconscious homosexuality and voyeurism, exhibitionism, and transvestism. The homosexual act may, like the heterosexual act, be the result of mutual consent and affection, or if it is purely sensual, it may be the result of seduction, violence, or compulsion. It is sometimes associated with sado-masochism. Homosexuality contains the full repertoire of sexual expression, but directed toward the same sex rather than the opposite one. Because of popular and legal condemnation, only the less savory aspects of the subject usually come to the public eye.

There are few subjects on which there is more general prejudice and lack of information. Comparable in intensity are the violence of race prejudice and the popular attitudes toward mental illness and mental institutions at the turn of the century. Yet homosexuality is far from rare. Professor Kinsey's studies arrive at the conclusion that 4% of the adult males are exclusively homosexual and have only homosexual activity, while 18% are more homosexual than heterosexual in their experiences after adolescence. In all, 37% after adolescence have had at least one homosexual experience leading to orgasm.[1] Kinsey, it is reported, has stated in private conversation that 50% of the male population has had some homosexual experience after adolescence. My own counseling experience tends to confirm this latter figure; yet most of these men make an adequate heterosexual adjustment. According to the famous anthropologist Dr. Margaret Mead, this sexual expression is observable in nearly all cultures, and in some of them it is a sign of distinction and honor rather than of degeneration and depravity.[2] Homosexual behavior is also observable among almost all mammals, although it is apparently only among human beings that there are individuals who direct their total sexual expression in this way.

While a small proportion of homosexuals do have bodily characteristics of the opposite sex, and some occasionally affect the mannerisms or clothes of the opposite sex, the great majority have no outer physical characteristics that identify them in their sexual predilections. Indeed, many feminine-appearing men are exclusively and enthusiastically heterosexual. The great majority of homosexuals, the best adjusted, pass through society with none of the heterosexuals knowing that they are different. It is the small percentage of identifiable homosexuals who create most of the prejudice, since the popular attitude has until recent years forced the adjusted homosexual to hide his variation.

The law in England, West Germany, and the United States has expressed this social horror. Sentences ranging from fines to life imprisonment are on the statute books of many American states for the punishment of one homosexual act. If people commit murder, their friends will probably come to visit them in jail, but if they are in jail for homosexuality, they may find themselves completely shunned by their heterosexual friends.

The object of the homosexual's affection may be an adult of the same age, an older adult, a younger adult, or a child. This sexual expression may take place in a fleeting and casual encounter in which the only important factor is sexual release, or the homosexual act may be merely one aspect of a relationship characterized by commitment, affection, and devotion, as well as sexuality, which may even have the quality of romantic love between the sexes. In fact, it is almost as meaningless to speak of homosexuality without defining its variation as it would be to refer to all heterosexual relationships as if there were no differences among them. We are well aware that these vary from the deepest kind of lifelong and affectionate relationship between a man and woman to, say, the violent rape of a young girl. Homosexual relationships are just as varied.

SEVERAL WAYS OF LOOKING AT HOMOSEXUALITY

In fact, the popular approach that sees no distinctions is only one of several different value judgments of homosexuality. It involves the view that these individuals perversely desire to be homosexual and are purposefully defying social conventions. Along with this attitude goes the belief that they must be changed, and since the perversity lies in the will, it is only through punishment that they can be brought to change. There is not a shred of evidence for this point of view. (Indeed, because of the social sanctions against homosexuality, many homosexuals have desired and tried to change, but without success.) This attitude is the basis of most of the antihomosexual statutes in this country. But I have yet to find one homosexual whose basic pattern was changed by legal punishment. Instead, punitive imprisonment simply places the individual in a situation that is more conducive to homosexuality.

The view of physical medicine, on the other hand, involves a judgment, accepted by many in this profession, that homosexuality is either a physical, glandular, or psychic predisposition about which little or nothing can be done. Homosexuality is then an anomaly, a physiological or psychic defect like a club foot or an extra toe. Of course, if this is true then there is little point to punishing homosexuals, except to protect the public who are offended by this particular human variation.

With the studies and theories of Freud we enter a new phase in the discussion of sexual variations. Freud hypothesized that human beings are essentially bisexual—capable of reacting sexually to either the opposite or the same sex. Nothing in his analytic experience ever gave him reason to doubt this hypothesis. He believed that changing the homosexual was seldom achieved, although through analysis the person could adjust to his situation. Younger men without a strong psychic predisposition might be changed more often than older men.

Although Jung usually put more emphasis upon psychic inheritance than did Freud, he seemed to stress the *environmental* causes of this variant behavior. In what can be gleaned from his scattered references, he saw male homosexuality as one result of a mother complex, of an identification with the feminine psychic framework that closeness to one's own mother could produce. His conclusions suggest that this early predisposing factor must first be present for homosexual feelings to develop as a result of seduction. In fact, one of my friends, whose practice is basically Jungian, protested to me the failure of the term *homosexual* to describe the actual fact; the expression for male homosexuality, he felt, should be "ascendancy of the feminine." Female homosexuality would be understood as a female identification with the father or the masculine.

In psychoanalytic theory homosexuality is also seen as one stage in the development of full heterosexuality. The individual is drawn first to the same sex, because it is easier to relate to the known than to the unknown. Homosexuality, in this third view, is a sickness in that it is a fixation at an immature stage of development, although this is using the term "sickness" in a loose way. The sickness described is due more to the inability to participate in heterosexual experience than to the presence of homosexual feelings or acts.

According to the various schools of depth psychology, this personality variation is extremely difficult to change, as it necessitates the change of one's essential identification with a psychic role. This may be possible where motivation is very great, where insight and ability

are also present; but under the best circumstances it requires excep-
tional effort on the part of both analyst and patient. Judging one who
backs away from this kind of effort hardly makes sense unless each of
us who does not put out the greatest effort in the development of his or
her own personality is ready to accept condemnation.

Still another psychiatric viewpoint was expressed by the late Dr.
Blanche Baker, who did a great deal of counseling with homosexuals
and worked with the Mattachine Society educationally. She once
stated in a radio interview: "I feel that a homosexual is, first of all, a
human being. Now that may seem to be a rather elementary statement, but I very much believe in the individual adjustment problem,
and I think that homosexuality may have many different kinds of
causes, and each individual case needs to be studied and interpreted
on its own merits. I do not look upon homosexuality as a neurotic
problem, but more a basic personality pattern reaction. Just as some
people prefer blondes and others prefer brunettes, I think that the fact
that a given person may prefer the love of the same sex is his personal
business. Now, this does not mean that homosexuals may not become
neurotic — I think that they often do, because society is so hostile to
them and their own families do not understand them, so they are
subject to a great many pressures and a great deal of unhappiness."[3]
My own view lies close to this, with the difference of a generally
Jungian approach, about which I shall say more later.

Finally, certain homosexuals express a view, in articles and novels,
that the homosexual adaptation is superior to the heterosexual — a
final, crowning mutation. This is a position from which the heterosexual world can be looked down on, although there is little objective
evidence to support the position that the homosexual is more advanced or superior psychologically.

ONE GOOD QUESTION

In this rather sketchy psychological survey, we have left one good
question that deserves to be asked. Is homosexuality a sickness? Certainly it is not a physical disability in the ordinary sense of the word,
and psychologically there does not seem to be any direct connection
with mental illness. Dr. Evelyn Hooker, one of the leading experts on
homosexuality, has made careful studies of both homosexuals and
heterosexuals. In her years of work on the subject, most of it under

federal grant, Dr. Hooker had access to a sufficient number of individuals for comparative study and worked with groups selected at random. Using the best testing tools available—the Rorschach, the MMPI, the TAT, which can pick out the psychotic and neurotic personality with uncanny accuracy—she found that these tests failed to distinguish the homosexual from the heterosexual. No significant variations were found, other than a slightly higher rating for the homosexual on general intelligence. Apparently they are no more psychotic or neurotic, and probably no more immature, than their heterosexual brothers and sisters. Dr. Hooker's conclusions are similar to those of Dr. Baker; her basic observation is that there is no easy understanding of this sexual problem.

It is true that homosexuals may be immature, and if they are unconscious homosexuals they may manifest neurotic symptoms, but for obvious reasons only a psychologist can put anyone in that category. More homosexuals probably come for help because of the difficulty of their situation, and so their immaturity is better known, while the best adjusted would never be seen in a psychiatrist's office. The American Psychiatric Association formally voted within the last several years to accept Dr. Hooker's view, and no longer lists homosexuality as a sickness. Finally, if we define sickness as the inability or unwillingness to conform to society's regulations, then many others besides homosexuals—including many religious groups, such as the Christians of the first centuries of our era—would come under this designation.

Homosexuals are subject to more sexual tension than are ordinary heterosexuals, in part simply because they are placed in so many situations that can only be compared to settling a heterosexual male down in a dormitory of chorus girls. There are sick heterosexuals and sick homosexuals. These latter have little control of their sexual impulses, and certainly they are more likely to express them in an antisocial way. Thus they clash with society, either by lack of control or through deliberate, rebellious flaunting of their difference before the public eye. Some people assume that all homosexuals must be like this, which is just as logical as the thinking of some old maids who, knowing only what they read in the newspapers, believe that all men are rapists. It is questionable whether we can evaluate homosexuality entirely in terms of sickness, any more than we can look at it solely as a problem of prostitution. Neither evaluation takes in the full scope of the homosexual's problems.

THE ORIGIN OF THESE ATTITUDES IN OUR CULTURE

The Judaeo-Christian attitude toward homosexuality during the last six centuries has been one of violent condemnation of any homosexual act. This was quite different from the attitude of the Great Mother cults of Asia Minor, of shamanism, and of other religious groups. The Christian Church took over and expanded the old Judaic laws against homosexuality that are found in Leviticus 18:22 and 20:13 and in Deuteronomy 23:17, which represent exactly the attitude expressed by Paul in Romans 1:25 ff., I Corinthians 6:9-10, and I Timothy 1:10. The same disapproval of the practice was also understood to be expressed in the story of Sodom in Genesis 19:5, and in a similar story in Judges 19:22. The penalty in the older Jewish code was death, and although there is a question as to how frequently it was invoked, the disapproval was as vehement as it was for nearly every other sexual variation, from bestiality to adultery, and even to the nearly universal practice of masturbation.

There is nothing in the teachings of Christ to continue the violence of this rejection; yet it appears that many leaders of the Christian Church took over a Jewish attitude without reexamination. The reason for this Jewish rejection has been rationalized on the basis that it would deter population growth if the male semen were not put to productive use. A more probable reason was the common practice of male homosexual prostitution in the Mother cult religions of the Near East and the fact that anything to do with these religions was rejected, whether it was the sacred groves, or divination, or interpretation of dreams by the foreign priests. In no place was the action viewed as a sickness or affliction over which the individual might have little or no control. It was viewed purely in moral terms.

As Christianity developed in the Graeco-Roman world, one of the greatest difficulties was in teaching control of the instinctual life. Lack of control led to lack of containment, and so to a lack of psychological growth and conscious direction of personality. Christianity stood for control and direction. Thus the early Church placed great emphasis upon sexual control, and gradually the attitude that sex was not quite nice crept into Christian thought, even though there was no basis for this in the teachings of Jesus. The only passage that could possibly indicate this point of view refers only to a specific situation.[4]

The devaluation of sexuality was common in gnosticism, which looked on the body as the prisonhouse of the soul. For the gnostic, since the goal of salvation was to free the soul from the body, the reverse, contributing to conception, was about as immoral a thing as one could do, because this was the way more soul became trapped in irredeemable flesh. Thus all sexual activity was surrounded by an aura of evil. Although this attitude toward sex was never officially accepted by the Church, it infiltrated Christianity through the writings of Augustine, who for many years belonged to the gnostic Manichean sect. The gnostics also believed that one could best find God through the mind, through religious intuition, through esoteric knowledge, and so anything to do with the emotions was quite inferior. Here the contrast is great: Jesus and Paul both maintained, along with the author of the letters of John, that we could not know or love God unless we loved the people we could see. Plato also clearly maintained (and here is one of the basic correspondences of Platonic thinking and Christianity) that the way men and women come to know the spiritual world is by divine madness, of which the most common form is the madness of love. I have discussed the relationship of Christianity and sexuality at greater length in *Caring: How Can We Love One Another?*

With the development of monasticism, the attitude that "sex" was really an evil thing was set. It was permitted in marriage as a concession to the weakness of the flesh and for begetting children. St. Augustine's treatise "On the Good of Marriage" expresses this point of view and has to be read to be believed. Some modern churches still hold to this point of view, which is at odds with anything said by Jesus, and was probably unconsciously formulated to help people gain control of their instinctual life. But in very recent years a part of the Church has come to see sexual activity as a fine and beautiful thing that ties people together in a deep psychological bond and that can be good apart from reproduction. This view is set forth clearly and well in *Toward a Quaker View of Sex,* published by the Friends' Home Service Committee in England. The author of the booklet understands that the original biological purpose of sexual feeling was to insure reproduction, but that sexual attraction has become more than this. Though the original use of vocal chords was to provide closure of the trachea, they can also be used in human speech and song, without getting in the way of this original purpose. In the same way, sex is more than reproduction. It is also one of the deepest ways in which the individual can express affection for another human being.

There is little reason to go into the unsavory history of the Church's attempt to stamp out homosexuality through law, punishment, and persecution. John Boswell has written a definitive study of this subject in his book *Christianity, Social Tolerance, and Homosexuality*.[5] Published in 1980 by a professor of history at Yale University, it maintains that the early Church was not as violent in its rejection of homosexuality as was the popular Christian attitude of the thirteenth century, which Aquinas legislated into dogma. The same age burned witches and heretics, fought infidels, and banished usurers. Boswell maintains that Greek had no word for homosexual and that many of the New Testament words translated as homosexual refer to a male prostitute. This work is a masterpiece of scholarship, and a necessity for anyone dealing with the subject of homosexuality in the Church.

It is certainly open to question whether the moral laws of our more recent Christian heritage have a place in our legal structure when they refer to a practice that may be a sickness or an involuntary condition or affliction rather than a moral problem. By the same logic we should also have laws against tuberculosis and the peptic ulcer. Samuel Butler's *Erewhon* describes an imaginary culture that puts the sick in prison and gives treatment to the criminal. It is hard to calculate the effect of such legislation. In homosexuals who are struggling with their own nature these laws can raise up rebellious attitudes toward society and so bring forth the worst side of homosexuality. Others, particularly the young, may become confirmed in homosexual practice as an expression of rebellion, as well as of their sexual feelings.

Why is there such horror of homosexuality in our culture today? It appears that the distaste for sexuality in general has been focused on this one expression of it. It also appears that while repressing the bisexual nature of human beings our society has come to fear that men and women will be more attracted to the homosexual way of life than to the heterosexual. What is denied any expression tends to become overvalued, and at the same time to be feared inordinately. In societies where there is no attempt to repress homosexual activity, cultural studies show that most young males pass through a homosexual phase to a heterosexual adjustment, only about 1% remaining homosexual. In societies with violent antagonism to homosexuality around 10% remain homosexual. Many societies, it is true, provide initiation rites to help the male make this transition from a feminine identification to a masculine one, while our society offers almost no

help in this area. The fear that young men will be lured into homosexual activity if the practice is allowed appears to be a neurotic fear
of repressed homosexuality. In part it comes from the terror most of us
have for the unknown, for anything that is strange or different. But in
the main it is a neurotic fear, in that it is not realistic, since there is
little evidence that persons who are not already predisposed will be
attracted.

THE CHRISTIAN ATTITUDE TOWARD SICKNESS

Christianity has had an attitude toward sickness and most aberrant
behavior quite different from that of many religious groups. As we
have already shown, most of the religious communities in the ancient
world, from the pagan to the Jewish, viewed sickness as a visitation of
the gods. The sick individual was the tainted one, to be avoided and
shunned as the moral leper. Christians understood sickness of mind
and body to be the result of some evil force in the universe, the
destructive, the uncreative breaking out in human beings. Their task,
instead of condemning or avoiding the sick, was to bring them the
healing available through the Holy Spirit and God and medicine.
There was no judgment upon the sick.

But as Teutonic pagan ideas filtered into the Church during the
dark ages, the Western Church forgot the basic teaching of Christ on
sickness, and adopted instead the idea that it is a punishment from
God that should be borne as a virtue. Thus the Church has no reason
to take it away. This is sheer nonsense in the light of Christ's teaching.
The clear task of the disciple of Christ is to preach, to teach, and to
heal, to defeat the forces of evil in every way. If homosexuality, then,
is a physical illness, there is no reason for the Church to condemn or
avoid it, but every reason to come forward to offer help and understanding. When the pagan emperor Julian made fun of Christians for
caring for the cripples and the poor, he left no doubt about the kind of
concern they showed. Christians would be offering the same concern
for this variation if they were consistent and their prejudices were well
in hand.

If homosexuality is a psychic illness, then the importance of acceptance and concern is even greater. Jesus seemed to have had considerable success in healing the mentally ill and demon-possessed, and
it was the healer and not the sick who came under condemnation if the

healing failed to take place. In Jungian terms, male homosexuality is understood as possession of the male personality by a feminine archetype; in other words, the feminine part of the psyche takes over and runs the whole show as an unconscious or autonomous complex. This is not the fault of the individual, since he is not responsible for this possession. If the writers who have seen a similarity between the demons Christ visualized and the autonomous complexes described by Jung are correct, it is the task of the Christian to transform these complexes, not to drive out the person who is possessed by them. Few people are released from bondage to any complex unless they are accepted as they are, and then, through love, given an opportunity to change. Hate and disgust only reinforce the bondage to unconscious possession; love offers freedom.

The same thing is true if homosexuality is a fixation at a lower level of maturity. Very few people are spurred by hate and contempt to grow and develop toward maturity; love and acceptance again offer the only route to healing. This is one reason for the emphasis on love in Christian practice and on loving concern in psychotherapy. The attitude of rejection is common in most churches and in most of society, and so both groups merely reinforce this problem, if it is indeed a sickness.

If homosexuality is merely a moral sickness—although, as we have noted, it is hard to find objective evidence for this that does not raise doubts about the "health" of most of us—still the same observations hold true. One does not change people by rejecting them and refusing to view them as valuable. Seldom is anyone transformed by judgment. Acceptance and love provide the tools for moral transformation, and so the Church's attitude can hardly be supported on this ground. Jung has pointed out that, although the Church often treats nonbelievers as contemptuously as an estranged wife, they are actually changed only when the Church becomes secure enough not to be threatened by these doubters, and to meet them with loving concern and interest. Likewise, when the Church is no longer threatened by the actions or rebellion of homosexuals, it may be able to offer them acceptance and help.

If, however, homosexuality is not a sickness, but merely an anomaly of nature, the attitude of Western society and the Church is cruel indeed. Whether the condition is psychic or physical or a little of each, whether it originates in the environment or from heredity, homosexuals are not responsible for these factors, and there is little they can do to change them. If this is the case, homosexuals are being judged morally on account of feelings for which they are no more responsible than they are for the color of their eyes. Or, if it is only their actions that are objectionable, is it possible to deny them an expression that is so large a part of other people's lives, simply because their constitution is such that homosexuality is their way of expressing sexual desire? The fact that sexuality is directed in a nonheterosexual expression in no way diminishes the power of the drive; among heterosexual males only a few heroic individuals are able to control and repress it completely. A very astute and honest heterosexual once said that a man and woman can remain friends only so long; the same essential truth applies to all but the most disciplined homosexuals, once they realize there is a mutual sexual feeling.

If, then, homosexuality is merely a variant type of personality, it is hardly open to moral question if it is not exercised with force, or upon those who have no right to consent, or in the open violation of public decency, rules that apply to heterosexual acts as well. In these circumstances it would seem that the task of the Church and society is to offer the homosexual understanding and help to change his pattern, or to come to control, sublimation, abstinence, or to a meaningful relationship, as individual circumstances dictate. They would thus be encouraged and helped not to use sex as an avoidance of relationship, but as a part of an abiding and meaningful one. And this brings us to the matter of relationship and love.

RELATIONSHIP AND LOVE IN CHRISTIANITY

Christianity has always placed a high value upon human relationship. One of the basic themes of the New Testament is that we cannot love God if we do not love our brothers and sisters. The experience of caring for others, of love, of *agape* (to use the Greek word for one form of love) is one way in which we are given genuine access to the realm of the Spirit. This is not accomplished by thinking or acting logically, but by something quite different. Unless we break through to an experience of God with love, even our experiences of the spirit may be confused and deluding. Love gives access to God and to another dimension of reality. This is the basic teaching of Jesus, of Paul, of John, particularly in the first Epistle, of St. Francis, and St. Catherine of Siena, of Martin Luther King and Mother Teresa.

It was undoubtedly this that made the philosophy of Plato so influential in the basic thinking of the very early Church. Plato's main concern was with the world of forms—the eternal, unchanging realities that lie behind the transitory things of this world. He did not believe that human beings reached this realm through intellect or imagination, but rather by divine madness—through the dream (or cathartic madness), prophecy, artistic madness, and the madness of love. A knowledge of the eternal realm was given in these experiences. In the *Symposium,* and particularly in the *Phaedrus,* Plato made this very clear. Friedlander, in his book *Plato,* and Pieper in his discussion of Plato, *Love and Inspiration,* both emphasize this.[6]

Love is a very mysterious force, and one with strange consequences. The Western Church has more or less forgotten this truth because for several centuries now it has had its thinking determined, not by the Platonic understanding, but by the rationalism of Aristotle and Descartes. With its emphasis on reason and the mind, the Church has become almost antagonistic to the irrational aspects of religious experience. These who speak in tongues or have visions and dream dreams come in for a rejection comparable to that inflicted upon the homosexual by the heterosexual. Where reason is enthroned as ultimate, all the divine madnesses—all the nonrational religious encounters that were so central to the thinking of Plato and so foreign to that of Aristotle—are inevitably devalued, love included.

In our time it is again possible to realize the importance of love. When a man and woman have come to a deep abiding relationship of physical, emotional, and spiritual love in which their lives are blended together into a harmony of closeness and yet distinction, there is expressed that mystical union which is between Christ and the Church. Charles Williams describes this in depth in his book *The Figure of Beatrice.* Most modern chuches romanticize marriage, but fail to see what it can be in honesty and reality. When we look at these facts, we must also realize that the love Plato was speaking about was love between men and men, and that this gave the same access to new levels of spiritual reality as we have seen in some examples of heterosexual love. In the deep commitment and sharing of lives that we call love, another dimension of reality does open up. There are homosexuals, as well as heterosexuals, who have experienced this breakthrough and spoken of it in our own time. We may not like to face these facts, but in spite of the condemnation of the Christian Church, they appear to be the religious facts.

Jung has given an interesting support to this thesis in a profound passage in which he discusses the positive side of a mother complex, which in his mind is related to homosexual activity. He wrote:

Since a "mother-complex" is a concept borrowed from psychopathology, it is always associated with the idea of injury and illness. But if we take the concept out of its narrow psychopathological setting and give it a wider connotation, we can see that it has positive effects as well. Thus a man with a mother-complex may have a finely differentiated Eros instead of, or in addition to, homosexuality. (Something of this sort is suggested by Plato in his *Symposium*.) This gives him a great capacity for friendship, which often creates ties of astonishing tenderness between men and may even rescue friendship between the sexes from the limbo of the impossible. He may have good taste and an aesthetic sense which are fostered by the presence of a feminine streak. Then he may be supremely gifted as a teacher because of his almost feminine insight and tact. He is likely to have a feeling for history, and to be conservative in the best sense and cherish the values of the past. Often he is endowed with a wealth of religious feelings, which help to bring the *ecclesia spiritualis* into reality; and a spiritual receptivity which makes him responsive to revelation.[7]

Although to the homosexual the problem of his sexuality may be his main concern, for good reason, Jung points out that it is rather a peripheral aspect of a whole personality development that is far from totally negative. Many homosexuals, active and latent, whom I have counseled have found in this passage a penetrating description of themselves and a source of hope within their own personality problems.

In another context Jung shows clearly that there is far more involved in homosexuality than simply a pathological problem. In discussing the general question of therapy he wrote:

The growing youth must be able to free himself from the anima fascination of his mother. There are exceptions, notably artists, where the problem often takes a different turn; also homosexuality, which is usually characterized by identity with the anima. In view of the recognized frequency of this phenomenon, its interpretation as a pathological perversion is very dubious. The psychological findings show that it is rather a matter of incomplete detachment from the hermaphroditic archetype, coupled with a distinct resistance to identify with the role of a one-sided sexual being. Such a disposition should not be adjudged negative in all circumstances, in so far as it preserves the archetype of the Original Man, which a one-sided sexual being has, up to a point, lost.[8]

In other places in his writings Jung expands the ideas that are basic to this understanding and suggests the reasons for the conclusions he states in these passages.

As one studies the whole subject of homosexuality objectively and dispassionately, it is difficult to come up with the totally negative reaction to it that is found in the popular mind, one that is not found among students of the subject. It is true that there are outer manifestations among certain rebellious and certain sick homosexuals that give rise quite understandably to these prejudices, but they are not an adequate sample of the homosexual population, nor do they represent the essential quality of homosexuality.

WHAT SHOULD BE THE ATTITUDE OF THE CHURCH?

What should be the attitude of the Church toward the homosexual and homosexuality? There are three areas of prophetic action to consider — educational, legal, and pastoral.

In the first place, the Church should work with interested groups in which individuals may be permitted to speak freely for the enlightenment of prejudices. Any blind prejudice is evil. The facts about homosexuals are no more totally negative than are the facts about blacks. In the same way that the Church stands against racial discrimination, it should stand against this kind of unenlightened sexual discrimination, wherever it exists. This is possible only as the leaders of the Church have the courage to find out what the facts are and to speak them forth in spite of the prejudices of congregations. Both homosexuals and the average minister should realize, however, that this is easier said than done. The Church, in fact, is not the force it appears to be, for many ministers are employees of their congregations, who will dismiss them if they run counter to their wishes. Ministers are authorities as long as they don't step on the prejudices of the people; the controversy surrounding Proposition 14 on the California ballot in 1964 is good evidence of this.[9] With the goal of living together long enough to know each other, homosexuals need also to respect the prejudices of their brothers and sisters who express a real fear by their very reticence on the whole subject.

In addition, the Church needs to provide guidance to families as to how to help young men make the shift into male identification. Whether some modern initiation rites are needed, or whether better family education on the nature of psychosexual growth or some other method would be best, some kind of education certainly needs to be provided in this area. Genuine family life itself is a deterrent to the development of the variation. But the Church, as Jung points out, can also provide a place where the developing male can make an identification with the "father" figure if he has an inadequate one at home. As things stand, the young man who is trying to find his way often finds a place to talk about his problems only in homosexual society. The Church ought to provide a place where the confused youth can discuss with openness his fears and doubts and aspirations, without censure or prejudice. The same kind of openness should be provided for sexually confused young women.

One sexual act does not make a homosexual. We have already shown the data to the contrary. Many younger and even older people still are caught by the old wives' tale that any homosexual act at any time indicates that one is essentially homosexual. Most people with this fear are greatly relieved when they can discuss these concerns in an unjudging and sympathetic atmosphere and discover that many "normal" heterosexual men and women have occasionally had homosexual feelings and have even committed such acts occasionally. Human beings are bisexual, and few of us are at either the totally homosexual or totally heterosexual extreme. Our sexual feelings are stretched out along a many-pointed continuum.

There are few groups that need more help than those quite conscious of their bisexuality. Many homosexual organizations and individuals deny the existence of a bisexual orientation and may even proselytize these people into making a homosexual declaration. Many heterosexuals are also unaware of this middle ground. Those burdened with this concern need a place where they can talk, be understood, and come to the best decision for their lives.

In the legal arena, the Church should also work for the repeal of the present unrealistic laws against homosexuality. If homosexuals by their actions are willfully causing damage to society, then it is up to the law to define such cases. But if homosexuality is a matter of private morals, it should not be punished by the law. And if it is a sickness or simply a variation, then the laws are absurd. The Church should follow the lead of the Woolfenden Report in England, the action of the Church of England, and the suggestions of the American Bar Association, which agree that there should be no legal sanctions against mutually consenting adults. The only punishment would be, first, for lack of public control so that the practice becomes indecent or a public nuisance, second, for its infliction by force, and third, for leading children into the practice. This last situation, however, should be more clearly defined than it is at present. Of course, in working to remove untenable laws the Church should be careful not to make a variant behavior normative.

Finally, in the pastoral ministry the Church should treat each homosexual as an individual. Nothing is more important in a matter so rife with prejudice than remembering the basic Gospel injunction, "Judge not, lest you be judged." Wherever homosexuality may be specifically mentioned in the New Testament, it is certainly not singled out; instead, each time Paul linked it with sins like greed, drunkenness, slander, envy, quarreling, intrigue, and similar vices. Although Paul was making the point that no one who is touched by these vices has the right to criticize or judge his brothers and sisters, the Church seems to have become far more tolerant of certain ones than of others.

It is our basic conclusion that homosexuality is not a moral matter, and whatever its origin and definition, moral judgment only makes it more of a problem. We simply do not know enough to be sure whether the origin is psychological or physiological, and it depends on how far we stretch the meaning of "sickness" whether it is a sickness or simply a variation. Therefore, the Church should provide competent counseling for homosexuals who are in doubt as to their sexual identification, or who wish to change. If, however, homosexuality is indeed an arrested state of psychosexual development then their very acceptance by the Church can help individuals through this stage and on into heterosexuality. Certainly judgment and condemnation do not help any of us in moving on to something else; instead, they set the fixation for good and all. This kind of help means encouraging discussion of sexual subjects when they arise in young people's lives, as in early adolescence. And this requires clergy who have dealt with their own psychosexual problems, since it is almost impossible to deal objectively with sexuality in others until we have come to terms with it within ourselves.

Furthermore, if the Church, instead of being threatened, understands the rebellion of the homosexual, and the rejection to which they are so often subjected, it can provide the best counseling situation for individuals who need to gain more control of their impulses, or need psychological help quite apart from the homosexual problem. As long as the state maintains its present legal sanctions against homosexuality, it will be difficult for the sophisticated homosexual to turn to state agencies for counseling and help, and private counseling is beyond the means of many people.

Finally, the Church should provide spiritual direction and welcome for the homosexuals who find that they cannot or really do not want to change their sexual orientation. There is no group in our society, with the exception of blacks in certain sections of the South, who is any more rejected and cut off from normal social life. Homosexuals need and are capable of knowing and serving God as much as any individuals, and the Church must provide them with the fellowship, sacramental life, and pastoral care that it offers other human beings. And who knows what creative possibilities may emerge in its attempts to carry out these actions?

NOTES

1. John W. Reavis, Jr., "The Rejected" (a transcript), A National Educational Television Network Presentation (San Francisco: Pan-Graphic Press, 1961), p. 11.

2. Margaret Mead, "The Rejected," p. 7 ff.

3. *The Homosexual in Our Society*, the transcript of a program broadcast on November 24, 1958, by radio station KPFA-FM, Berkeley, Cal., (San Francisco: Pan-Graphic Press, 1959), p. 6.

4. Matthew 19:12.

5. John Boswell, *Christianity, Social Tolerance, and Homosexuality* (Chicago, University of Chicago Press, 1980).

6. Paul Friedlander, *Plato: An Introduction*, tr. by Hans Meyerhoff (New York: Harper & Row, for the Bollingen Foundation, 1964). Josef Pieper, *Love and Inspiration: A Study of Plato's Phaedrus* (London: Faber & Faber, 1964).

7. C.G. Jung, *Collected Works*, Vol. 9, Part 1, *The Archetypes and the Collective Unconscious* (New York: Pantheon Books for the Bollingen Foundation, 1959), pp. 86 ff.

8. *Ibid.*, p. 71.

9. This proposition was a referendum to repeal an act of the California legislature penalizing certain real estate practices considered by the legislators to discriminate against minority races.

Chapter 11
_____

MINISTRY TO THE VIOLENT

PART ONE: AGGRESSION AND RELIGION

Among thinking people today there is real concern over the problem of controlling human aggression. Because of our skyrocketing population and new techniques of communication, the world is shrinking into a tight little ball. People cannot get away from each other as they once did. The very efficiency of our systems, even in sports, seems to reduce the acceptable outlets for aggressive energy. And so it boils over in riots and crime, in organized vandalism, in civil war and international conflicts. Even worse, with nuclear power in our hands, the final result may well be the destruction of the human race itself.

No wonder so many students of human nature have begun to study aggression in human beings. Not liking the prospect of global suicide, they have tried to see how we can be helped to control its violent aspects. To deal with any element of human behavior, one must first understand its nature. This requires a theory or hypothesis that fits what one knows about this particular element of behavior into a total understanding of humanity. *Homo sapiens* is a complex creature, and no element of our nature is easy to understand—particularly one like aggression that we need to learn to control. The most adequate theory generally turns out to be the one that lines up all the factors in the simplest and most understandable relationships. At best it will be none too simple.

The way I propose to study the nature of aggression is to look at the spadework done by various thinkers, considering five representative theories and asking what each offers, or fails to offer, to an understanding of our subject. We will look first at a point of view that sees aggression as a reaction that each individual learns through experiences of frustration and denial, rather than as a natural or instinctive propensity. Next we will examine a naturalistic theory that the aggressive reaction is essentially instinctual—the theory of Konrad Lorenz. Third, we will consider the complex understanding of Freud, the theory that aggression is an extraverted expression of the death wish. We will also discuss a modification of this view, represented by Anthony Storr, which integrates the biological data of Lorenz and others with the thinking of Freud. Finally, we will conclude with a theory based on the thinking of C. G. Jung, which gives a comprehensive understanding of the data involved.

THE TABULA RASA THEORY

It may come as a surprise to find the followers of Aristotle and St. Thomas linked with Watson and Skinner, Maslow and Rogers, in the study of human aggression, but these thinkers have at least one thing in common. They all hold a basic understanding of human beings that puts the essential stress on consciousness and rationality, and practically eliminates instinct as a meaningful concept in discussing human life. They believe that each human being starts life as a *tabula rasa,* a clean slate or blank piece of paper, upon which experience writes what the person is to become. Individuals are determined by the input of their experience. If their conditioning is adequate, a happy, well-adjusted human being is the result; if not, then society must suffer for their aggressiveness.

This theory leaves no room for either a psychically structured unconscious or the physiologically determined instincts to influence us. The unconscious and the instincts are both rejected, either because they cannot be observed scientifically, or because theoretically they limit human freedom. Humans are malleable, and when subjected to the right input, the proper human being will result. This is the thesis of Skinner's *Walden II*—a materialistic utopia sketched out by one of the most sophisticated behavioral thinkers of all time. Obviously, the only need is to understand what kind of conditioning is required, subject human beings to it, and the problem of aggression is solved.

The task of the educator in this framework is to shape experiences so that the desired behavioral results are accomplished. Thus one provides programmed learning. Since affect and emotion are considered destructive and dangerous, little attention is given to them; usually they are to be eliminated in favor of reason. I have discussed this matter at greater length in my book *Can Christians Be Educated?* By the same token, values too must be eliminated in teaching, because they are related to emotions, and neither one can be viewed as "scientific" in the behaviorist sense.

This point of view was carried to the absurd in child raising some thirty years ago. The school of thought popular at that time ruled that, to resolve problems like aggression in adults, the only thing necessary was to start them out right as children, and raise them with openness and complete permissiveness. The result, however, was not well-adjusted men and women, but frightened and self-centered adults. Life without limits is terrifying to both children and adults, and raises far greater hostility and aggression in them than reasonable restraints.

We sometimes forget how far scholastic and traditional education went in the opposite direction. Schools in Europe often functioned on the principle that information had to be beaten into the child, and they provided negative rather than positive conditioning. Hermann Hesse's *Beneath the Wheel* is a tragically accurate description of this kind of education. In this educational framework there is little thought of providing the conditions that make it possible for individuals to develop to their potential; instead, the idea is to provide a set goal and force its achievement. Parts of the Jansenistic and Puritan tradition even viewed the child as a malicious little brute who had to be shaped into a decent and civilized human being. The brutishness was simply the result of our animal nature, which we had to transcend.

One of the most influential and important schools of modern psychology is humanistically oriented. Its leading exponents, Carl Rogers, Viktor Frankl, Abraham Maslow, Adrian Van Kaam, and Rollo May, have reacted against the deterministic attitudes of both the behaviorists and the Freudians. They have followed the bent of philosophical existentialism in stressing the value and importance of the will, and in the process have either ignored or denied any innate aggressiveness in human beings. C. W. Tageson has described Carl Rogers' way of accounting for evil, violence, and destruction as "the distortion of the more basic inherent drive towards self-realization of the human organism . . . by a faulty socialization process which tends progressively to eliminate the self from its deepest organismic strivings and experience." Anything in our essential nature contributing to violence and aggression is eliminated.

The backside of this theory of human behavior is its denial that there is any substantive reality to evil. This view, established by Aristotle and St. Thomas, sees evil as the absence of good, the *privatio boni*. In us humans it is an accidental lack of perfection, which can be more and more avoided as we come closer to keeping our lives perfect. There can, therefore, be no drive within us that leads to destruction and evil, and nothing that really stands in the way of human perfectibility. In Chapter V of *Aion*, C. G. Jung has noted the dangers — individual, social, and religious dangers — that can arise from this doctrine,[1] and I have discussed the same problem in my book *Discernment*.

It is not hard to see what this view of evil does to our understanding of people's aggressive actions. If there is no substantive evil that works through us, then conditioning is the only handle we have on the aggressive, hostile, and even demonic behavior that comes out of us. The trouble is that conditioning alone doesn't seem to solve the problem. It doesn't even account for all the facts. How do we explain the quiet, exemplary boy scout in New Jersey who got up one night and killed his whole family? Was it just frustration that made an earnest student like Charlie Whitman go up into the tower and shoot at random across the campus at Austin, Texas? Or how about the well-meaning and probably well-adjusted men who directed the use of napalm and the mass killings in Vietnam? Sometimes this aggression is turned inward in suicidal feelings or depression. Sometimes the same force separates the individual from reality and results in schizophrenia. There is little evidence that altering conditions changes these aggressions. Either we know too little about how to condition human beings, or else it is simply beyond our power to remove enough frustrations to start the wheels turning toward change.

Still, this theory presents an important side of human nature. Frustration, and conditioning to it, can be effective means of raising up hostility, violence, and hatred in us, and any comprehensive theory of aggression will take them into account. But this theory of aggression, which considers the human being only as a *tabula rasa*, soaking up conditioning like a dry sponge, fails to be comprehensive. It fails to account for all of the data, and may even neglect some of the most relevant facts. Carl Gustav Jung has written that the concentration camps of totalitarian countries can hardly be described as examples of the accidental lack of perfection of our moral nature.

John Sanford, in his book *Evil,* suggests that failure to realize the existence of evil within the individual may be disastrous indeed: "As long as we are convinced that there is no tendency to evil in us we are not capable of individual morality. Good intentions are not enough. To become an individual means facing our own inclination to evil — our own imperfection and falling short — and taking personal responsibility for it. There is a dark aspect within everyone of us, an 'adversary' or 'opponent' . . . which we must face and declare."[2]

AGGRESSION AS A BIOLOGICAL INSTINCT

Those who line up with the physical scientists take quite a different view of the subject. They see us primarily as "human" animals, dependent upon our biological instincts. One of the best known spokesmen for this group is Konrad Lorenz, who has amassed a great amount of material on the aggressive propensities of animals, and applies his information rather uncritically to the human animal. His study *On Aggression*[3] is a very bad book from a general point of view, and yet an important one. Lorenz is a strict Darwinian naturalist, who holds that our greatest problem in handling aggression is our lack of humility in acknowledging our purely animal heritage.

Thus this theory is based on the understanding that there is an aggressive instinct in animal life that can be traced in all the higher species. It has continued in human evolution, developing through the process of natural selection and survival of the fittest. Lorenz believes that we will be able to deal with our problems of aggression only as we come to understand this instinct and its biological meaning. The first step is to understand the expression of the aggressive instinct in animals; only this will shed real light on the same behavior in humankind.

To begin with, aggressive behavior in animals is carefully distinguished from the predatory activity of animals that kill for food. Confusion about this is seen as hindering an understanding of aggression. Under natural conditions, predatory animals seldom, if ever, eat their own species. Instead, Lorenz sees us as the only higher vertebrate that enjoys cannibalism, but apparently not for its nutritional value.

It seems to be performed among humans for ritualistic reasons, rather than because of hunger.

It is the numerous examples of other hostilities among animals belonging to the same species that give us clues about our own behavior. These are acts that have meaning from a biological point of view. For instance, they provide territorial separation, keeping members of the same species in a balanced distribution over the available environment. Aggression also serves to help the processes of evolution along. The fights between males over mating with the female of the species is one way that natural selection works to insure the survival and propagation of the strongest individuals. Perpetuation of the species itself depends upon the aggressive instinct and the power it gives to defend the young. In addition to these values, aggression seems to be linked with motivation and drive, and to be involved in the love relationship among both animals and humans.

Thus in the natural state aggression serves a valuable purpose. It even seems to provide its own inhibiting instinct, so that the strongest and most dangerous will not destroy each other. Through natural selection among animals with strong beaks or dangerous teeth or claws this counterbalancing instinct develops, so that fighting among them is ritualized and becomes almost a game. In the natural state it very rarely results in killing.

According to this theory, the basic problem in human beings is that we started as relatively innocuous and harmless creatures, and physically we are still not particularly dangerous to our fellows. We cannot kill with the glancing blow of a paw, a scratch, the bite of carnivorous teeth, or the pecking of a beak. Therefore we developed no natural instinctive mechanism to inhibit our natural aggressiveness. Then suddenly, through the development of our associative and reasoning powers, we were able to create tools far more deadly than any of these natural weapons. Over the centuries we developed first the stone ax, then the bow and arrow, gunpowder, and finally atomic fission. In each case we became farther and farther removed from the victim, and our killing became more and more impersonal. Our problem comes from the fact that we retain the same animal instinct for aggression, but lack both the natural restraint of the carnivore and the inhibiting instincts that keep animals from destroying their own kind.

Thus the problem of controlling human aggression is one of building into human beings a set of inhibiting instincts. This presents a bleak picture, but Lorenz does not give up hope. He seems to feel that, by selection, this can be accomplished, even quickly. By the use of reason and through realizing the essential truth of Kant's categorical imperative, we can help the process along. Rituals can be created; sports can be encouraged, a sense of humor developed, contact kept open with people of other societies, and these will all tame the natural aggressive instinct in us. We must avoid militant enthusiasm, however, because this gets out of control. And since spiritual ideas about human nature lead to this enthusiasm, we must therefore restrict ourselves to the nature we have inherited with our physical structure, and many of our pet conceptions about ourselves must go.

This point of view contains excellent and thought-provoking material, much of it relevant to the problem. But as a one-shot approach it has several serious shortcomings. Its complete naturalism sees us as nothing but another animal, and thus our higher emotional as well as rational abilities are neglected. It also overlooks the fact, indicated by most modern studies, that we become increasingly free of control by the instincts the more conscious we become. Something else may be more important than a new instinctual control, and for the same reason it is next to impossible simply to create effective rituals. Whether their purpose is to shift gears on the instincts or on some other force, such rituals must rise out of meaning within us if they are to mesh. As we shall see later, it is not an easy matter to plumb the depths of human beings and come up with a conscious solution to aggression.

FREUD AND THE DEATH WISH

Much thinking about aggression has been done among psychologists with a clinical orientation, and, quite understandably, this has been largely influenced by the theories of Sigmund Freud. Although Freud has little to say about aggression in his earlier writings, overall he left us one of the most comprehensive pictures of the human being ever produced. Originally he saw all aspects of human life as derived from the erotic libido, the pleasure principle. The strange deviations that are seen in human psychology could be explained by the fact that this force came up against outer reality and the ego, or superego, was blocked and rerouted. But later Freud became aware that not everything could be explained on this single basis.

Once he had become deeply involved emotionally in World War I, and had seen the futility of his involvement, he began to look for another force operating within the human psyche. As a starting point, he realized that he had never been able to explain terrifying dreams on the basis of the pleasure principle alone. This suggested the existence of another psychic agent, as basic as sexual libido. We have already referred to two books, *Beyond the Pleasure Principle* and *Civilization and Its Discontents*, which were written to postulate this primal force, and which Freud called the death wish, or *thanatos*. In essence it is the inner drag of the nonliving within the individual, drawing a person back into an inorganic state and death.

Just as *eros* is first directed towards the self, and then extraverted out to the world, so the death wish, *thanatos*, is first of all directed inward, towards the individual, and only later directed towards the outer world in aggression. Aggression, then, was understood by Freud to be the extraverted expression of the primal death wish, redirected from its basic form against onself and turned outwards against persons in the external world. Within the psyche a struggle goes on between blind *eros*, striving towards union and life, and blind destructive *thanatos*, drawing the organism back into disintegration, dissolution, and death. As we have already noted, even the most perfect love relationship is seen as tainted with this destructive instinct as well. It is clearly an everpresent force. But *thanatos* is also elusive, and the important place to discover it is within the individual himself—not after it has been unleashed outwardly as aggression.

The death wish is seen most nearly naked in the depressed state, when the individual is overwhelmed by this primal force and wishes to die. If the subject is also seen as an object, and the aggressive desire to kill is added to depression, then suicide is possible. In fact, if the psychic causes are present, death may even occur without the overt act of suicide. This is well corroborated by medical studies among both primitive groups and animals. Studies of native tribes show that men and women who have broken a taboo can simply die for no other reason than the psychic state that results. In the case of animals, rats were placed in a situation that was frightening because their normal way of reacting was disrupted, and many of them died—simply from fear, as the postmortems showed.[4] Indeed, medicine lends much interesting support to Freud's basic idea.

In *Man Against Himself*, Karl Menninger has worked out the medi-

cal implications of the death wish. As he shows, it is expressed in many
ways, and the most interesting of them are masked; often they look
like physical cause and effect. Yet the death wish is responsible not
only for psychoneurotic disease, for anxieties and phobias. By working
through the psyche upon the body, it contributes to a host of physical
illnesses, organic as well as psychosomatic and neurotic. Things like
allergies, ulcers, and heart disease can be traced to the influence of
this destructive element, and there are other ways it can be expressed.
Drug addiction and alcoholism, accidents, the need for repeated
surgical intervention, self-mutilation, asceticism and martyrdom, perversion, criminality, and psychosis can also be traced to the destructive
power of the death wish when it is ignored and avoided.

It is only a little less complex to see the death wish related to its outwardly directed forms. When the wish is projected outwards, then one
desires, not one's own death, but that of other persons, and the result
is aggression in some form, from antisocial social behavior to war.
There are enough of these outer expressions available, and we often
enough mask our aggressions as necessity, to make it difficult to pin
responsibility for them onto the individual. In the case of sadism this is
easier to see. When the death wish is mixed with *eros* and turned outwards, sadism results—the individual derives erotic pleasure from the
suffering of another. Menninger suggests that this is better than the
straight desire to kill, even though sadism often seems more
despicable. At any rate, it is inescapably individual.

Thus far the understanding of Freud offers a great deal to our
thinking about the problem of aggression. But when it comes to possibilities for action, there is a different turn. In 1933 Albert Einstein
wrote to Freud, asking him for a psychological explanation of human
hatred and destructiveness, an understanding of our stupidity in
allowing ourselves to be led into war. In this reply Freud recapitulated
his theory and then wrote:

The willingness to fight may depend upon a variety of motives which may
be lofty, frankly outspoken, or unmentionable. The pleasure in aggression
and destruction is certainly one of them. The satisfaction derived from these
destructive tendencies is, of course, modified by others which are erotic and
ideational in nature. At times we are under the impression that idealistic
motives have simply been a screen for the atrocities of nature; at other times,
that they were more prominent and that the destructive drives came to their
assistance for unconscious reasons, as in the cruelties perpetrated during the
Holy Inquisition. . . .

The death-instinct would destroy the individual were it not turned upon objects other than the self so that the individual saves his own life by destroy-ing something external to himself. Let this be the biological excuse for all the ugly and dangerous strivings against which we struggle. They are more natural than the resistance which we offer them.

For our present purposes then it is useless to try to eliminate the aggressive tendencies in man.[5]

Freud's pessimistic tone is questioned even by his disciple Mennin-ger, who quotes him. But there is a thoroughly pessimistic tone throughout Freud's view of the human being. The best that can be expected of the most conscious person is a cold-war standoff between supergo, id, and *thanatos* on the battleground of the ego. Many of Freud's followers, Erich Fromm in particular, for this or other reasons, have abandoned the idea of the death wish.[6] Yet there still occurs the puzzling clinical experience of the many persons who come seeking help because they are unable, on their own, to keep from destroying themselves. There has been an attempt to provide an alternative to Freud's theory of aggression and the death wish, but one that would still see a direct link between them — a sort of expressway traveled by the instincts and various kinds of human experience.

A COMPOUND THEORY OF AGGRESSION

This understanding has been offered by the British psychotherapist Anthony Storr, who has attempted to incorporate the materials pro-vided by Lorenz within a modified psychoanalytic framework. In his book *Human Aggression,* he suggests that a combination of purely biological and psychological factors is responsible for this trait and its problems in human beings.[7]

He lays out first, in some detail, the physiological base for aggres-sion, describing how the human body reacts to a threatening situation. When a threat is perceived, automatically, without any conscious in-tervention, the body is mobilized for either flight or fight. The sympathetic part of the autonomic nervous system goes into action in the hypothalamus, just above the spinal column, secreting a chemical that activates the pituitary gland. From there the chain of command moves to the adrenal glands, and the messages go out in rapid fire. For good reason, Aldous Huxley suggested in *The Devils of Loudun* that people who can't control their tempers are adrenalin addicts. Instantly the whole body prepares for violent action. The heartbeat and blood pressure rise. The liver orders sugar released into the blood for fuel, and the bronchial tubes expand, taking in more oxygen. The digestive organs all shut down. And finally, perhaps the most interesting touch, the blood clotting time goes down so that, in case of a wound, the loss of blood will be minimized.

Except for a few expert practitioners of yoga, these physiological responses take place in every human being in a threatening situation. The mouth may lie about the presence of emotion, but as the polygraph or lie-detector shows, the body never does; given a threat, the system reacts. Furthermore, the trigger is not always a "real" situation. This response can be activated by a dream, and studies of heart attacks occurring during sleep strongly suggest that they may often be caused by a dream that sets off these reactions. Even animals show much the same kind of response when they sleep. And in humans this same aggression system can be set in motion by images and memories, and even ideas. Most amazing of all, it can even be touched off by ideas and fears of which we are completely unconscious, by images and attitudes we do not even know exist in us. Once in action, this biological system seems to stimulate itself, adding fuel to the reaction by bringing up new images of oneself in anger or aggression. Thus it can become circular in buildup.

The standard human being comes equipped with three capacities that alter and intensify the biological response of aggression, and make it far more dangerous and unpredictable. These were added through the development of the human ability to conceptualize and the development of memory, which goes hand in hand with this. First, human beings are able to relive events of their past, and often react to them as if they had happened within the hour, and they can do this in the absence of any discernible outer stimulus. A dream or association can set off a hostile reaction quite out of the present context.

Next, the capacity to *project*, which is apparently not found among animals, enables human beings to read into the situation at hand attitudes and emotions they have experienced through other persons in other situations. And this can occur whether there is any actual similarity or relation between the two or not. For instance, one can see in a perfectly friendly person the attitude of a rejecting parent or hostile teacher, recalled from childhood. By projection we even burden strangers with inappropriate emotions, so that anger and guilt are often transferred to people we do not even know.

And then, through the human ability to *identify*, individuals are able to select the choice characteristics, or the choice role in the group, and then adopt them as their own. By identification human beings see themselves as the righteous ones, and even enjoy the sufferings of those on whom aggressions are committed. So activated, they believe—in fact, know without question—that the punishment of the victim is deserved. Thus the victim who is hanged or lynched or burned at the stake carries the projections of the spectators, while they in turn identify with the guiltless, and are free to discharge their pent-up aggressive feelings and unconscious guilts. We are very quick to call the practices of German concentration camps abnormal, but let us not forget that it has been only a few years since traitors in Britain were publicly castrated before they were finally dispatched. As Storr writes, "The catalogue of human cruelty is so long and the practice of torture so ubiquitous that it is impossible to believe that sadism is confined to a few abnormals."[8]

Aggression, supercharged with memory, projection, and identification, can be turned back upon the individual. Then one is presented with depressive reactions and suicide, or with schizoid, paranoid, or psychopathic reactions. These human problems are caused, not by a death wish, but by an aggressive reaction gone amok and turned in upon oneself, rather than upon the world. In other words, Storr comes to just the reverse of Freud's theory of the death wish as basic. Instead, he sees aggression as the primary force, a reaction built into our physical nature and encouraged by our psychological structure.

He makes several suggestions for the control of aggression. The raising of children is important. Children raised with love and limits, and exposed to a minimum of violence and aggression, appear to be less violently aggressive. There are research studies that bear out this contention.[9] The impersonalization caused by great masses in urban centers contributes to violence. To deal with this, something needs to be done, first, about the very important factor of overpopulation. Then, individuals need to develop sensitivity to other human beings; developing imagination can also help by bringing one closer to the actual suffering caused by violence. For example, a person who might drop napalm on villages with hardly a second thought would find it much harder to line up men, women, and children and burn them alive.

Last of all, Storr suggests draining off the aggressive drive in sports and other constructive competition. He notes that Jung, commenting on the ability of the Swiss to remain neutral, has suggested that by cantonal squabbles they take out among themselves what other nations take out on each other in war. This idea is being carried a good deal farther in a seminar on creative or fair-fight aggression at the University of California, Los Angeles, with laboratory training for individuals and couples.[10] Storr concludes his study hoping that human beings will use intelligence and planning to solve a problem so complex and threatening that these measures seem hardly enough.

His material linking certain psychological activities of human beings with their physical reactions in aggression is valuable. And perhaps the greatest value of this theory is its understanding that, when these reactions occur and are not released appropriately, they can be turned back upon the person and produce psychological illness. A depression or schizoid reaction is certainly not reasonable human behavior, but psychopathological reactions are what the therapist sees every day. The problem is to find an approach that does not limit the facts that one can see and consider.

To consider an example, for the past five years or so I have been seeing a middle-aged man from a very wealthy family. He had an alcoholic father who left him alone, and a mother who had been interested in his older brother and sister, but not in him. As an adult he suffered periods of intense depression, and had once made a serious suicide attempt. This behavior would then change, and he would become incredibly cruel to people. He even believed that his wife and child and friends deserved to be treated in this way. Then once more he would slip out of emotional contact with the environment, almost like falling into a pit without light, except that his dreams showed what was going on. In his depression a primal rage was focused on himself, and this was only relieved when it shifted away from him, onto his family and others. In the end, once he began to see this hostility as a force separate from his ego, working on and through him, he was able to start dealing with it and to bring some order into his life and outer actions.

Yet Storr's point of view and the others we have discussed make it difficult to understand such a case. Each of them makes assumptions about the nature of human beings that fix aggression as our natural birthright, with nothing to oppose it except our reason. They reduce aggression to a natural disposition built into our very being. It is a fixture permanently installed in either our physiology, our instincts, or our psychology in a way that keeps it from being affected by any other force working through our nature. Thus these thinkers develop only one real approach to the threat of our destructiveness. They see us solely responsible for protecting ourselves from our own violence, and in spite of the rapid increase in irrational behavior today, their only suggestion is that we decide consciously upon reasonable courses of action and follow them. They do not really look to see whether anything besides a purely physical nature (and the psychological factors derived from it) lies deep underneath our reason *and* our irrationality—anything that might also account for our aggression, and even our other drives.

There is one other view of the subject, however, which sees the problem in quite a different way. This is the view of Jung, who rejects these strictly naturalistic assumptions, and offers instead, as we have noted before, a teleological understanding of the human being. Let us define this view and look at the basis for it, and then see what it offers in coming to terms with human aggression.

JUNG AND HUMAN AGGRESSION

The idea of teleology or ultimate purpose in getting a picture of human personality suggests that we are not driven simply by blind mechanisms, but that there is meaning or purpose in the phenomena themselves that affect us, as well as in the way we react to them. Jung did not always look at things this way, as we shall see. He came to this view only after several experiences that he would have been quite happy to call coincidences and forget, except that there were strange connections that frequently had a startling effect on people's lives. For one thing, he was forced to admit that dreams sometimes spoke of the future with uncanny, and often painful, accuracy.

Thus when Jung discovered, during the years of peace before Hitler showed up, that every one of his German patients was having disturbing mythological dreams of violence and cruelty that made no sense on the basis of their personal approaches to life, he had quite a clear understanding of what this meant. In these particular people at least, an element of personality was being heard from that most Germans ignored as if they had outgrown it. Something forgotten was stirring—very much like a caged beast—and the same kind of things began to show up in the dreams of other Western Europeans. Jung noted that there were likely to be devastating consequences for society as a whole.

One may say "political guesswork," but, like most of Jung's thinking, this conclusion was backed up by facts about human beings, understood from the standpoint of a consistent, well-considered world view. With the help of the diagram which we introduced earlier let us see the implications of this point of view in regard to violence.

A MODEL OR SCHEMA

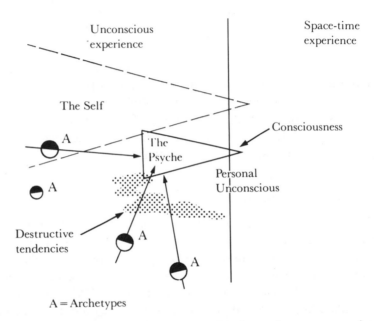

A = Archetypes

Besides contacts with the physical world through sense experience, we are in touch with psychic contents from the unconscious known as archetypes (the small circles with arrows). These are figures, or groups of images, in drama form, that operate independently of our conscious life and act upon it through dreams and various experiences like intuitions and fantasies. Archetypes work on a direct level to produce feelings, direct reactions, and even whole patterns of behavior, and they are nearly always bipolar in nature, as well as autonomous. In other words, they contain both constructive and destructive elements, which can be thrown at us without warning, usually through the more primitive parts of our central nervous system. In relating to these contents, the ego has real value because it is able to let the energy of the archetype work through the human psyche while filtering out its destructive aspect.

One of the most important archetypes is the configuration Jung calls the shadow, which often appears in dreams as a pursuing or hostile figure. This content represents aspects of the unconscious the individual does not want to deal with, which therefore seem threatening and destructive. But let the person confront these aspects consciously, and the shadow often turns out to be 90% pure gold; it can and does collect some of the most valuable elements of the psyche. At the same time other archetypal figures may be coming to the surface, like the dazzling feminine figure or the prophetic leader, which can contain much real destructiveness.

In addition, there appears to be an element in the unconscious that is destructive, in itself annihilative, a force (represented by the shaded area at the bottom) which seeks to draw people away from consciousness and to encourage possession by archetypes, rather than letting a person find relationship to them. This force appears to have more knowledge and cunning than the human ego. It is interesting how many people try to deny that such a reality exists, by calling it a lack of something else. But far from being just the absence of something, this is a substantive, destructive force that works by attraction, and can appear in dreams as an angel of light. The way it acts is described in Golding's *The Lord of the Flies*, to pick one out of many such novels, and by Jung in his work *Aion* and in Chapter 6 of his *Memories, Dreams, Reflections*, as well as in his analysis of the German mass psychosis in *Civilization in Transition*. John Sanford, in his book *Evil*, does a brilliant analysis of this reality using Stevenson's story *The Strange Case of Dr. Jekyll and Mr. Hyde*.

When people are possessed by this force, the net result may be that it leads the individual into depression and self-annihilation. Or the destructiveness can be projected out upon other individuals and groups, leading to a cult of hate and anything from neighborhood hostilities on up. The same force can seize individuals so that they run amok, as in so many newspaper stories of sprees of murder and destructiveness. Sometimes it may come out in subtle ways, by indifference and isolation, or our separating ourselves from others who need us. Or it can lead to war; it can seize a whole culture as it did the Germans under Hitler, the Mongolians under Genghis Khan, the Macedonians under Alexander, or the Romans under various leaders. Yet this force is not characterized so much by brute strength as by cunning, pride, and separation from the positive. It has been identified in this way by many religions—for instance, by Persian religion as

Ahriman, the supreme spirit of evil, and in the Judeo-Christian tradition as Satan or the Evil One.[11]

Jung, however, came to his conclusions through the experiences of his practice. This power, he found, is more than human; it cannot be tamed by purely human methods. In the same way, by listening to dreams and fantasies, the inner experiences and intuitions of people, he discovered that this is not the only force found coming into the human personality from outside it. There is also a creative, integrating power impinging on the psyche that is probably responsible for our survival as people, and certainly holds the one final answer to the problem of human aggression. This is the power, the psychic reality that he described as *the self* (denoted by the upper, open-ended triangle).

Neither of these ideas came easily to him, as we have already noted in an earlier chapter. In fact, when Jung started in practice, he came to his patients with much the same attitude as Freud, the reductive attitude of nineteenth-century German medicine in which he was trained. But gradually he came to see that these theories did not account for the facts. In spite of his personal inclinations, he had to accept the reality of first one and then the other of these two forces at work in human lives. Scientific understanding was still his real interest, however, and in order to keep these findings free of the once-and-for-all, settled interpretations of religion, he used the word *self* for this second, integrative force, rather than any of the more standard religious terms. In other words, if an idea like that was accepted before it was ever investigated, how could one decide whether he was touching a bit of truth, or only fingering an assumption that pleased him (or made him very mad)?

And so Jung set to work to investigate this new insight. Beginning in *Psychology and Alchemy*, and throughout his later writings, particularly in *Aion*, he brought out the evidence for the reality of such a power, which is more intelligent and creative than the human ego. Basically, what he discovered is this: that when the human psyche is centrally motivated by this reality, it becomes whole and creative, truly effective. It is only the *self* that can sift out the negative contents from the shadow and the other archetypes, integrate their creative power, and keep the dark destructiveness of raw, primal evil at bay. The function of the *self* in the psychic economy is to integrate into the psyche what can be integrated, and to give protection against the things which we cannot handle.

If this understanding, which Jung reached through nearly sixty years of working with people and their problems, is anything like a true picture of our nature, then it suggests a much more complete way of dealing with the problem of aggression. We have a bigger and far more important task, and at the same time a more hopeful one, than most other thinkers have envisioned. Besides the direct approaches that others have proposed, we have the task, according to Jung, of coming to know and develop capacities within ourselves that we scarcely imagine at present.

In the first place, Jung's suggestions start from the understanding provided by these other points of view, behaviorist and naturalist, as well as Freudian. Far from denying these basic scientific discoveries, and the necessity of acting on them, what Jung proposes is a way of going on from there. His thinking takes it for granted that the individual will avoid unnecessary frustration of others, particularly children, in whom traumatic memories can have such tragic results, and that we will do what we can to express the physiological drive of aggression harmlessly. In fact, he considers that the first, indispensable step towards psychological maturity is the development of a sound ego and learning to make good use of it in ways like these. Without this much, there is little hope of controlling our destructiveness.

The real problem is next to discover and identify the destructive elements operating within oneself, and this often involves unexpected and painful experience. The task is essentially the same for either aggression directed inwardly, seeking to destroy the individual, or that directed out towards the world. In the first case, one is probably already involved in the difficulty and pain. And where the violence and rage are projected out, one has undoubtedly laid aside a part of oneself and let it become unconscious. As Jung has remarked:

Anything that disappears from your psychological inventory is apt to turn up in the guise of a hostile neighbor, who will inevitably arouse your anger and make you aggressive. It is surely better to know that your worst enemy is right there in your own heart.[12]

In either case, if aggression is to be controlled, individuals must know and confront—whether through active impulses, or in dreams or imagination or meditation—things within themselves that they do not want to face consciously.

We must then do all that we can accomplish by our own ego power

to withstand the forces that are awakened when we confront the unconscious. But once we have perceived the opposites within ourselves
the human ego is powerless to resolve the conflict alone. Finally, as we
call upon something from beyond our own consciousness, the power of
the *self* breaks through to integrate the opposites; instead of aggression, we are left with an experience of psychic totality and creativity.

RELIGION AND AGGRESSION

Even though this is described in nonreligious language, this is clearly what all the great religions of the world have attempted to describe
in one way or another. It is particularly close to the idea of patristic
Christianity. Certainly we stand today against forces that we cannot
adequately handle. Only as we find another power accessible to us,
willing to give aid, and then bind ourselves to that force can we survive
personally or socially. Only the religious inner journey (in the broad
sense) frees us or the group. The basic meaning of religion, from the
word *religio*, is to bind to, to relate to. The human task is first to know
ourselves and face the destructive powers within us, and then to come
to know this saving power, to tie to it and relate to it. This power alone
can handle metaphysical evil. Those who would handle aggression in
themselves or in others have more than a humanistic task. It is not that
militant enthusiasm is bad, but our attachment had better be to the
creative force, and not to some bipolar archetype or the supposed
angel of light. (I have offered ways of learning to relate to God in *The
Other Side of Silence.)*

My own experience—within myself, in working as counselor with
others, in observing society, and in reading and thinking—leads me to
believe that Jung's basic theory is necessary to explain the complex and
diverse problems involved in dealing with human aggression. I also believe that it provides the most fruitful solution to the problem. The
question is whether it can be accepted today as anything like a true
picture. But is it so absurd to posit a realm of spiritual reality? It is
good to remember the logical difficulty of establishing a negative
proposition. This is particularly true when experience does not fit into
neat naturalistic and reductive categories. As difficult as it is for people brought up in a naturalistic and materialistic culture to consider
the ideas of C. G. Jung, it seems that his is the best analysis of the
demonic powers of human hatred and violence.

In less conscious societies, destructive tendencies are held in check by group mores, while in other cultures the living religions have given men and women a means of understanding and coping with these incredibly powerful forces. But modern people who can no longer accept the traditional religious framework are forced to go on an inner journey if they are to deal creatively with these destructive forces. We are in contact with them whether we like it or not, and we must find consciousness and our own religious way. When they are not dealt with, these forces usually find unconscious expression within or through the individual. A tremendous burden and opportunity is laid today upon those of us who would find a nonviolent way. The value of a conscious, remythologized Christian faith is incalculable. Let us look now at how a group can take the first steps in confronting their own inner violence.

NOTES

1. C. G. Jung, *Collected Works*, Vol. 9, Part II, p. 41 ff.
2. John A. Sanford, *Evil* (New York: Crossroad, 1981), p. 65.
3. Konrad Lorenz, *On Aggression* (New York: Bantam Books, 1970).
4. Discussed by Jerome D. Frank, *Persuasion and Healing* (New York: Schocken Books, 1963), p. 39 ff., and Herman Feifel, *The Meaning of Death* (New York: McGraw-Hill Book Company, 1959), p. 302 ff.
5. Albert Einstein and Sigmund Freud, *Why War?* (Paris: International Institute of Intellectual Cooperation, 1933), quoted by Karl Menninger, *Man Against Himself* (New York: Harcourt, Brace and Company, 1938), p. 411.
6. The most comprehensive neo-Freudian discussion of the subject without reference to the death wish is Fromm's *The Anatomy of Human Destructiveness* (New York: Holt, Rinehart and Winston, 1973).
7. Anthony Storr, *Human Aggression* (New York: Atheneum, 1968).
8. *Ibid.*, p. 98.
9. Martin Hoffman, "Childrearing Practices and Moral Development: Generalizations from Empirical Research," *Child Development*, 1963, 34, pp. 295-318.
10. Conducted by George R. Bach. His methods are discussed in the book he wrote with Peter Wyden, *The Intimate Enemy: How to Fight Fair in Love and Marriage* (New York: William Morrow and Company, 1969).
11. I have discussed this at great length in my books *Discernment* and *Myth, History and Faith* (New York: Paulist Press, 1978 and 1974).
12. C. G. Jung, *Civilization in Transition*, (New York, Pantheon Books for the Bollingen Foundation, 1964), p. 225.

PART TWO: CONFRONTING INNER VIOLENCE

Shortly after the peace march in the spring of 1971, as Washington began to clean up the Mall and monuments and impromptu prisons, I talked at some length with a young man who had been there. This student, whom I knew fairly well, had taken part in the protest and been jailed in the mass arrest. It was the first experience he had ever had with the kind of heady emotions that were generated in both protestors and police. As the situation had grown more and more volatile and the police were pressed further and harder, my friend had found himself swept with an unexpected experience of rage and violence. He spoke of this frankly. "I'd never dreamed," he told me, "that there was so much violence and hatred inside me. But there they were, just spilling over, when I saw the things the police did. Feelings just spouted that I had no idea I was capable of."

Such feelings of violence are much more general than is usually recognized, particularly in persons who are concerned with taking a nonviolent stance. For instance, one psychiatrist friend of mine remarked that there is a "quiet Quaker rage" he has observed in certain people who are consciously trying to follow a peaceful, nonaggressive life-style like that of the Quakers. It appears, in fact, that impulses towards violence lie deep within each of us, no matter how positive one's conditioning has been. And on the other side of the coin, there is good evidence that our chances of holding to a consistently nonviolent course of action are far better if we become aware of this inner violence and deal with it.

How do we deal with our inner violence? Let us be very practical and look at an actual attempt to deal with inner violence. Although this class was part of a college curriculum, it could be recreated in any parish in which a group wanted to deal with their inner violence.

This was the experience of a group in the Program for Nonviolence at the University of Notre Dame, in a seminar designed for students with some background in the program. Entitled "Nonviolence Perspectives," the course was developed to deal with the subject affectively as well as cognitively, in order to give these young people an opportunity to explore their own inner attitudes freely. Originally it was set up by Charles McCarthy, former director of the program, because he suspected that some of the students in the Program for Nonviolence had come into it for violent reasons. The seminar was constructed to help students come to terms with their inner violence, with the aim of enabling them to live and act in harmony with the life-style they have chosen—in other words, to express nonviolence in spite of provocation. Those who started this program realized that handling personal violence takes more than rational understanding or intellectual maturity. It takes emotional maturity as well.

After first describing briefly the composition of the group and certain characterics of those who made it up, we will outline something of its development over the two semesters that this particular group met. We will then indicate what changes took place, both in the group and within these individuals, concluding with some general comments about the direction of such groups among people of all ages today.

THE GROUP—ITS FIXED POINTS AND VARIABLES

There were twelve in the first semester group—seven seniors, four juniors, and one sophomore. All were good students, with an overall grade point average of about 3.25. At least four ranked among the most capable in the university, and several graduated with honors. The Myers-Briggs Type Indicator Test was administered, and all but two scored as introverted feeling intuitives. The others were extraverted intuitive feeling types, who were only mildly extraverted. At the same time some of the introverted types were just barely so.[1]

At the second semester nine more students were added, six of whom were seniors and three graduate students, of similar academic background. These students all tested out in type as introverted feeling intuitives. One of this number dropped out of the group meetings because the group stimulated too frequent and too violent responses in him; he continued seeing the facilitator on a weekly basis instead. Out of the twenty-one, three were women. Fifteen of the group were good representatives of the frame of mind and life-style which Reich described as "Consciousness III" in *The Greening of America*. All but three had had some experience with the drug culture, and some had more than casual experience.

It is impossible to say how representative this group would be of the college community as a whole. Compared with other student groups with which I have been connected, and particularly with a group of preprofessional students for whom I have been the facilitator in a seminar on death and dying, my educated guess would be that this group was slightly less conservative than the average student on the Notre Dame campus and more nearly the norm on the average college campus. They all expressed deep concern over the mechanization of modern living and searched for spiritual reality without knowing where to turn. It never occurred to most of them to seek in the Church for experiences of another dimension of reality.

The group met once a week for about three hours in my living room, with a fifteen-minute break halfway through the session. My wife acted as cofacilitator with me. The larger group during the second semester was divided into two sections, and my wife and I spent half of our time with each, switching during the break . Rather than dividing the group on the basis of old and new members, the more extraverted students were placed in one section, and those who were more introverted in the other.

At the first session, a sheet was distributed to each member that outlined the parameters of the group experience. Since these instructions were brief, I include them *in toto:*

The purpose of the course is to explore the roots of violence within each of us, using the insights and general methods of Jungian analysis in this process. We shall make use of several different techniques for this exploration.

1. The class interaction is of primary importance. Within a group situation we come to see ourselves as we react with others, often seeing ourselves in truer perspective than we do when alone. The group reveals parts of ourselves of which we are often unconscious. Attendance at the class is of the greatest importance; it is the primary obligation of those taking this course. The nature of the group changes with the absence of just one member. If it is impossible to be present, please inform the instructor before class time.

2. If the interaction of the class is to be meaningful, we must bring as much of ourselves as we feel comfortable bringing. The keeping of a journal is essential to the whole process of developing deeper consciousness of one's self. The journal will contain some of the following items, many of which we shall discuss during class time:

    a. One's dreams and an attempt to understand them;
    b. Reflections of any kind that seem pertinent to one's life in general;
    c. Reflections on previous class periods or materials;
    d. Attempts to understand one's projections;
    e. Reflections on various life situations in dorm or home relationships;
    f. Fantasies or imaginings, written down to keep them from being lost;
    g. Drawings or doodlings;
    h. Poetry;
    i. Copies of important letters.

3. To provide a common understanding of the depth of our psyche, we

shall use the following books by C.G. Jung as our base. The student should own the four paperback volumes of Jung, because it is helpful to read, mark, and inwardly digest these four:

Man and His Symbols;
Modern Man in Search of a Soul;
Memories, Dreams, Reflections;
Two Essays on Analytical Psychology;
Civilization in Transition; Collected Works, Vol. 10, pp. 177–243.

Also the following by Morton T. Kelsey: *Encounter with God.*
4. The instructor will make at least one appointment each month with each of the seminar members to go over personal materials, to give guidance in further reading or to discuss any matter pertaining to the seminar that the individual may wish to discuss.
5. At the conclusion of the seminar the students will present, either as a paper or in some other way, their reactions to the seminar, suggestions for change, improvement, analysis of personal changes, etc.

It was hoped that the original group, who had been asked to do some reading before the seminar, would have started reading Jung, but this was the usual overoptimism of teachers, and so the books were read and a terminology acquired along with the classes. Jung's *Answer to Job* was also added to the list, and during the second semester the new students read these books while the others went on to read Jerome Frank's *Persuasion and Healing,* Jung's *Psyche and Symbol,* and the rest of *Civilization in Transition.* They could then read three of the following, or other books approved by the instructor: Morton T. Kelsey, *Tongue Speaking* and *Dreams: The Dark Speech of the Spirit,* and John A. Sanford, *The Kingdom Within* and *Dreams: God's Forgotten Language.* At no time did the different levels of accomplished reading interfere with either the group discussion or interaction.

THE DEVELOPMENT OF INTERACTION

It is about as easy to detail the growth of viable relationships within a group as it would be to paint a picture of all that goes on in the cell as new life begins. Still, in the seminar group certain stages of development did occur; there were crucial movements within the group life, and these we have tried to note and record.

Although the first session brought a rather spirited interchange, and even expression of feeling, the second meeting was characterized by long periods of silence. Indeed, one of the most striking aspects of the group, in the early stages of its development, was the frequent inability to begin group interaction, and real discomfort in the presence of silence. We came to see that the silence stemmed largely from fear of expressing significant feelings or even ideas. "Why would anyone want to hear what I have to say?" was a common attitude. On the other hand, the lack of interest in the feelings and ideas of others on the part of many of the group members, and their inability to listen with any real interest, gave some basis for this fear.

I came to know each of the individuals of the group in depth in personal interviews, and to realize that all shared the same desire for genuine relationship, real intimacy. Yet at the same time they were afraid of close relationships. It was very difficult for them to move in either direction—either to express a desire for the interest of the group, or to reach out towards another member with concern. It came as a shocking realization to most of them that they really did not care about the others, and that they all shared in the violence of indifference to each other by failing to listen closely and rarely picking up an interesting lead. For the most part they were so caught up in their own preoccupations and fears that they could not or did not hear what others were saying. Thus they contributed to the violence of not caring. One student remarked that he had wept when he realized how little he cared and how seldom he reached out to another who needed him.

The group attempted to resolve the problem by giving one person at a time the center of focus (and nearly everyone wanted it), and then allowing the group to question and relate to this individual. By the last few weeks, however, the group had become comfortable with silence and could allow it to continue. The reason was unquestionably that they had to come to know, respect, and trust one another. Silence was no longer a threat because it no longer represented hostility.

As we came to know each other better, the fears came tumbling out. Fears of every kind were expressed, and this opened the way for expression of anger, hostility, and feelings of violence. As is true of most of us, the violence and anger were a defense against hurt and fear, and once the fears were expressed, the turbulent affect could be expressed more easily and with less guilt.

Most prominent at first were the fears of sexuality, fear of being too free sexually, of not being a real man or a real woman, of homosexuality, and of inability to love at all. In most of the students there was also a fear-hostility reaction to their parents. Only three of the twenty-one were comfortable with parental figures. Among the men, most of this anger was directed towards the mother, and my wife found it very difficult to step out of the mother-role and be a person in the eyes of the students. There was an obvious connection between this parental problem and their sexual fears.

There were fears about society's attitude towards drugs, coupled with anger that the authorities were so opposed to their use. As we have noted, a large number of the students had experimented with drugs, but not too many deeply. Their major concern was about the attitude towards marijuana and certain hallucinogens; there had been little experience with hard drugs. The drug experience for most of them was one of trying to expand consciousness and discover more about reality and its nonphysical dimensions, rather than an attempt to avoid reality.

At the deepest level, every one of the group was afraid of rejection. They placed little value upon themselves as persons, and many of them at times felt a sense of utter isolation. In spite of casual friendships — and there were several in the group who had roomed together through most of these years — they found it difficult to share these deep feelings of valuelessness and isolation with each other. But it was easier to do this within the group or with the facilitator. One evening the subject of suicide came up and several were able to speak of their fears of self-destruction or of an early death. Five or six of the students had known a sense of real depression because of these feelings and fears, and they were able to recognize and speak frankly about some of the things that may have been responsible for this inner heaviness.

Isolation and the lack of a common collective viewpoint within which they could communicate were undoubtedly factors. Many of the students had had more education than their parents and were separated from the worldview of their families; this added to their isolation. They were isolated from peers, parents, authorities, and had no collective religious point of view. The vice president for student affairs made a point of telling me of a suicide that had occurred on campus. In order to investigate, the administration had tried to question the young man's close friends, only to find that he had had none; he had had no real relationship with anyone.

With these fears and angers expressed, it was easier for members of the group to see why they had been so afraid of one another, so suspicious of each other. They found the presence of the facilitator a stabilizing factor within the group, and were able to express more feelings when he or she was present than in any discussions on their own. They also found that by talking individually with the facilitator they could speak even more freely about these very fears, and that this sometimes enabled them to discuss things of importance in the group setting. What had happened within the group was also sometimes the stimulus for the individual discussions.

My experience with adults in a parish or conference setting has revealed the same sort of isolation and (with the exception of drug use) the same fears. The Church needs to help its people with these inner concerns.

The theoretical framework of C.G. Jung, described earlier, provided a meaningful base for dealing with inner hostility and its outer expression. Jung's model made sense to the students, as it does to most people I meet at workshops and conferences. It was not only congruent with their own experience of hostility and isolation within the group, but it met the deep need for some meaningful worldview. Only three of the twenty-one had come into the group with any religious or philosophical base. Although most had been raised in the parochial school system of the Catholic Church, most of them had rejected its views as inadequate, and so had nothing to turn to. Reading Jung's *Answer to Job* also suggested a creative pattern for expressing the violence and anger within them. This is the work that Jung wrote after an encounter with agony and a near brush with death, letting loose his feelings upon God. The young people quickly grasped its significance, and saw that God is not hurt by our expression of negative feelings and violence, while most human beings are.

This led to a realization of the importance of affect and emotion. We had already realized in the group how much easier it was to deal with our ideas than with our feelings, and how little effect ideas usually had upon our actions or our relations with other people. Until affect was expressed there was no real relationship within the group. And certainly there was little chance of relating to a transpersonal meaning when we did not care one way or another.

The students also realized that it was far more threatening, to oneself at any rate, to express positive affect than negative. When we showed that we really cared, then we were out on a limb and vulnerable, open to rejection and ridicule. In expressing hostility, on the other hand, we were already in a defensive position, and not so vulnerable. Occasionally it was necessary for the facilitator to step in when hostility was expressed that might have been damaging to an individual. For the most part, however, his or her task was to call the group back to feelings when it had slipped back into the safety of cognitive ideas.

From the first, the students brought their significant dreams. They knew enough about Jung, and they also knew the facilitator's interest in and work with dreams, and this gave them a marvelous way of offering themselves tentatively, without being too specific in the beginning. Later they brought the dreams because they wanted the intuitive understanding of the group. Often the other members offered significant insights into the dream material. In this way discussions and interactions were opened up on all sorts of subjects. Indeed, the dreams that were offered formed a bridge by which the students reached others and bypassed the fears that had separated them.

Finding how much meaning came from their own dreams also brought them an appreciation of the depth of the unconscious and the reality of an inner world. For one thing, those most committed to a nonviolent stance found they had dreams of terrifying violence so often that it seemed this might explain, at least in part, their reason for taking this stance. It appeared that, consciously or unconsciously, they realized the kind of violence that could erupt from them if they did not take a stand against it. They appreciated Jung's formulation even more, realizing that they could not — and *did* not — stand against such destructiveness simply by willing to do so. They needed inner reinforcement if they were to succeed.

The best way, they found, to open themselves to such reinforcement — in other words, to this kind of positive, transpersonal force — was by caring as best they could for those around them. Nonviolence could be achieved, in nearly every instance, only as the actual violence within the individual was replaced by a genuine and positive caring for people. Hatred, they say, is the zero of love, and only real love, genuine caring, will displace violence.

No problem or feeling was forbidden group expression; yet there were very few instances of inappropriate subjects or timing. For the most part, personal and touchy subjects were held back for individual discussion with the facilitator. But towards the end of the year many very personal subjects were brought up and discussed within the group. One young man was even able to speak of his homosexual fears and feelings, and he received real support and understanding. The few times when personal hostility became apparent, and a discussion had to be cut off during the group session, the situation was handled by bringing those involved in later for a private discussion with the facilitator.

There were certain subjects that aroused almost universal hostility, particularly the subjects of nuns and parents. The nun was apparently the most convenient symbol on which to hang all their distaste for prudish restrictions and curbs. Once their pet hates had been sorted out, they realized that nuns might as well have been pegs on the wall for all they had really seen them, and they began to see the nun as a person in her own right. In much the same way, most of the group came to realize that their parents, who were caught up in a different worldview, also needed to be approached and understood as individuals.

The presence of a mature woman interacting within the group added an interesting dimension. Although it was relatively easy for the group members to call me by my first name, it was very difficult for them to do the same with my wife. She picked up the mother images of many of the students. Only slowly were they able to detach them and view her as an individual person. As they did so, they were more likely to see their parents in the same light.

CHANGES WITHIN THE GROUP

The question naturally arises: Was this group experience merely an interesting pastime, even something of an exercise in self-indulgence, or did it result in actual changes in the individuals? Although it is impossible to state with absolute certainty that the changes that occurred were a direct result of the group experience, there is good reason to believe that the group did facilitate very real and discernable growth and change in the students. This conclusion is based on our own observations and the student evaluations.

Probably the most startling change came from the realization by most of the members of the group of how little they had listened to each other in the beginning. Being unable to listen, they were unable to care. The visible change was clear; they made the effort to listen, out of a desire, as they expressed it, to do better both in this and in caring for other people. By following up these students after the seminar was over, I could see that this change had remained operative. A large number of these students have kept in touch with me.

The freedom to vent hostilities about church, religion, and parents allowed some of the students to form more creative relationships in these areas. Several of the members found that they could begin to communicate with their parents with a good deal of understanding, while a number of them found that church services became meaningful to them once again.

In general, the students became far more comfortable with themselves and with their freedom. Their statements showed clearly that they found this exercise of coming to know themselves and each other one of the most helpful experiences in their academic careers. They were grateful that the academic community had provided this kind of opportunity.

At least five of the group had successfully repressed their hostilities, and so these unconscious feelings had surfaced as depressive, and even suicidal, fantasies. The ability to discuss these things within the group and to receive group support, realizing that others confronted the same conflicts, as well as the opportunity to talk these matters over with the facilitator, resulted in a marked decrease in their pain and anxiety over these feelings. Each of them also worked at the roots of these feelings, and by the end of the year they appeared much less subject to mood swings.

Several students who had been heavily involved in the drug scene came to realize that their use of drugs was reducing their effectiveness, and either stopped or curtailed their use. They also realized that hallucinogens often became a substitute for relating to other students, and in this sense were a form of violence. These realizations struck home, whereas a moralistic approach would have been rejected.

Six of the students were either married or about to be married, and these young people found the insights of the group helpful in making these relationships work. They found the same forces operating within marriage as they found within the group, and all of them discovered that they were better able to deal with the marriage relationship as they found themselves comfortable within the group.

A great majority of the group realized how far they had to go in order to express the idea of nonviolence fully in their own lives. This could not be done by conscious choice alone, but only as the whole personality became known, was examined, and brought into play. Once they could see how divergent they were from the ideal, they began to work at personal integration and bringing this whole person into service of the nonviolent ideal.

For instance, one student wrote a novel describing his inner experience of dismemberment and his coming together, which had been possible only as he dealt with his inner violence. The group gave him some aid in working through this experience, which was very similar to the initiation required to become a shaman. Another of the group, who recognized his need for outer steps, expressed it by taking in a graduating senior who had no place to go, and sharing with him.

Several students worked on coming to terms with military service. They found the group interaction of great help in formulating their individual solutions to this problem, which was universal for the male seniors with low draft numbers. One joined the Peace Corps, another the army reserve. Several filed papers for status as conscientious objectors, and others sought and obtained deferment on other grounds.

These class experiences were offered each year for several years. The same kind of positive response was obtained in all groups but one, and in that one I had allowed too many students into the group.

CONCLUSIONS

This kind of opportunity for free interaction can offer today's college students a valuable supplement to their development through academic work. Most students can benefit from such an opportunity, and it can even add to the value of their academic work and the use they are able to make of it. It would probably do the most good to offer these groups during the first years of college, so that the relationships that developed would have a chance to continue.

The same kind of program could be offered in a well-developed parish education program. I have seen such courses operate in several parishes. The effect of such study has been to raise the level of consciousness of the whole parish.

The group interaction is most likely to be fruitful if an effort is made to understand it within some particular frame of reference. The approach that is chosen will determine to some extent the direction the interaction takes. For several reasons we have found the Jungian framework the most helpful. It is the one most specifically related to the inner development of the individual. At the same time, it allows the greatest latitude of interpretation of experience, and it also allows a discussion of the religious aspect of experience, which can be very important to the college-age group. At least a basic understanding of the dynamics of group interaction, of course, is needed, as well as a leader able to shift gears when a situation starts to get out of hand.

For good or ill, the influence of facilitators will have a great effect upon the results. If they are accepting and genuine, this attitude will pervade the group, while if they are hostile or defensive, this too will be experienced. The most important qualities for the group leaders are a depth of knowledge of and acceptance of themselves and some knowledge of the group process. If the deeper areas of human relationship are to be explored, the leaders need to be comfortable with these, and willing to take individuals beyond the group experience when this is indicated. They will most likely be needed for individual listening. In *Freedom to Learn*, Carl Rogers describes the ideal teacher as genuine, caring, and sympathetic. This applies to anyone leading such a group experience. Roger's book *On Encounter Groups* is a good introduction to group process.

There is much fear and hostility, as well as a need to care and to be cared for, just below the surface of the college student — just as there is in most adults. This tends to isolate the individual, and either to break out in active hostility or outer indifference, or to be turned inwards in self-directed hostility. When people, through group interaction, become less afraid of themselves, they tend to become open to real relationships, both among themselves and with the leader. This can add a dimension that is lacking from both the ordinary college campus and most churches. It can create an atmosphere of confidence and more open communication that comes with acceptance of self and of others, and even to a greater openness to vital Christianity, as well as to academic learning.

In a time of such traumatic change as we are experiencing, it is the rare parent who is able to provide open communication. Groups such as these can help to keep communication open and make growth creative. The presence of an older woman, properly qualified as a leader, can help to constellate the mother image, giving students (and even adults) a chance to work it through.

For those whose interest in nonviolence is more than cerebral and academic, experiences such as these can be especially helpful, turning the idea of nonviolence into a genuine stance that works in actual situations. In the long run, a group has the best chance of accomplishing this when its experience is directed towards the attempt to become caring and concerned about others. The implications of this caring need to be pointed out with some regularity to participants in the group if they are to see the possibilities involved. As one of the group so aptly put it, "As long as I was not very conscious of my feelings, or of 'just not caring' I was about the first to react violently, and usually the last one to recognize it."

NOTES

1. For a basic understanding of these terms see the Manual by Isabel Briggs Myers, *The Myers-Briggs Type Indicator*, and the handbook *Introduction to Type* (Consulting Psychologists Press, 577 College Ave., Palo Alto, Calif.). A more complete treatment is found in *Gifts Differing*, by Isabel Briggs Myers (Consulting Psychologists Press, 1979).

Chapter 12

MINISTRY TO THE DYING

Not many thinkers—with the exception of Plato in ancient times—have dealt with the problem of death as fully and directly as Dr. C.G. Jung. He not only struggled to give an understanding of the human psyche, including the inevitable human problem of dying, but he also wrestled with the possibility that the individual psyche may persist after this life. He did not approach this question as a classical philosopher or theologian, but as a psychiatrist, a doctor of the soul. His was the practical task of helping people as they confronted psychic pain and meaninglessness.

He attempted to share something of his broad experience, the understanding he had gained, with patients who were often overwhelmed by the thought of death, and so by a sense of meaninglessness. Since these people had found little or no help in the usual religious circles, Jung realized that it was up to him, as a physician, to try to offer them the understanding and confidence that brings relief. "Meaninglessness," he wrote, "inhibits fullness of life and is therefore equivalent to illness."[1] He tried to get at the roots of this illness, and to do so, he tackled the problem in several ways. The ministry of the Church has the same concern, and can learn much from him.

First of all, he carefully outlined a worldview that took into account the broad range of facts he had encountered. In other words, he put together an hypothesis about the nature of the world we live in, and then he went on accumulating data. In this view, which we have already described, the human psyche does not appear to be merely an epiphenomenon of a material universe; rather, it has a central reality which must be reckoned with. In fifty years as a therapist he amassed quite a bit of evidence about the phenomenology of the human spirit and its religious dimensions, and about the nature of death. He then came to some plausible conclusions about this, and about the probability of some kind of life after death.

In his book *Jung, Gods, and Modern Man,* Fr. Antonio Moreno — although he was not very happy with some of Jung's theological conclusions — wrote that

> Scientists should very carefully consider Jung's priceless contribution to the phenomenology of religion, his best empirical work in a field which until recent years has been almost untouched. Neither scientists nor those engaged in pastoral theology and religious psychology can afford to ignore the material and the observations gathered by him in sixty-five years of pioneer work.[2]

Jung was able to accumulate this material because he had a worldview in which people's experiences are important. He could listen to the accounts they gave without deciding that what they were saying was silly. Because people are quite sensitive to such openness in another, and also because Jung had a personal charisma, many persons were able to open up the deepest levels of themselves to him.

In addition, when Jung was in his middle sixties he had a personal confrontation with death. In an accident he broke his foot and had to crawl to a town to find help; as a result of severe complications, he lingered between life and death for several weeks, and during this time he was confronted with a series of extraordinary experiences. This episode altered Jung's attitude towards death.

It also changed the entire direction of his psychological investigations and development. In the last part of his life he was concerned with questions that would ordinarily be considered religious, except that they were carefully dealt with from his critical, scientific point of view. Only in one place — in his *Memories, Dreams, Reflections* — did he abandon this criterion and speak as Jung, the suffering human being. And he expressly requested that these personal reflections not be included in the corpus of his collected works.

His general studies of death and renewal are scattered throughout the twenty volumes of these works. The very philosophical framework he proposed and supported in them has implications for the idea of some kind of survival after death, and it was evident almost from the beginning that Jung held a point of view quite different from the naturalism of most of his scientific colleagues. His first specific treatment of the subject in a published work was written in 1934, and from then until his death articles and books that touched on his ideas about death continued to appear.

The volumes that relate most centrally to this thinking are *The Structure and Dynamics of the Psyche* and *Psychology and Religion: West and East*, Volumes 8 and 11 of his collected works. In addition, some of his most mature thinking on the subject is found in the two works completed just before his death—*Memories, Dreams, Reflections* and his introduction to the provocative study *Man and His Symbols*. These also represent his only attempt to put his views in a popular form. Many of the references to fate, death, and renewal from the collected works have been gathered together by Jung's friend and collaborator Jolande Jacobi, in one section of the book she edited, *Psychological Reflections*. To have a grasp of these conclusions in terms of actual experience, it is essential to understand Jung's basic worldview, which we have already described at some length.

LIFE AFTER DEATH

Jung's worldview has significant implications for the consideration of death. Once the human psyche is considered as having the same level of reality as the physical world, the problem of death is shifted to another plane. If we are indeed caught between two realms of experience—each at least as real as the other—then the dissolution of our physical bodies (the cessation of our concrete participation in the space-time world) need not imply that the psyche itself ceases to exist. Since one cannot confirm the idea that death destroys the psyche by any critical or scientific reason, there is then no critical *a priori* reason for denying our continued existence. Instead, we are free to take up the evidence with an open mind. We can look at the red six of spades. We can consider the rare but significant data that occur from time to time, and listen to the intimations of our own hearts, as well as the almost universal beliefs on the subject. Of course, it may be that Jung is wrong, and these attitudes and the data itself are the result of self-deception, of the neurosis that we call civilization. But in that case, most of what we call "objective knowledge" today would also have to be reexamined, and much of it would probably go by the boards.

If it is true, however, as Jung's data suggests, that the human psyche has the ability to transcend or move beyond the strictly space-time world, this would seem to indicate that the psyche is not totally conditioned by this world. Most of the religions of humankind have offered such evidence through the centuries until the rational materialism of the nineteenth century swept it aside in cavalier fashion. If there is truth here, and if we can be open to it, then there are ways in which we can deal creatively with the data, on the basis of Jung's view.

Jung sees human life as a meaningful development from an unconscious matrix towards a growing consciousness. This is very different from Freud, who sees human beings caught in a cold war between meaningless, irrational forces, with the rational ego barely able to keep a tenuous balance and survive. For Freud, civilization is merely the product of this neurotic tension, and the only compensation we get for living through this meaninglessness. In the end, the best we can hope for is to face death with fatalistic stoicism, as Freud did with magnificent courage.

Jung also sees us propelled forward by a tension of opposites, but towards a meaningful end. This process starts as we become more conscious and begin to face, first, the unaccepted side of ourselves, and then a pervasive destructiveness operating deep within us. Only through a genuine catharsis, usually with another person, can we realize fully the chaos within ourselves. This stage of self-knowledge leads towards a real relationship, in which the courage to bear the darkness and the pain of growth is given by one who has passed through similar experiences. A stage of self-development follows, of self-education, as we try to bring together the fragmented and opposing parts of our own personalities. But we find that this unifying can seldom be accomplished by ourselves. Instead, it is usually given. The resolution comes to a person in such conflict much as it did to Job out of a whirlwind. In hundreds of patients Jung observed what seemed to be a transcendent function that brings us together, resolving our problems and fears.

Thus the human psyche appears to be a special "interest" of this creative center. This appears, as Jung saw it, to be the same reality spoken of by religions in terms of experiences of deity. The same resolution of problems is often described in the purely religious process. This is brought out with startling clarity by John Sanford in *The Kingdom Within,* where he discusses the way of individuation and wholeness, comparing it to the best in the Christian tradition.

When life is seen as a teleological, purposeful process, there is reason, as Jung suggests, to look for its continuance. In his paper "Stages of Life," Jung suggested that old age, as a time of withdrawal, of reflection and introversion, prepares for the next step forward, the next mutation, as it were. This very way in which life moves forward purposefully from stage to stage makes us look ahead to some extension, some further expansion of our psychic being after death. The best preparation for this expansion is living life as deeply, fully, and consciously as possible.

This process of individuation is not easy. Indeed, it involves a kind of death. Our ego must die to allow for a new center of being. The worst thing about death is the utter giving up of ourselves to something else. Indeed, those who go this way are usually subject to negative incursions of the unconscious like those described with terrifying reality by Jung in Chapter 6 of *Memories, Dreams, Reflections,* and by Carlos Castaneda in *The Teachings of Don Juan. To be open to this kind of suffering is death.* In the midst of it, we wonder if we can face it through; we would gladly exchange it for simple dissolution into meaningless molecules. Asking for such an experience, Jung has written in his "Psychological Commentary on *The Tibetan Book of the Dead,"* is like "meddling with fate, which strikes at the very roots of human existence and can let loose a flood of suffering of which no sane person ever dreamed."[3] Yet the person in the individuation process must pass through this experience. St. John of the Cross describes the same reality in his book *Dark Night of the Soul.*

Physical death, then, becomes a symbol for a confrontation with something far *more* terrifying. Those who have experienced this confrontation with the negative side of the unconscious usually lose much of their fear of death; there is nothing left to fear. The understanding expressed in *The Tibetan Book of the Dead* is that there is no avoiding the growth process—those who do not make the confrontation in their life process must make it in the existence that follows death.

The nihilism of much modern thought is a far easier way out for twentieth-century people; it makes fewer demands on the individual and might actually be motivated by unconscious fear of life. There are also people unaware of the depth of the psyche, who have a sentimental idea of death as an easy transition to a life of bliss, harping on the clouds. This naiveté is rightly ridiculed by existential thought. It debases not only death, but life, as a simple, unconscious, basically undirected process. But because these generally fearful people pervert the reality is no reason for rejecting the truth, and falling into a blatant *ad hominem* fallacy.

Dreams of death are often best understood in the total context of the individual's life as a place for rebirth. Psychic growth implies that something has died and been reborn. The same is true of dreams of coffins, sarcophagi, and tombs.[4] Often, with understanding of such dreams there is a new widening and development of consciousness, new awareness and understanding. New developments in the person's outer life often take place at these times also. Such initiation ceremonies as the Eleusian mysteries and others are attempts to introduce people to much this same experience of death and rebirth. Baptism has the same meaning, and the Eucharist is, in part, a celebration of this reality. Jung laments that about the only place one can experience this reality of initiation in these days is in the office of an analyst. The Church seldom provides it. Few clerics seem to have the confidence to pass through psychic death or neurosis with the suffering individual. Instead, such sufferers are referred to analysts. This is something the Church should be doing. If we do not deal with the depth of human suffering, we will not be ready to help them at death and in bereavement.

EXPERIENCES AND PROBABLE CONCLUSIONS CONCERNING LIFE AFTER DEATH

One of Jung's most impressive precognitive experiences occurred in the autumn of 1913, when he was in his late thirties. He was seized by an overpowering vision of a monstrous flood sweeping down from the north and covering all of Europe except Switzerland. Its mighty yellow waves reduced everything to rubble, and then turned to an ocean of blood over Europe. The vision lasted for an hour. Two weeks later the same vision recurred, even more vivid, and since this kind of vision often precedes psychotic collapse, Jung feared for his sanity. In the spring and early summer of 1914 Jung dreamed three times of a Europe devastated by frost and ice. When World War I broke out on August 1, Jung was forced to look inward and try to understand how the psyche can speak in such a way.[5]

This turning inward occurred only after his break with Freud. With no person to whom he could turn, his introversion resulted in the kind of experiences reported in shamanistic initiations and religious experiences. It seemed that "gigantic blocks of stone were tumbling down upon [him]."[6] For nearly eight years he lived in this inner difficulty, at the same time seeing his patients and keeping up his ordinary life and family relationships. When he finally passed through it, he had gained a confidence in the objectivity and reality of the psyche that remained with him as long as he lived.

In 1944 Jung experienced another invasion of the unconscious. Following the accident to which I referred earlier, he hung between life and death for three weeks. In this condition he was presented with a flood of visions. One of the most impressive of them seemed to portray his departure from this world in the most universal images, and then his return. Of these experiences, he wrote, "It was not a product of imagination. The visions and experiences were utterly real; there was nothing subjective about them; they all had a quality of absolute objectivity."[7]

One of the last chapters of Jung's *Memories, Dreams, Reflections* is entitled "On Life After Death." Here Jung offers the probable conclusions of his years of study and personal experience. He presents his own experiences and those of others. I have had people bring me similar experiences, and I have also found these experiences recounted by the Church fathers; some of them are related in my book *Afterlife: The Other Side of Dying*. Jung suggests that these rare but significant experiences may be the evidence for which people are looking, and that they are probably not as rare as the spontaneous occurrences of disintegrating atoms. In addition, he tells many examples of intuitions and dreams in which the psyche seems to foresee its death and prepare for it. Jung presents a series of such dreams in *Man and His Symbols*. These dreams suggest the psyche's independence of the space-time world and also its concern for its transition through death to something else. Indeed, the dream seems to view the physical event of death as relatively unimportant.

One such experience came to my attention quite recently, when I was visiting some very sophisticated people in New Haven, an attorney and his wife. The husband had just lost his mother. Several times over the past year he had dreamed that she would die when he was returning from a trip to the West Coast, and that he would find her lying on the floor of her home. This was precisely what happened. On his return from such a trip, he went directly to see her, and found her lying in the position of which he had dreamed. Diane Pike tells of the same kind of experience after Bishop Pike's death. Indeed, this is the kind of evidence waiting to be considered once it is realized that the psyche is not bound to the physical body, but has an existence of its own.

Something of the psyche seems to persist. Just as there are all degrees of development among human beings before death, so there are all degrees of development of these persisting psyches. Unfortunately, most of the so-called communications with the deceased are somewhat naive and puerile and, if genuine, indicate a rather low development of the psyche. The deceased seem to be speaking in an undeveloped kind of consciousness. Jung warned against spending much time seeking these experiences. Acknowledging their reality, he added, "On the other hand, too much traffic with these germs of myth is dangerous for weak and suggestible minds, for they are led to mistake vague intimations for substantial knowledge, and to hypostatize mere phantasms."[8]

Jung concludes that the world is unitary, and that the same process of tension of opposites that leads to psychic growth in the space-time world will continue in the life after death. He wrote:

> The world into which we enter after death will be grand and terrible, like God and like all of nature that we know. Nor can I conceive that suffering should entirely cease [9]

In his own visions his experienced liberation and perception of meaning brought bliss, but on the other hand a strange cessation of human warmth. The place to which he came was dark and of hardest granite. One is reminded of the imaginative discussion of the afterlife by C. S. Lewis in *The Great Divorce,* in which hell consists of the gray meaninglessness of living within one's desires while heaven, being firm, hard, and real, requires our adaptation to it and continued human growth.

Jung also took up the idea of reincarnation, which is the belief of so many of the world's peoples. He remarked that he had no idea whether or not he had lived before, pointing out that Buddha also left the question open. Reincarnation is certainly one way of explaining one's present situation, and Jung considered that it might be better explained as a participation in the collective unconscious.

> I know no answer [he added] to the question of whether the karma which I live is the outcome of my past lives, or whether it is not rather the achievement of my ancestors, whose heritage comes together in me.[10]

The important thing is not our speculations, but how we live life. This, he wrote, will have some lasting effect: "When I die, my deeds will follow along with me — that is how I imagine it. I will bring with me what I have done. In the meantime it is important to insure that I do not stand at the end with empty hands."[11] It is better to put our efforts into living, as Buddha taught his disciples, than in speculating about the possible outcome.

In the very last pages of his memoirs, Jung gave a clue as to the way life is to be lived. At the end of the chapter "Late Thoughts," he set down a paean of praise to *Eros. Eros* he conceives as the daimon of Plato, the same reality of love that Paul praised in the thirteenth chapter of I Corinthians. The people who allow love to move through them participate in the most meaningful and lasting reality of the universe. Jung saw this kind of love as not just wishing or desiring, but as the very creative force of the universe, the source of cognition, understanding, the very quintessence of divinity itself. In his words:

. . . we are in the deepest sense the victims and the instruments of cosmogonic "love". . . . [Man] is at its mercy. He may assent to it, or rebel against it; but he is always caught up by it and enclosed within it. He is dependent upon it and is sustained by it. . . . "Love ceases not" — whether he speaks with "the tongues of angels," or with scientific exactitude traces the life of the cell down to its uttermost source. Man can try to name love, showering upon it all the names at his command, and still he will involve himself in endless self-deceptions. If he possesses a grain of wisdom, he will lay down his arms and name the unknown by the more unknown . . . that is, by the name of God. That is a confession of his subjection, his imperfection, and his dependence; but at the same time a testimony to his freedom to choose between truth and error."[12]

Jung would conclude that the people who build such reality into their lives probably build it in permanently and this probability is as good as that of quantum mechanics. He would probably agree with these words of Karl Jaspers, which occur in a little book called *Death to Life,* and are very reminiscent of Plato:

The consciousness of immortality needs no knowledge, no guarantee, no threat. It lies in love, in this marvelous reality in which we are given to ourselves. We are mortal when we are without love, and immortal when we love. . . . I achieve immortality to the extent that I love . . . I dissipate into nothingness as long as I live without love, and therefore in chaos. As a lover I can see the immortality of those who are united to me in love.[13]

It does not take much imagination to see the implications of Jung's conclusions for Christianity. If one translates his terminology to that of patristic Christian theology, it is easy to see that they are saying much the same thing. There may be a change of key, but the tune is still the same. Jung's critical thought and detailed experience gives modern and much-needed support to the early Christian view of the afterlife. A critical modern Christian can affirm with confidence the following belief: When we live in Christ, who is Love incarnate, then we allow the reality that Christ incarnated to operate in and through our lives. When we live in this way we build permanence into our lives that extends into a mysterious and continued growth in a life to come.

The people in churches need to hear this message again and again. Church groups need to discuss the data about an afterlife. Yet we hear little concerning the nature of afterlife from theologians. Indeed, some even deny any continuing life after physical death. I wrote my book *Afterlife: The Other Side of Dying* to provide a basis for preaching, teaching, and pastoral care to all Christians, but for the ministry to the dying and bereaved in particular.

NOTES

1. C.G. Jung, *Memories, Dreams, Reflections,* recorded and edited by Aniela Jaffe (New York: Pantheon Books, 1963), p. 340.

2. Antonio Moreno, *Jung, Gods, and Modern Man* (Notre Dame: University of Notre Dame Press, 1970), p. 110.

3. C.G. Jung, *Psychology and Religion: West and East,* Vol. 11 of the *Collected Works* (New York: Pantheon Books, 1958), p. 520.

4. Edgar Herzog, *Psyche and Death* (New York: Putnam, 1967) is an excellent study of this subject.

5. C.G. Jung, *Memories, Dreams, Reflections,* p. 175ff.

6. *Ibid.,* p. 177.

7. *Ibid.,* p. 295. A full description of this experience is to be found in the appendix of my book *Afterlife: The Other Side of Dying.*

8. *Ibid.,* p. 316.

9. *Ibid.,* p. 321.

10. *Ibid.,* p. 317. I have discussed the whole subject of reincarnation at length in *Afterlife: The Other Side of Dying.*

11. *Ibid.,* p. 318.

12. *Ibid.,* p. 354.

13. Karl Jaspers, *Death to Life* (Chicago: Argus Communications, 1968), p. 34ff.

Chapter 13

FACING DEATH AND SUFFERING

There are many ways of dealing with a subject such as death. Ideas about it can be drawn from literary and historical materials, and discussed in historical perspective. We can reflect upon such a subject in various ways philosophically. We can analyze the source of our ideas about it, or their meaning, or we can reflect upon personal experience and deduce the philosophical implications. We also can research the subject sociologically and compare the ideas and reactions of various groups.

But there is another approach besides these, which may cast even more light on the subject of death and dying. We human beings are interested in this subject not only from a cognitive point of view, but affectively as well. Our individual reactions to death and suffering are important to us, and they also offer an important means of exploring the subject—which is the story this chapter has to tell. It is the record of what happened when a group of intelligent young men and women opened themselves to their own reactions to suffering and death. In order to make the somewhat unusual situation clear, we shall relate how the group got together, how it was constituted and structured, and in general how the reactions developed. We shall conclude with an evaluation, and some general observations about such a group.

HOW IT ALL STARTED

In the spring of 1970 I was approached by a group of students at Notre Dame who were soon to enter their final year of premedical studies, and who had some serious questions about the profession they had chosen. They had been awakened to the realities of suffering and death by courses given by Charles McCarthy in the program on nonviolence, and they wanted a seminar in which they could explore their own reactions to the subject. The concern of these students is best told in their own words, the words of the two of them who described this background, and then their experience in the seminar that resulted, for the college newspaper *The Observer:*

We were concerned about the lack of attention given by medical education to the psychological suffering of the dying patient in a world where advanced technology and science, although prolonging his life, often tend to depersonalize the patient.

We were worried not only about the care of the dying; the effect of daily contact with enormous suffering seemed to have taken its effect also on the medical profession itself. Some of the more obvious signs of the resulting emotional instability are revealed in the high rates of suicide, drug addiction, and alcoholism within the profession. Since the greatest portion of a medical student's education is concerned with the scientific aspect of medicine, most young physicians seem emotionally unprepared to face the suffering, especially the intense emotional pain found in the terminally ill patient. Surely, American society, with its numerous denials of and escapes from death, offers little support to those people who must be faced daily with the care of the sick and dying.

Although it is not always the case, many doctors relate to a patient in only a scientific manner, which often results in the objectification of the patient. Medicine becomes then only a business—the more intangible, emotional needs of the patient, especially the terminally ill patient, are often overlooked. When a doctor does try to open himself in a more humane manner to the dying individual, he must wrestle with his own sanity because of his anxieties about death that can be stirred up by such an encounter. The common occurrence of impersonal health care and the existence of such frightening statistics as the above seem to say that many physicians have not been able to adequately resolve their relationship to the patient's emotional suffering.[1]

What these young men have expressed about the medical profession can be said about most of the rest of us as well when we find ourselves face to face with suffering and death. But what is more interesting is the fact that they did something about it. I will go on with the story rather than quote from their briefer account.

With enthusiastic support from both the late Dr. Lawrence H. Baldinger, then chairman of Preprofessional Studies, and my own Department of Graduate Studies in Education, a course was planned in which we would discuss and attempt to face in depth the problems involved in caring for the terminally ill patient. By the following fall the initial group had grown to sixteen.

THE GROUP AND ITS STRUCTURE

For the first semester the group was limited to sixteen students, who met once a week for three hours in an informal atmosphere. At the first session each member received a brief description of what was intended, along with a bibliography, which is appended to this chapter. It was stated that: "The purpose of the course is to explore — 'with no holds barred' — the meaning of death and suffering within the modern cultural situation." It was also stated that this was a group exploration, in which class interaction was of prime importance; therefore each individual was important, and his or her presence had a direct effect upon the quality of the group. In other words, the group itself was there to facilitate an effective treatment of the subject.

A few other suggestions were made: first, that each member keep some record or journal of his or her own personal reactions that were related to the class material, including feelings and dreams; second, that the instructor would be available at least once a month for each class member to discuss special readings, personal concerns, and anything else too far afield for group discussion. In place of a final examination, each of the group was to make a careful examination of the seminar and what he or she had learned — its value, the possibilities for improvement, etc. The grade was to be established by the student on a basis of introspection and thought, plus individual reading and group participation.

Ten more students came into the group for the second semester, and two of the original members dropped out. During this period the meeting schedule was varied, partly because of the time pressure on the instructor. The twenty-four students were divided into four groups of five and one group of four, each with a student leader from the first-semester class. These smaller groups met each week for discussion and then came together every three weeks for a full session with the instructor.

The reading started with a review of the literature in recent periodicals, including *Psychiatric Opinion,* April 1970, *Patient Care,* May 31, 1970, *Bulletin of Suicidology,* Spring 1970, and *Psychology Today,* August 1970. Next, we turned to the then recently published

book by Elisabeth Kübler-Ross, *On Death and Dying.* Two books by
Carl Jung — *Memories, Dreams, Reflections* and *The Answer to Job* —
were then read and discussed, giving us not only a common terminology in which we could discuss the psychological implications of our
subject, but also a powerful modern study of the meaning of suffering.
Certain articles by the instructor (later published as *Encounter with
God*) were also distributed. In addition, the work edited by Herman
Feifel, *The Meaning of Death,* and Jerome Frank's *Persuasion and
Healing* were read. These gave, respectively, a cross-cultural approach
to death and a study of the psychological factors in illness. In general,
the readings provided a basis for discussion, which at times stayed
quite close to the written ideas, and at times went far afield.

Two tests were administered to the students, the Myers-Briggs
Personality Indicator and a questionnaire from the August 1970 issue
of *Psychology Today* on the subject of "You and Death." From these
tests, and from personal conversations and group discussion, the
following characteristics of the group emerged:

1. All of them had achieved at least a 3.0 grade point average up to the end of the
second semester of their senior year and the overall average was nearer 3.5. All but
two of the twenty-five premedical students had been accepted in medical school by
May 1971 (one student in the second semester was not in premedical studies). They
were gifted intellectually.

2. In personality type they exemplified for the most part the usual variety of type
structures found among physicians, as described in the Myers-Briggs Indicator
Manual (1962). Among the students, however, there was a somewhat greater number
of individuals of an introverted, intuitive-feeling type.

3. Most of the students considered themselves stable and quite well adjusted, although two had experienced suicidal thoughts at one time and one was having such
thoughts at the present time.

4. All had been raised in practicing Catholic homes, and all but two had been educated entirely in Catholic schools.

5. The majority of the group showed very much the same general attitude that
Charles Reich has described as Consciousness III in *The Greening of America.*

6. All but two had been raised in comfortable, middle- or upper-middle-class
homes.

7. They had all been raised with the traditional Catholic heaven-hell concept of an
afterlife, and all twenty-six had rejected it. This idea had been replaced with nothing
at all.

8. Several of the group had experienced immediate encounters with death or near-
death when the seminar began or during it. Three had lost parents within the prior
ten years. Two had parents seriously ill when they came into the group; another
parent died during the seminar, and still another had a serious heart attack towards
the conclusion of it. During the first semester the chairman of Preprofessional Studies,
who had been advisor for many of the students, died, and four of our group served as
pallbearers at his funeral.

In addition, two students had spent the previous summer working in a dispensary in Haiti, one the year before in Peru, and several had had experience in hospital emergency rooms.

THE DEVELOPMENT OF THE SEMINAR

At the first session, held in the science building, the class plan sheet was distributed; then each of the group spoke of their expectations of the class and of their experiences with death and suffering. After this, all other meetings were held informally in the living room of the group leader, with the students sitting on the floor. At all but one class my wife was also present, acting as cofacilitator. In this relaxed atmosphere the students gradually began to discuss what really concerned them. At first they were either hesitant to speak of personal fears of suffering and death, or else unaware that they had them.

But as one after another mentioned some experience and the feelings it had aroused in him or her, others found that they could do the same. By the fourth meeting of the group it was clear that none of them was alone in having such concerns and anxieties. Later in the year, the experience of acting as pallbearers for the chairman of their department, and attending his funeral, evoked open concern and anguish. The class met on the evening of the funeral in a hushed and tense atmosphere.

Dr. Kübler-Ross's book opened the eyes of the students as much as any of the readings. The ones who had had to deal with death in their own families realized how inadequately they had handled these confrontations with the fact of suffering and dying. Most of them had denied its reality. Dr. Kubler-Ross lectured at Notre Dame during the fall semester, and had dinner with the students. As a person she conveyed a comfortableness with death, a concord or congruity with what she expressed in her writing. She showed a personal interest in the students, and invited several of them to visit her in her Chicago home. From her book they realized that something was known about the process of dying, and that there are actual stages—from denial and depression to acceptance and hope—through which the patient needs to be allowed to pass. They realized that dying patients are usually quite aware of their condition, and that most of all they need honesty, understanding, and care.

In several of the sessions role-playing was introduced. This involved two students, one taking the role of doctor and the other that of the dying patient. As each of the group tried to play these roles, they discovered how much better they could play the patient than the doctor. They realized that, even in role-playing, they had little understanding or stability or security available to offer to another person. One student broke down as he tried to act out the doctor's part and could not continue. This role-playing brought home in a poignant way their confusion and uneasiness when confronted, even imaginatively, with a dying person. It became easier to understand and be tolerant of physicians who so often denied and withdrew from such situations.

One of the most interesting and unexpected developments in the class was the expression of total lack of belief in any form of afterlife by this group of students brought up staunchly within the Church and its educational system. Most of the students were angry about the teaching on hell they had been given, and the emphasis on fear of hell. They felt they had been trained and not educated, that they had not been prepared to deal with the skepticism of college. One of the reasons for rejecting an afterlife was their eagerness to remove all trace of the concept of hell. They were willing to throw the baby out with the bathwater, and they voiced the fear that, like their parents, they might return to the old beliefs if threatened by death.

The ideological framework of these young people was fashioned more by materialism and existentialism than by Catholicism when it came to their view of death. Nearly all had ceased going to Mass. One or two said in private that they still attended occasionally and still had some belief. But so strong was the group attitude, and that of their college peers in general, that they felt they did not dare express these views within the group!

After voicing their angers and resentments, the members of the group were open and even eager to see if something could be presented to fill the void that the rejection of their religious "mythology" had left. Many of them were deeply impressed by the philosophical point of view expressed by C.G. Jung, and particularly by his conclusions on life after death, and by the way he had arrived at them (which is presented in the previous chapter). A summary of this material was presented by the instructor in one of the two sessions that resembled lectures; the other session had to do with funerals and dealing with funeral directors. The material from Jung aroused heated discussion, and there were some results that we shall consider later.

The whole group was impressed by August Kasper's discussion of the characteristics of the doctor and his problems with death — "The Doctor and Death" in Feifel's book — particularly by his accurate portrayal of the emotional qualities of medical students.[2] They were half embarrassed and half amused at how well they had been depicted. Most of the young men had not had adequate relationships with their fathers and yet had experienced a close relationship with their mothers within the family. They admitted to a certain "mothering" interest in going into medicine.

After reading Jung's books and Jerome Frank's *Persuasion and Healing,* they began to realize that there was a close relation between emotions and health. They began to talk about the necessity of dealing with the whole person, rather than with symptoms alone, and this involved at least learning to listen. This was not limited to dying patients, but was only particularly true of them. It came as quite a shock to the students, as they reflected upon their group discussion, how little they listened to one another, and how unready they were to listen to their potential patients. They realized how hard it is to listen, and how much concern and caring, in fact, love, it takes truly to listen to one another. They were similar in these reactions to students in the nonviolence program.

As they began to listen a little more, many of the members of the group began to express their own doubts, fears, and anxieties about death and about other subjects. This led to an open and liberating atmosphere. Many of the students made it a point to say that they had not found this kind of open, honest, and relevant discussion before in their college careers. The ability to talk about their fear of death released them so that they could talk about other things that concerned them. The result was a group cohesiveness and mutual support that brought into focus many things they had to deal with.

One of the things this group met head-on was the meaning of suffering. Most of the orthodox Christian theories were rejected. Some suggested that there was no meaning to suffering; the world itself was meaningless. Others were drawn to the Oriental view that suffering was a necessary part of the cyclical process of life, and not evil in itself. None of them could see the possibility of a classic Christian solution to the problem of suffering and evil in general. Only after a viable worldview was presented in which both good and evil had a realistic metaphysical role could they take in such a possibility.

During the second semester the large class group was divided into those who had been together during the first semester and those who were new. The new members followed the same pattern of reading as had the first-semester students. The others drew up their own reading lists on some aspect of suffering and death. During this period two films were presented: *Face to Face with Dr. Jung* and a film made for Dr. Kübler-Ross of her interviews with dying patients.

In one of the last classes the subject of the supernatural was brought up by the students. During the discussion nearly every one of the group contributed some experience or story. Gone was the materialistic assurance that nothing of this sort could be real or meaningful.

THE CHANGES IN ATTITUDE AND RESULTS

Were there any results that could be observed from the outside or reported by the individuals who were engaged in this experience of facing death and suffering? The students' own evaluations stated overwhelmingly that there had been changes in attitude and behavior, and these changes could be observed by the instructor and the group during the last meetings of the class. According to their evaluations, the reading and role-playing, the free and open discussion, all had contributed to a change in point of view.

The most important change was a lessening of the fear of talking about suffering and death. What had been taboo subjects, or at best handled only at arm's length, could now be spoken of with reasonable comfort. Having resolved, or at least faced, their own fears of suffering in a possibly meaningless universe and of dying, they no longer found these subjects impossible to talk about. All of the students expressed appreciation for the opportunity to discuss them. The future doctors, in particular, realized that this might be their only opportunity to explore their attitudes and feelings about death before they entered medical training and practice, and that within months they would be faced with death in the unpleasant form of a cadaver. They knew that we had only opened the door to the study of the subject, and that there was much more to be done by each of them. Most of them intended to go on working in the area that had been opened up.

Something else happened once these young people began to recognize their own fears of death, and admit that they had anxieties about the world around them, particularly when faced by suffering. They began to deal with other, connected pockets of fear. Many of them spoke of intense personal suffering that they had experienced, but had not been able to talk over with anyone until this class provided the opportunity. They knew more about suffering than they had admitted at first. How relieved they were to find that their peers shared the same fears and emotional discomfort; none of them was unique. The result was that they saw communication in a new light.

Most of them had not even realized that their closest friends sometimes entertained the same fears that possessed them. Thus there had been an isolation and lack of communication because vital personal subjects had been avoided. When these students realized their isolation, and the dynamics that had caused it, they began to discover the depth and complexity of the human psyche, and so of human communication. They found a new openness among each other and began to look forward to the task of communicating with each other and with patients.

Some members of the group, however, found fears in themselves that they felt were too personal to be discussed among the group, which they were led to talk over with the instructor. Two of these students said that they had come to a church-oriented college hoping that they would find someone to relate to, with whom they could communicate about these long-standing fears, and that they had found this only in the last semester of their senior year. They found it because the openness of the class and the instructor had enabled them to discuss these problems that had been pressing upon them for many years. One student realized that he was not constitutionally fitted to deal with suffering and dying people and decided to go into another profession.

Nothing was more appreciated by this group of preprofessional students than the availability of the group leader, and his willingness to listen to them on any subject that troubled them. Fears of parents, sexuality, and personal value, as well as fears of death and suicide, came out. In most cases merely the opportunity to discuss the fears and be listened to was enough to put things into perspective. In several instances, however, longer and deeper counseling was necessary. These sessions with the instructor were not only helpful personally, but also were described by several of the group as an object lesson in the kind of personal concern they would like to provide as they became physicians. Most of them had not experienced this concern before in sixteen years of education.

Nearly every student had come into the class with a fear that there was no way for the "intelligent modern" to believe in life after death. The Aristotelian-Thomistic worldview in which they had been raised had not been able to stand up against the impact of a mechanistic scientific worldview, of behaviorism, and of nihilistic existentialism. They were not even aware that there was any other viable option. They were amazed to read Plato, and to realize that many modern scientists of the highest rank had embraced a somewhat Platonic point of view. They were most impressed with the views of Heisenberg, Max Knoll, Kurt Gödel, Wolfgang Pauli, and Carl Jung, and they realized that their agnosticism would have to be reworked. Most of the students stated that without a worldview that has a place in it for an afterlife, they would be crippled in dealing with dying patients and their families. They realized that they had a large task ahead of them to work out such an understanding and integrate it into a religious framework. They began to see that religion is a necessary base for an adequate life, and particularly necessary for the physician dealing with suffering and dying people.

Several of the students commented that the group experience had taught them how difficult it was actually to care about one another, and how often their lack of care had been manifested by a failure to listen. If they continued to treat people as they had treated one another, their patients would not be heard. As one student put it very aptly, "I have been 'hearing' without listening." Before the sessions ended it was obvious that each of us, the instructor included, found it easier to listen and respond acceptingly to others.

Another thing noted by most of the group was their realization of the importance of feelings and emotions as well as thought, particularly in relation to death. They understood that patients might often sense what is being felt by the doctor, and their own reactions made it clear that thought and feelings are not necessarily congruent, or even remotely in harmony. These students indicated in their statements that unless they became comfortable with their feelings about death and suffering they were likely either to put on a callous facade or else be overwhelmed with unconscious fear. Since neither of these is very helpful to the doctor or the patient, most of the group saw that what was needed was an honest facing of their fears within a framework that has a place for ultimate meaning.

In addition, there were some excellent suggestions about other experts who might meet with the class from time to time. While a few members felt that more of the materials should have been introduced in lecture form, most of them considered that the free-flowing give-and-take of the seminar was the only way of achieving the objective of the group. As some of them expressed it, they had seen important changes take place within themselves; they felt that these depended upon the care and concern that became the attitude of the group, and that this could not have occurred in a more formal classroom atmosphere.

As leader, I also changed. I realized the loneliness that existed among the most successful and sophisticated college seniors, and their need to relate to an adult who can be emphatic and, at the same time, accepting and caring. The value of people with this attitude on the campus and in the Church can hardly be overestimated. The alienation that one sees so often in the world has already begun in this age group, but here the problem is easier to reach and alleviate. I found an idealism and a sensitivity to personal hurt, as well as a spiritual seeking, which are refreshing and encouraging. I also discovered that these capable, self-reliant, and independent students would take advantage of as much of my time as I could spare.

It may seem difficult to believe that changes could occur in individuals in this way. But these students were hungry for personal concern, which they felt they did not receive from their professors in general. These were the reactions they described in their own evaluations, and which were observed in their actions by others in the group.

Many of the students in these classes have kept in touch with me and my wife in the eleven years since these classes began.

GENERAL CONCLUSIONS

The group experience was creative, and both eye-opening and heart-opening for most of the participants. They became more comfortable with suffering and death and also with themselves. They began to see the human possibilities in the medical profession, as well as the merely physical ones.

A variation of this seminar was offered every year until my final leave of absence. Seminarians, graduate students in psychology, and undergraduates from every department attended. Each class was unique, but each left an impact on the students and me. The reading list changed over the years to add new and relevant books. It is this later list which is provided in the appendix.

Such an experience would be creative for any mature group of adults, college or older, who wanted to understand more about the alienation of modern human beings. Unfortunately, people do not talk comfortably until they can discuss the matters that trouble them most, and unless the hearers are comfortable they will not permit such subjects to be brought up. A college course of this kind might go far towards alleviating the loneliness that is so common among students of American universities and is commented on by deans and educators from one coast to the other. Such a course could not be required, however, because fears may be aroused that are more than some individuals can handle. The required nature of such a course would also impede its freedom.

Such a group discussion of vital personal matters requires a facilitator who is relatively comfortable and secure with death and suffering him- or herself, both emotionally and cognitively, both affectively and philosophically. If instructors are not comfortable, their anxieties will be passed on to the group. They must also be genuinely interested, or the students will likewise detect it. Carl Rogers has pointed out the importance of the teacher's attitudes of genuineness, prizing, and empathic understanding in his fine book *Freedom to Learn*. If this is true of the ordinary teacher, how much more true it is of the teacher in an open situation such as we have described. The students will try in every way to test instructors to be sure that they are congruent with what they say before full openness can be achieved within the group.

It is important that instructors have a viable philosophical framework from which to give some kind of meaning to life after death. Without this, death is an unsolvable problem, which can be handled only with stoicism. Humanism and concern for the student are not enough. One of the basic reasons that death has become such a taboo subject is that our society has been brainwashed by a mechanistic and materialistic philosophy that makes men and women afraid of life, as well as of death. Earlier I presented one such meaningful and possible framework. It is the one from which I operate, and which, according to the students, opened doors to them for belief. What began as a course in preprofessional studies became in the last analysis pastoral care, in the best sense of the expression.

It is also important that the group facilitators be comfortable with the personal problems that will emerge in such an honest discussion. If they find that these personal concerns are more than they are able to handle, then it is necessary to have someone else on tap who can step in and deal with these. Otherwise, the experience may cause individual problems to surface that are then left hanging.

The basic structure of the course seemed quite adequate. The reading provided a springboard for discussion, the role-playing gave affective content, the discussion provided openness, and the personal interviews allowed loose ends to be tied up. In later courses, I invited funeral directors and doctors, and had tapes played of conversations with dying persons. Some of the students also visited rest homes and talked with the terminally ill.

Meeting and discussing death and suffering in an open atmosphere, with a "no holds barred" attitude, led the group to discuss not only these crucial human topics, but the very nature of human existence and human relationships. The group provided an opportunity for growth as students, as human beings, and as religious searchers, and it provided an experience of human warmth that has become rare in either secular or religious classes in our present era. It could be replicated in any parish where someone on the staff had adequate training.

NOTES

1. Pat Lamb and Frank Capobianco, "Suffering, Dying and Death," *The Observer*, Notre Dame University, Notre Dame, Indiana, Monday, April 26, 1971, p. 5.

2. Herman Feifel, ed., *The Meaning of Death* (New York: McGraw-Hill, 1965), pp. 263 ff.

APPENDIX

READING LIST FOR CLASS ON WORKING WITH THE DYING
(NUMBERED BOOKS ARE TO BE READ IN THE ORDER SHOWN)

PERIODICALS:

13. *Psychology Today,* August 1970.
13. *Medical World News* (McGraw-Hill publication), May 21, 1971.
13. *Psychiatric Opinion,* Vol. 7, No. 2, April 1970; Vol. 7, No. 5, Oct. 1970.
13. *Patient Care,* May 31, 1970, "Managing the Dying Process."
13. *Bulletin of Suicidology,* National Institute of Mental Health, No. 6, Spring 1970. (Other issues also relevant.)
13. "The Dying Patient," *Psychosocial Dimensions of Family Practice,* Roche Laboratories, Nutley, N.J. 07110).
13. *Event,* American Lutheran Church magazine, Dec. 1972, issue on Life and Death.
13. *The Marriage and Family Counselor's Quarterly,* Vol. 7, No. 2, Winter 1972, "Terminal Illness Counseling — The Death Experience."
13. *Notre Dame Lawyer,* Vol. 45, No. 2, Winter 1970, "Undue Influence, Confidential Relationship, and the Psychology of Transference" (Dean Shaffer).

PSYCHOLOGY AND SUFFERING:

C.G. Jung *et al., Man and His Symbols* (Doubleday, 1964, or Dell paperback), sections by Jung, Jacobi, and von Franz.
1. C.G. Jung, *Memories, Dreams, Reflections* (Random House, 1963), with particular attention to Chapter 6, "Confrontation with the Unconscious."
8. _____, *Two Essays on Analytical Psychology,* Collected Works, Vol. 7 (or Princeton University paperback).
_____, *Modern Man in Search of a Soul* (Harcourt Brace, paperback).
12. _____, *Answer to Job,* Collected Works, Vol. 11, pp. 355–470 (or Princeton University paperback).
Peter Steinfels and Robert M. Veatch, eds., *Death Inside Out* (Harper paperback, 1975).
4. M.T. Kelsey, *Encounter with God* (Minneapolis: Bethany Fellowship, 1972, paperback).
11. _____, *Healing and Christianity* (Harper paperback, 1973).
_____, *God, Dreams, and Revelation,* Chapter 9 (Augsburg, paperback 1973).
S. Freud, *Beyond the Pleasure Principle,* Complete Works, Vol. 18, (or Norton paperback).
_____, *Civilization and Its Discontents* (Norton paperback).
Jerome Frank, *Persuasion and Healing* (Schocken paperback).
10. Adolf Guggenbühl-Craig, *Power in the Helping Professions* (Spring Pub.).
6. Karl Menninger, *Man Against Himself* (Harcourt Brace paperback).

GENERAL DISCUSSION OF SUFFERING:

The Book of Job in a modern translation.

Alan Paton *et al.*, *Creative Suffering: The Ripple of Hope*, (United Church, 1970).

Aldous Huxley, *The Devils of Loudun* (Harper paperback). A study of man's inhumanity to man.

Anne Walters and Jim Marugg, *Beyond Endurance* (Harper, 1954). What it is like to come through polio and be in an iron lung.

Kurt F. Reinhardt, *The Existentialist Revolt* (Ungar, 1960, or later ed.), chapters on Kierkegaard and Nietzsche.

Baron F. von Hügel, *Essays and Addresses on the Philosophy of Religion*, 1921 (Dutton, 1963), 1st Series, pp. 98-116; 2nd Series, pp. 167-213.

Miguel de Unamuno, *Tragic Sense of Life* (Dover paperback).

GENERAL DISCUSSION OF DEATH AND DYING:

2. Elisabeth Kübler-Ross, *On Death and Dying* (Macmillan, 1969).

    _____, *Death: The Final Stage of Growth* (Prentice-Hall, 1975, paperback).

    _____, *Questions and Answers on Death and Dying* (Macmillan, 1974, paperback).

7. Herman Feifel, ed., *The Meaning of Death* (McGraw-Hill, 1959, also paperback).

    Robert Kastenbaum and Ruth Aisenberg, *The Psychology of Death* (Springer Pub., 1972).

    Group for the Advancement of Psychiatry, *Death and Dying: Attitudes of Patient and Doctor* (Mental Health Center, 1967), pp. 615 ff. (Samuel Feder, "Attitudes of Patients with Advanced Malignancy.")

    Leo Tolstoy, *The Death of Ivan Ilych* (New American Library paperback).

    Plato, *Phaedo*. On the death of Socrates.

    Geoffrey Gorer, *Death, Grief, and Mourning* (Doubleday paperback). On the value of rituals at the time of death.

    Alfred Worcester, *The Care of the Aged, the Dying and the Dead* (Thomas, 1961).

3. Ernest Becker, *The Denial of Death* (Free Press, 1973).

    John Hinton, *Dying* (Penguin paperback).

    Bernard Schoenberg *et al.*, eds., *Loss and Grief: Psychological Management in Medical Practice* (Columbia University Press, 1973).

    Marjorie Mitchell, *The Child's Attitude to Death* (Schocken, 1967).

    Kurt R. Eissler, *The Psychiatrist and the Dying Patient* (International University Press, 1955).

    Notre Dame Journal of Education, Vol. 5, No. 2, Spring 1974, pp. 121 ff. (McNeill, "Learning and Teaching Experiential Theology: An Intergenerational Journey.")

    Earl Grollman, ed., *Explaining Death to Children* (Beacon paperback).

DEALING WITH DEATH, GRIEF, AND LIFE AFTER DEATH:

Albert Camus, *The Plague* (Modern Library paperback).

Karlis Osis and Erlendur Haraldsson, *At the Hour of Death* (Avon paperback, 1977).

C.S. Lewis, *A Grief Observed* (Seabury, 1963). Personal discussion of grief.
Alan Paton, *For You Departed* (Scribner, 1969). Personal discussion of grief.
Glen W. Davidson, *Living with Dying* (Augsburg paperback, 1975).
Baron F. von Hügel, *Eternal Life* (Edinburgh: T&T Clark, 1929).
_____. *The Mystical Element of Religion* (Dutton, 1928), Vol. 2, Chap. 12, pp. 182–258.
Bernadine Kreis and Alice Pattie, *Up from Grief: Patterns of Recovery* (Seabury, 1969).
Evelyn Waugh, *The Loved One* (Dell paperback). A satire on Forest Lawn mortuary.
Emily Gardiner Neal, *In the Midst of Life* (Morehouse-Barlow, 1963).
Helen Chappell White, *With Wings as Eagles* (Rinehart, 1953). A woman's story of recovering from her son's death.
Edgar Herzog, *Psyche and Death: Archaic Myths and Modern Dreams in Analytical Psychology* (Putnam, 1967).
Dante, *The Divine Comedy*, Sayers translation (Penguin paperback, 3 volumes).
14. Helen Luke, *Dark Wood to White Rose* (Pecos, N.M.: Dove). The meaning of Dante.
 5. Raymond Moody, *Life After Life* (Mockingbird Books, 1975; also Bantam paperback).
_____, *Reflections on Life After Life*. (Mockingbird Books, 1977; also Bantam paperback).
Arthur Ford (as told to Jerome Ellison), *The Life Beyond Death* (Berkley paperback).
Journal for the Scientific Study of Religion, Vol. 12, No. 2, June 1973, pp. 209 ff. (R. Kalish and D. Reynolds, on "Post-Death Contact")
Death to Life, Papers by biologists, theologians, and philosophers (Chicago: Argus Communications, 1968).

THE PROBLEM OF EVIL IN GENERAL:

 9. Elie Wiesel, *Night* (Avon paperback).
Eldridge Cleaver, *Soul on Ice* (Dell paperback). Evil, suffering, and the blacks.
Malcolm X, *Autobiography* (Dell paperback). Evil, suffering, and the blacks.
John H. Griffin, *Black Like Me* (New American Library paperback). Evil, suffering and the blacks.
Herbert Kohl, *36 Children* (New American Library paperback). Urban evil and suffering.
Jonathan Kozol, *Death at an Early Age*. (Bantam paperback). Urban evil and suffering.
Kerényi et al., *Evil*, ed. by Curatorium, Jung Institute, (Northwestern University, 1967).
Charles Williams, *Shadows of Ecstasy, War in Heaven,* and *Descent into Hell* (Eerdmans paperbacks). Three novels depicting the reality of evil.
C.S. Lewis, *Out of the Silent Planet, Perelandra,* and *That Hideous Strength* (Macmillan paperbacks). Trilogy dealing with the roots of evil.
 9. _____. *The Lion, The Witch and the Wardrobe* (Macmillan paperback). An amazing children's allegory of evil.
J.R.R. Tolkien, *The Lord of the Rings*, 3 vols. (Houghton Mifflin paperbacks).
Leon Christiani, *Evidences of Satan in the Modern World* (Macmillan, 1962).

SUICIDE AS ULTIMATE SUFFERING:

Maurice L. Farber, *The Theory of Suicide* (Funk and Wagnalls, 1968).

N.L. Farberow and E.S. Shneidman, *Cry for Help* (McGraw-Hill paperback).

E.S. Shneidman, ed., *Essays on Self-Destruction* (Science House, 1967).

H.L. Resnik, *Suicidal Behaviors: Diagnosis and Management* (Little Brown, 1968).

H. Peck and A. Schrut, "Suicide Among College Students," *Proceedings of the Fourth International Congress for Suicide Prevention* (Delmar, 1968).

A. Schrut, "Suicidal Adolescents and Children," *Journal of the A.M.A.*, 188: 1103-1107, 1964.

A. Schrut, "Some Typical Patterns in the Behavior and Background of Adolescent Girls Who Attempt Suicide," *American Journal of Psychiatry*, 125:1, 1968.

Louis Dublin, *Suicide: A Sociological and Statistical Study* (Ronald Press, 1963).

Erwin Stengel, *Suicide and Attempted Suicide* (Penguin paperback).

E.S. Shneidman and N.L. Farberow, eds., *Clues to Suicide* (McGraw-Hill paperback).

James Hillman, *Suicide and the Soul* (Harper, 1965).

James J. Lynch, *The Broken Heart* (Basic Books, 1977).

BIBLIOGRAPHY

(Note: A separate bibliography for chapters 12 and 13 is to be found in the appendix of chapter 13.)

Assagioli, Roberto, *Psychosynthesis*. New York: Hobbs, Dorman and Company, Inc., 1965.

Ayer, A.J. *Language, Truth and Logic*. New York: Dover Publications, Inc., 1952.

Baba Ram Dass. *Be Here Now*. Distributed by Crown Publishers, New York, 1971.

Bach, George R. and Wyden, Peter. *The Intimate Enemy: How to Fight Fair in Love and Marriage*. New York: William Morrow and Company, Inc., 1969.

Banks, Ethel. *The Great Physician Calling*. San Diego: St. Luke's Press, n.d.

Berdyaev, N. *The Meaning of the Creative Act*. New York: Collier Books, 1962.

Boswell, John. *Christianity, Social Tolerance, and Homosexuality*. Chicago: University of Chicago Press, 1980.

——————. *The Myers-Briggs Type Indicator*. Consulting Psychologists Press, Palo Alto, California.

Bristol, Claude. *The Magic of Believing*. Englewood Cliffs, N.J.: Prentice-Hall, 1948.

Bruner, J.S., and Postman, Leo. "On the Perception of Incongruity: A Paradigm." *Journal of Personality* 18 (1949): 206–23.

Bunyan, John. *The Pilgrim's Progress*. 1678–1684.

Burrell, David. *Exercises in Religious Understanding*. Notre Dame, Indiana: University of Notre Dame Press, 1975.

Butler, Samuel. *Erewhon*. Hong Kong: Golden Press Pty Ltd., 1973.

Canale, Dr. J. Andrew. "Dealing with Pain from the Perspective of Wholeness," *Unitarian Universalist Review*, 1st issue, 1977.

——————. *Masters of the Heart*. New York: Paulist Press, 1978.

Carroll, L. Patrick, and Dyckman, Katharine M. *Inviting the Mystic, Supporting the Prophet*. New York: Paulist Press, 1981.

Castaneda, Carlos. *The Teachings of Don Juan: A Yaqui Way of Knowledge*. Berkeley: University of California Press, 1968.

——————. *Journey to Ixtlan: The Lessons of Don Juan*. New York: Pocket Books, 1974.

——————. *A Separate Reality: Further Conversations with Don Juan*. New York: Simon & Schuster, 1971.

——————. *Tales of Power*. New York: Simon & Schuster, 1974.

Cox, David. *Jung and St. Paul*. New York: Association Press, 1959.

Dante (Alighieri). *Divine Comedy*. Translated by Dorothy L. Sayers and Barbara Reynolds. Baltimore: Penguin Books, Vol I: *Hell*, 1949; Vol. II: *Purgatory*, 1955; Vol. III: *Paradise*, 1962.

d'Aquili, Eugene and Laughlin, Charles, Jr. "The Biopsychological Determinants of Religious Ritual Behavior," *Zygon*, March 1975.

Dearmer, Percy. *Body and Soul*. London: G. Bell and Sons, 1899.

de Castillejo, Irene. *Knowing Woman*. New York: G.P. Putnam's Sons, for the C.G. Jung Foundation for Analytic Psychology, 1973.

Dunbar, Dr. Flanders. *Emotions and Bodily Changes*, 4th ed. New York: Columbia University Press, 1954.

Edwards, Tilden. *Spiritual Friend: Reclaiming the Gift of Spiritual Direction*. New York: Paulist Press, 1981.

Einstein, Albert and Freud, Sigmund. *Why War?* Paris: International Institute of Intellectual Cooperation, 1933.

Eliade, Mircea. *Shamanism: Archaic Techniques of Ecstasy*. Princeton, N.J.: Princeton University Press, 1970.

Eliot, T.S. *Cocktail Party*. New York: Harcourt, Brace and World, 1950.

_____. *Four Quartets*. New York: Harcourt, Brace and World, 1943.

Farnsworth, Dana and Braceland, Francis. *Psychiatry: The Clergy and Pastoral Counseling*. Collegeville, Minn.: St. John's University Press, 1969.

Feifel, Herman. *The Meaning of Death*. New York: McGraw-Hill Book Company, 1959.

Frank, Dr. Jerome. *Persuasion and Healing*. New York: Schocken Books, 1969.

French, R.M., ed. *The Way of a Pilgrim* and *The Pilgrim Continues His Way*. New York: Harper and Row, n.d.

Freud, Sigmund. *Beyond the Pleasure Principle*. Translated by James Strachey. New York: Liveright Publishing Company, 1961.

_____. *Civilization and Its Discontents*. Translated by Joan Riviere. Garden City, New York: Doubleday and Co., n.d.

_____. *The Future of Illusion*. Translated by W.D. Robson-Scott. London: Hogarth Press, 1949.

Friedlander, Paul. *Plato: An Introduction*. Translated by Hans Meyerhoff. New York: Harper & Row for the Bollingen Foundation Inc., 1964.

Friends' Home Service Committee. *Toward a Quaker View of Sex*. Friends House, Euston Road, London, N.W.1. 1963.

Fromm, Erich. *The Anatomy of Human Destructiveness*. New York: Holt, Rinehart and Winston, 1973.

Frost, Evelyn. *Christian Healing*. London: Mowbray, 1954.

Golding, William. *The Lord of the Flies*. New York: Coward-McCann, 1962.

Gratton, Carolyn. *Guidelines for Spiritual Direction*. Denville, N.J.: Dimension Books, 1980.

Guggenbühl-Craig, Adolf. *Power in the Helping Professions*. New York: Spring Publications, 1971.

Harding, Esther. *The Way of All Women*. New York: G.P. Putnam's Sons for the C.G. Jung Foundation, rev., 1970.

Heisenberg, Werner. *Physics and Philosophy: The Revolution in Modern Science*. New York: Harper & Row, 1958.

Heron, Dr. Woodburn. *Sensory Deprivation*. Cambridge: Harvard University Press, 1971.

Hesse, Hermann. *Beneath the Wheel*. Translated by Michael Roloff. New York: Farrar, Straus & Giroux, 1968.

Hillman, James. *Emotion.* Evanston: Northwestern University Press, 1961.

––––––––––––. *Suicide and the Soul.* London: Hodder & Stoughton, 1964.

Hiltner, Seward. *Pastoral Counseling.* New York: Abingdon Press, 1949.

Hoffman, Martin. "Childrearing Practices and Moral Development: Generalizations from Empirical Research," *Child Development* 1963, p. 34.

Holmes, Urban T. *A History Of Christian Spirituality, An Analytical Introduction.* New York: Seabury Press, 1980.

Hostie, Raymond. *Religion and the Psychology of Jung.* New York: Sheed & Ward, 1957.

Howes, Elizabeth and Moon, Sheila. *Man the Choicemaker.* Philadelphia: Westminster Press, 1973.

Huxley, Aldous. *Doors of Perception.* New York: Harper & Row, 1970.

––––––––––––. *The Devils of Loudun.* New York: Harper & Row, 1979.

I Ching or *Book of Changes.* (The Richard Wilhelm translation). Translated by Cary F. Baynes. New York: Pantheon Books for the Bollingen Foundation, 1952.

Introduction to Type. Consulting Psychologists Press, 577 College Ave., Palo Alto, California, n.d.

Jackson, Edgar. *Parish Counseling.* New York: Jason Aronson, 1975.

Jaffé, Aniela. *From the Life and Work of C.G. Jung.* New York: Harper & Row, 1971.

James, William. *Varieties of Religious Experience.* New York: Longmans, Green & Company, 1925.

St. John of the Cross. *The Dark Night of the Soul.* Garden City, N.Y.: Doubleday & Co., 1959.

Johnson, Robert. *He!.* King of Prussia, PA: Religious Publishing Company, 1974.

––––––––––––. *She!* King of Prussia, PA: Religious Publishing Company, 1976.

Johnston, William. *The Still Point.* New York: Harper & Row, 1970.

Jung, C.G. *Collected Works.* New York: Pantheon Books for the Bollingen Foundation.

Vol. 5, *Symbols of Transformation,* 1956.
Vol. 7, *Two Essays on Analytic Psychology,* 1953.
Vol. 8, *The Structure and Dynamics of the Psyche,* 1960.
Vol. 9, Part 1, *The Archetypes and the Collective Unconscious,* 1959.
Vol. 9, Part 2, *Aion: Researches into the Phenomenology of the Self,* 1959.
Vol. 10, *Civilization in Transition,* 1964.
Vol. 11, *Psychology and Religion: West and East,* 1958.
Vol. 11, *Answer to Job.*
Vol. 12, *Psychology and Alchemy,* 1953.
Vol. 14, *The Mysterium Coniunctionis,* 1963.
Vol. 16, *The Practice of Psychotherapy,* 1954.
Vol. 18, *The Symbolic Life,* 1976.

––––––––––––. *Man and His Symbols.* Garden City, N.Y: Doubleday and Company, Inc., 1964.

––––––––––––. *Modern Man in Search of a Soul.* New York: Harcourt, Brace and World, Inc., 1933.

––––––––––––. *Memories, Dreams, Reflections.* rec'd and ed. by Aniela Jaffé. New York: Pantheon Books, 1963.

Kalish, R.A. and Reynolds, D.K. . "Phenomenological Reality and Post-Death Contact," *Journal of the Scientific Study of Religion.* 12, no. 2 (June 1973).

Kant, Immanuel. *Critique of Pure Reason*. Translated by Norman Kemp Smith. London: Macmillan and Company, Limited., 1929.

Kazantzakis, Nikos. *The Saviors of God*. Simon & Schuster, 1960.

Kelly, Thomas. *A Testament of Devotion*. New York: Harper and Brothers, 1941.

Kelsey, Morton T. *Adventure Inward*. Minneapolis, Minn.: Augsburg Publishing House, 1980.

—————. *Afterlife: The Other Side of Dying*. New York: Paulist Press, 1979.

—————. *The Art of Christian Love*. Pecos, N.M.: Dove Pamphlets, 1973.

—————. *Can Christians Be Educated?* Mishawaka, Ind.: Religious Education Press, Inc., 1977.

—————. *Caring: How Can We Love One Another?* New York: Paulist Press, 1981.

—————. *The Christian and the Supernatural*. Minneapolis, Minn: Augsburg Publishing House, 1976.

—————. *Discernment: A Study in Ecstasy and Evil*. New York: Paulist Press, 1978.

—————. *Dreams, A Way to Listen to God*. New York: Paulist Press, 1978.

—————. *Dreams: The Dark Speech of the Spirit*. Garden City, N.Y.: Doubleday and Company, Inc.: 1968.

—————. *Encounter with God*. Minneapolis: Bethany Fellowship, 1972.

—————. *Finding Meaning: Guidelines for Counselors*. Pecos, N.M.: Dove Pamphlets, 1974.

—————. *God, Dreams, and Revelation: A Christian Interpretation Of Dreams*. Minneapolis, Minn: Augsburg Publishing House, 1974.

—————. *Healing and Christianity*. New York: Harper & Row, 1973.

—————. *Myth, History and Faith*. New York: Paulist Press, 1974.

—————. *The Other Side of Silence*. New York: Paulist Press, 1976.

—————. *Tongue Speaking: An Experiment in Spiritual Experience*. Garden City, N.Y.: Doubleday and Company, Inc., 1964.

Kirsch, James. *Shakespeare's Royal Self*. New York: G.P. Putnam's Sons for C.G. Jung Foundation, 1966.

Krieger, Dolores. *The Therapeutic Touch*. Englewood Cliffs, N.J.: Prentice-Hall, 1979.

Krippner, Stanley. *Song of the Siren: A Parapsychological Odyssey*. New York: Harper & Row, 1975.

Kübler-Ross, Elisabeth. *On Death and Dying*. New York: Macmillan, 1969.

Kuhn, Thomas S. *The Structure of Scientific Revolutions*. 2nd ed. Chicago: University of Chicago Press, 1970.

Lame Deer and Erdoes, Richard. *Lame Deer: Seeker of Visions*. New York: Simon & Schuster, 1972.

Leech, Kenneth. *Soul Friend: The Practice of Christian Spirituality*. San Francisco: Harper & Row, 1980.

LeShan, Lawrence. *Alternate Realities*. New York: Evans & Co., 1976.

—————. *The Medium, the Mystic and the Physicist: Toward a General Theory of the Paranormal*. New York: Viking Press, 1974.

Lorenz, Konrad. *On Aggression*. New York: Bantam Books, 1970.

Loyola, Ignatius, *The Spiritual Exercises*. Garden City, N.Y.: Doubleday and Co., Inc., 1964.

Luke, Helen. *Dark Wood to White Rose*. Pecos, N.M.: Dove Publications, 1975.

—————. *The Way of Woman Ancient and Modern*. Privately published,

208   PROPHETIC MINISTRY

Apple Farm, Three Rivers, Michigan, n.d.

Lynch, James. *The Broken Heart: The Medical Consequences of Loneliness.* New York: Basic Books, 1977.

MacMillan, William J. *Reluctant Healer: A Remarkable Autobiography.* New York: Thomas Y. Crowell Co., 1952.

Macquarrie, John. *Twentieth Century Religious Thought.* New York: Harper & Row, 1963.

Mahoney, Maria F. *The Meaning in Dreams and Dreaming.* New York: The Citadel Press, 1970.

Masters & Johnson. *The Pleasure Bond.* Boston: Little, Brown & Co., 1974.

May, Rollo. *Love and Will.* New York: W.W. Norton & Company, Inc. 1969.

McGlashan, Alan. *Gravity and Levity.* Boston: Houghton Mifflin Co., 1976.

_____. *The Savage and Beautiful Country.* Boston: Houghton Mifflin Co., 1967.

Menninger, Karl. *Man Against Himself.* New York: Harcourt, Brace and Company, 1938.

Miller, Arthur. *After the Fall.* New York: The Viking Press, 1964.

Montagu, Ashley. *Touching: The Human Significance of the Skin.* New York: Columbia University Press, 1971.

Moreno, Antonio. *Jung, Gods, and Modern Man.* Notre Dame, Ind.: University of Notre Dame Press, 1970.

Nagel, Ernest and Newman, James R. *Gödel's Proof.* New York: New York University Press, 1964.

Naranjo, Claudio. *The Healing Journey: New Approaches to Consciousness.* New York: Pantheon Books, 1973.

Neihardt, John G. *Black Elk Speaks: Being the Life Story of a Holy Man of the Oglala Sioux.* Lincoln: University of Nebraska Press, 1961.

Newcomb, Franc Johnson. *Hosteen Klah: Navaho Medicine Man and Sand Painter.* Norman: University of Oklahoma Press, 1964.

New York Times "Medicine Men Successful Where Science Falls Short" July 7, 1972. Cover Story, section D.

Ornstein, Robert. *The Psychology of Consciousness.* San Francisco: W.H. Freeman, 1973.

Otto, Rudolf. *The Idea of the Holy.* New York: Oxford University Press, 1958.

Panati, Charles. *Supersenses: Our Potential for Parasensory Experience.* New York: Quadrangle/New York Times Book Co., 1974.

Peale, N.V. *The Power of Positive Thinking.* Englewood Cliffs, N.J.: Prentice-Hall, 1952.

Pieper, Josef. *Love and Inspiration: A Study of Plato's Phaedrus.* London: Faber & Faber, 1964.

Plato. *Dialogues.* Translated by B. Jowett. New York: Random House, 1937.

Prayer Book Studies III: The Order for the Ministration to the Sick. The Standing Liturgical Commission of the Protestant Episcopal Church in the United States of America. New York: Church Pension Fund, 1951 (pamphlet).

Provonsha, J.W. "The Healing Christ," *Current Medical Digest,* December 1959.

Reich, Charles A. *The Greening of America.* New York: Random House, 1970.

Rice, Edward. *The Man in the Sycamore Tree.* Garden City, N.Y.: Doubleday-Image Books, 1972.

Riesman, David. *The Lonely Crowd.* New Haven, Conn.: Yale University Press, 1973.

Rogers, Carl. *Carl Rogers on Encounter Groups.* New York: Harper & Row, 1970.

_____. *Freedom to Learn.* Columbus, Ohio: Charles E. Merrill Publishing Co., 1969.

Sanford, Agnes. *The Healing Light.* Minneapolis: Macalaster Park, 1947.

Sanford, John. *Dreams: God's Forgotten Language.* Philadelphia: J.B. Lippincott Co., 1968.

_____. *Evil, The Shadow Side of Reality.* New York: Crossroad, 1981.

_____. *Healing and Wholeness.* New York: Paulist Press, 1977.

_____. *The Kingdom Within.* Philadelphia and New York: Lippincott Co., 1970.

_____. *The Man Who Wrestled With God.* King of Prussia, PA: Religious Publishing Co., 1974.

Sargant, William. *Battle for the Mind.* Baltimore: Penguin Books, 1961.

Simonton, Carl and Stephanie. *Getting Well Again.* Los Angeles: J.P. Tarcher, 1978.

Skinner, B.F. *Beyond Freedom and Dignity.* New York: Alfred A. Knopf, 1971.

_____. *Walden Two.* New York: Macmillan Co., 1960.

Stearn, Jess. *Yoga, Youth and Reincarnation.* New York: Doubleday and Co., Inc., 1965.

Storr, Anthony. *Human Aggression.* New York: Atheneum Publishers. 1968.

Suenens, Cardinal. *A New Pentecost?* New York: Seabury Press, 1975.

The Dimensions of Healing, A Symposium. The Academy of Parapsychology and Medicine, 314 Second Street, Los Altos, California 94022, 1972.

The Homosexual in Our Society. The transcript of a program broadcast on November 24, 1958 by radio station KPFA-FM Berkeley, California (San Francisco: Pan-Graphic Press, 1959).

The Interpreter's Bible. Vol. 1-13. Nashville, Tenn.: Abingdon Press, 1953.

The Prayer of Jesus. (anon.) New York: Desclee, 1967.

The Tibetan Book of the Dead. W.Y. Evans-Wentz, ed. New York: Oxford University Press, 1957.

Toben, Bob and Sarfatti, Jack. *Space-Time and Beyond.* New York: Dutton, 1975.

Toulmin, Stephen. *The Philosophy of Science: An Introduction.* New York: Harper & Brothers, 1960.

Toynbee, Arnold. *Half the World: The History and Culture of China and Japan.* New York: Holt, Rinehart and Winston, 1973.

Villasenor, David. *Tapestries in Sand: The Spirit of Indian Sandpainting.* Healdsburg, California: Naturegraph Co., 1966.

Von Hügel, Baron Friedrich. *The Mystical Element of Religion as Studied in St. Catherine of Genoa and her Friends.* London: J.M. Dent and Sons Limited, 1927.

_____. *The Reality of God and Religion and Agnosticism.* London: J.M. Dent and Sons Limited, 1931.

Watson, Lyall. *Supernature: A Natural History of the Supernatural.* New York: Bantam Books, 1974.

Weil, Dr. Andrew. *The Natural Mind.* Boston: Houghton Mifflin, 1972.

Weiss, Edward, and Spurgeon, O. *Psychosomatic Medicine: The Clinical Application of Psychopathology to General Medical Problems.* Philadelphia: Saunders, 1943. (2nd ed. 1949; 3rd ed. 1957.)

White, Victor. *God and the Unconscious.* Chicago: Regnery, 1953.

Wickes, Francis. *The Inner World of Childhood.* New York: Appleton Century, rev. 1966.

Wilkerson, David. *The Cross and the Switchblade.* London: Hodder & Stoughton, 1967.

Williams, Charles. *The Figure of Beatrice.* New York: Octagon Books, 1980.

Wink, Walter. *The Bible in Human Transformation.* Philadelphia: Fortress Press, 1973.

——————————. *Transforming Bible Study.* Nashville: Abingdon. 1980.

Wise, Carroll. *Pastoral Counseling, Its Theory and Practice.* New York: Harper & Brothers, 1951.